MW01627735

The EYEWITNESS HISTORY *of the* CHURCH

Volume Two

SACRIFICE BRINGS FORTH THE BLESSINGS OF HEAVEN

1833–1844

COMPILED BY

JENNIFER JOHNSON, CLAIRE KOLTKO, CELESTE PITTMAN, RACHEL COPE

CFI
Springville, Utah

ISBN: 1-55517-926-6
v.1

Published by CFI,
an imprint of Cedar Fort, Inc.
925 N. Main Springville, Utah, 84663
www.cedarfort.com

Distributed by:

Cover design by Nicole Williams
Cover design © 2006 by Lyle Mortimer

Printed in the United States of America
10 9 8 7 6 5 4 3 2 1

Printed on acid-free paper

Contents

Acknowledgments

We feel blessed to have had the opportunity to read and collect firsthand accounts for this second volume of *The Eyewitness History of the Church*. It has been both humbling and inspiring to read the powerful testimonies and experiences left by faithful Saints, and to see the unfolding drama of this final gospel dispensation through their eyes. There are many people we would like to thank for their invaluable contributions.

Thank you to Dr. W. Jeffrey Marsh for his direction and help with this student-mentoring research project sponsored by Brigham Young University.

Collecting these wonderful first-person narratives has taken us to historical archives at BYU, the University of Utah, the Daughters of the Utah Pioneers Museum, the LDS Church Archives in Salt Lake City, the archives of the Reorganized Church of Jesus Christ of Latter Day Saints (now known as the Community of Christ) in Independence, Missouri, and Church history sites in New York, Ohio, Illinois, Nebraska, Iowa, and Utah. Thank you to all the archivists and historians who helped make these treasured records available to us.

Natalie Ross, Cami Moore, and Kristen Kelley tirelessly searched through archives and the microscopic print of aged manuscripts to reproduce the original texts that helped make this book possible.

We gratefully acknowledge the contributions of those at Cedar Fort, especially Lyle Mortimer and Lee Nelson, for their willingness to publish volume two of *The Eyewitness History of the Church*. Thanks also to Michael Morris and Mindy Higginson for their insightful editing, and to Nikki Williams for her beautiful work on the cover and layout of the book.

We would also like to offer special thanks to William W. Slaughter and those at the LDS Church Archives for their help in securing permission for us to use the photographs seen throughout this book.

Most especially, thank you, dear reader, for your willingness to join us on this exciting journey through the eyewitness history of the Church.

Introduction

As the miraculous events of the Restoration were unfolding, the Prophet Joseph Smith pled with the Saints to record their experiences. He envisioned the rich heritage and living legacy of faith and devotion that these experiences would bequeath to future generations: "Our name will be handed down to future ages; our children will rise up and call us blessed, and generations yet unborn will dwell with peculiar delight, upon the scenes that we have passed through, the privations that we have endured, the untiring zeal that we have manifested, the all but insurmountable difficulties that we have overcome, in laying the foundation of a work that will bring about the glory and blessing which they [our children] will realize" (*History of the Church* 4:609).

The Eyewitness History of the Church, Volume Two draws together, for the first time, hundreds of first-person accounts from those who walked and talked with the Prophet Joseph Smith, allowing you to experience Church History in an exciting new way—through the eyes and ears of those who were there. This book allows you to eavesdrop on the miraculous events of the Restoration, giving an "armchair-view" of the unfolding drama that ushered in the dispensation of the fullness of all times. You will experience what the early Saints saw and felt during some of the most significant moments in Latter-day Saint Church history, as if you were present when it occurred. These eyewitness accounts not only take us back to relive the *them-there-then* experiences of the early Church, but they also empower us to persevere through the *we-here-now* realities we encounter as we build on the foundation they established.

Volume One of *The Eyewitness History of the Church* covered early milestones leading to the Restoration, and important events in the rise and progress of The Church of Jesus Christ of Latter-day Saints. This second volume picks the story up in the early 1830s, beginning with the spiritual outpourings in Kirtland, and follows the Prophet Joseph Smith to his final moments at Carthage Jail, in 1844.

As early as March 1831, John Whitmer was designated by revelation to serve as a Church historian and recorder (D&C 47) and was instructed to "travel many times from place to place . . . that he may the more easily obtain knowledge—preaching and expounding, writing, copying, selecting, and obtaining all things which shall be for the good of the church, and for the rising generations" (D&C 69:7–8). Obviously the Lord is interested in having His children travel to Church-related sites and bear record of Church history so that others—particularly the "rising generations"—may come to know of the spiritual significance of what took place.

We owe these early Saints an incredible debt of gratitude for the spiritual heritage and faith-promoting history they left us. We must never forget the legacy we have inherited. With resolute faith and undaunted courage, the early members of the Church struggled to establish communities of faith amidst persecution, to take the restored gospel of Jesus Christ to the ends of the earth, and to build up the kingdom of God wherever they were commanded to tarry.

The work they began was foreknown and foretold. It is now up to us, under the direction of living prophets, to put the capstone on the Zion they introduced. Isaiah said that this latter-day Zion would rise like an ensign, or banner, on a high mountaintop, to wave to all the world and prepare the earth for the coming of the Lord and Savior Jesus Christ. To those early Saints who began this work, and to Saints now living, the Savior declared:

> Thou shalt declare glad tidings, yea, publish it upon the mountains, and upon every high place, and among every people that thou shalt be permitted to see. And thou shalt do it with all humility, trusting in me, reviling not against revilers. And . . . thou shalt declare repentance and faith on the Savior, and remission of sins by baptism, and by fire, yea, even the Holy Ghost. (D&C 19:30–31)

As prophesied, the Church is beginning to roll across the earth like a stone cut out of a mountain without hands. We look to the Prophet Joseph Smith and the early Saints with gratitude and respect, and because of them, we look forward to the future with greater faith in the Lord Jesus Christ.

Note: Whenever a citation is attributed to the Prophet Joseph Smith from the *History of the Church* or from the *Teachings of the Prophet Joseph Smith* (which was compiled using the *History of the Church* as its source), it should be remembered that the volumes contained in that history were compiled from a variety of journals, diaries, and accounts by a committee called by the Prophet to help him write his history. Most of the *History of the Church* was completed after the death of the Prophet.

1

Kirtland Revelations

In Kirtland, Ohio, the Lord revealed many truths about Himself and the eternal possibilities for His children. Many of the Saints living in Kirtland beheld visions and entertained angels. During this time, a book containing revelations received by the Prophet Joseph Smith, known as the Book of Commandments, was readied for the press (see Chapter 5). This chapter highlights several of the spiritual experiences of the Saints and some of the revelations received by the Prophet Joseph Smith at Kirtland, Ohio.

The Law of Consecration

The law of consecration is a divine principle of the gospel whereby the members of the Church voluntarily devote their time, talents, and means to help sustain and build the kingdom of God (D&C 42:30–39; 51:2–19; 58:35–36). This law was practiced in the church anciently, during both New Testament and Book of Mormon times (Acts 2:44–45 and 4 Nephi 1:3). In response to a revelation given February 9, 1831, the Saints were asked to live this same law and consecrate all their "properties . . . with a covenant and a deed which cannot be broken," requiring them to "impart . . . substance unto the poor . . . before the bishop of [the] church" (D&C 42:30–31). "Individuals shared property, goods, and profits, receiving these things according to their wants and needs (D&C 51:3; 78:1–15; 104)" ("United Order," *The Guide to the Scriptures* [Salt Lake City: The Church of Jesus Christ of Latter-day Saints, 1993], 249).

Lyman Wight

In conformity to this covenant I moved the next February [1830] to Kirtland, into the house with Bro. Morley. We commenced our labors together with great peace and union. We were soon joined by eight other families. Our labors were united both in farming and mechanism, all of which was prosecuted with great vigor. We truly began to feel as if the millennium was close at hand (as cited in Richard L. Anderson, "The Impact of the First Preaching in Ohio," *BYU Studies* [1970–71]: 484).

Wilford Woodruff

(On December 31, 1834, Wilford Woodruff consecrated all his time, talents, and earthly possessions to the Lord.)

Believing it to be the duty of the Latter-day Saints to consecrate and dedicate all their property, with themselves, unto God in order to become lawful heirs to the celestial Kingdom of God, I therefore, with this view, consecrated all I had (though but little) before Edward Partridge, the Presiding Bishop of the Church, in Clay County, Missouri, in this form: "Be it known that I, Wilford Woodruff, do freely covenant with my God, that I freely consecrate and dedicate myself, together with all my properties and effects, unto the Lord, for the purpose of assisting in the building up of His Kingdom and His Zion upon the earth, that I may keep His law. I lay all before the Bishop of His Church, that I may be a lawful heir to the celestial Kingdom of God" (Wilford Woodruff, *Wilford Woodruff, His Life and Labors,* comp. Matthias F. Cowley [Salt Lake City: Deseret News, 1916], 44–45).

Leo Tolstoy

(Leo Tolstoy made an observation about the economic principles introduced by the Prophet Joseph Smith.)

Count Leo Tolstoy, Russian author and statesman, in conversation with Andrew D. White, United States foreign minister to Russia, in 1892 said, . . . "I want to know about the American religion. . . . The church to which I refer originated in America and is commonly known as the Mormon Church. What can you tell me of the teachings of the Mormons?"

Dr. White said, "I know very little concerning them."

Then Count Leo Tolstoy rebuked the ambassador. "Dr. White, I am greatly surprised and disappointed that a man of your great learning and position should be so ignorant on this important subject. *Their principles teach the people* not only of heaven and its attendant glories, but *how to live so that their social and economic relations with each other are placed on a sound basis. If the people follow the teachings of this church, nothing can stop their progress—it will be limitless."*

Tolstoy continued, "There have been great movements started in the past but they have died or been modified before they reached maturity. If Mormonism is able to endure, unmodified, until it reaches the third and fourth generation, it is destined to become the greatest power the world has ever known" (Thomas J. Yates, "Count Tolstoi and the 'American Religion,'" *Improvement Era* [February 1939]: 94; as cited in David B. Haight, "He Is Not Here. He Is Risen," *Ensign,* May 1980, 11; italics added).

John Whitmer

(While attempting to live the law of consecration at Kirtland, a few Saints misunderstood and misapplied the principle.)

The disciples had all things common, and were going to destruction very fast as to temporal things; for they considered from reading the scripture that what belonged to a brother belonged to any of the brethren, therefore they would take each other's clothes and other property and use it without leave . . . for they did not understand the scripture (John Whitmer, *From Historian to Dissident: The Book of John Whitmer,* ed. Bruce N. Westergren [Salt Lake City: Signature Books, 1995], 27; punctuation standardized).

John Whitmer
(Courtesy of the Church Archives, The Church of Jesus Christ of Latter-day Saints)

Levi Hancock

(Describing another incident when the law of consecration was applied.)

Brother Harvey Redfield took us to Brother Isaac Morley's who was a cooper by trade and one of the most honest, patient men I ever saw. The company he maintained looked large enough to bring on a famine. I do not know if they lived on him all the time or not.

Levi Hancock
(Courtesy of the Church Archives, The Church of Jesus Christ of Latter-day Saints)

While I was in the room at "Father Morley's" as we all called him, . . . Hermon [Heman] Bassett [Basset] came to me and took my watch out of my pocket and walked off as though it was his. I thought he would bring it back soon but was disappointed as he sold it. I asked him what he meant by selling my watch.

"Oh," said he, "I thought it was all in the family."

I told him I did not like such family doings and I would not bear it (Levi W. Hancock, *The Life of Levi W. Hancock* [L. Tom Perry Special Collections, Harold B. Lee Library, Brigham Young University, Provo, Utah], 27; punctuation standardized).

The United Order

In both Kirtland and Missouri the Prophet Joseph Smith introduced an ideal form of community living, known as the United Order. This order was not after the pattern of men, but after the pattern of God, and was established as a mercantile cooperative— a business organization through which the Saints in the early days of the restored Church sought to live the law of consecration.

Rules That Were to Be Observed by Members of the United Order

[*Rule 1:*] We will not take the name of the Deity in vain, nor speak lightly of his character or of sacred things.

[*Rule 2:*] We will pray with our families morning and evening and also attend to secret prayer.

[*Rule 3:*] We will observe and keep the Word of Wisdom according to the spirit and the meaning thereof.

[*Rule 4:*] We will treat our families with due kindness and affection, and set before them an example worthy of imitation. In our families and intercourse with all persons, we will refrain from being contentious or quarrelsome, and we will cease to speak evil of each other, and will cultivate a spirit of charity towards all. We consider it our duty to keep from acting selfishly or from covetous motives, and will seek the interest of each other and the salvation of all mankind.

[*Rule 6:*] We will observe the Sabbath day to keep it holy, in accordance with the revelations.

[*Rule 7:*] That which is committed to our care, we will not appropriate to our own use.

[*Rule 8:*] That which we borrow we will return according to promise, and that which we find we will not appropriate to our own use, but seek to return it to its proper owner.

[*Rule 9:*] We will, as soon as possible, cancel all individual indebtedness contracted prior to our uniting with the order, and, when once fully identified with said order, will contract no debts contrary to the wishes of the board of directors.

[*Rule 10:*] We will patronize our brethren who are in the "Order."

[*Rule 11:*] In our apparel and deportment we will not pattern after nor encourage foolish and extravagant fashions, and cease to import or buy from abroad any article which can be reasonably dispensed with, or which can be produced by combination of home labor. We will foster and encourage the producing and manufacturing of all articles needful for our consumption as fast as our circumstances will permit.

[*Rule 12:*] We will be simple in our dress and manner of living, using proper economy and prudence in the management of all entrusted to our care.

[*Rule 13:*] We will combine our labor for mutual benefit, sustain with our faith, prayers, and words, those whom we have elected to take the management of the different departments of the "Order," and be subject to them in their official capacity, refraining from a spirit of fault-finding.

[*Rule 14:*] We will honestly and diligently labor and devote ourselves and all we have to the "Order" and to the building up of the Kingdom of God (B. H. Roberts, *A Comprehensive History of The Church of Jesus Christ of Latter-day Saints,* 6 vols. [Provo, Utah: Brigham Young University Press, 1977], 5:485–86).

Brigham Young

(Commenting on some of the difficulties encountered while trying to live the United Order.)

If we were to divide up our substance now equally amongst this people we would have to do it all over again in a year from now, for the thrifty and careful would have a surplus while the extravagant and shiftless would be without hope and in debt. For . . . you remember what Bishop Hunter used to say, "there are the Lord's poor and the devil's poor and the poor devils, and we have all three kinds in this Church" (Susa Young Gates, *The Life Story of Brigham Young* [New York: The Macmillan Co., 1931], 201).

REVELATION FORETELLING THE CIVIL WAR AND OTHER WARS

On December 25, 1832, during a time of much reflection concerning slavery and the African-American people, Joseph received a revelation foretelling a rebellion and conflict between the northern and southern states, beginning in South Carolina. The fulfillment of this prophecy (D&C 87) commenced on April 12, 1861, when the first shots of the American Civil War were fired on Fort Sumter. During the Civil War, several individuals acknowledged that the prophecy Joseph Smith made in Kirtland, regarding the war, had indeed come to pass.

Civil War Soldier

(A soldier who had fought in the Civil War reported to a Mormon elder the following incident.)

One evening after fighting all day, one of the soldiers got up on the stump of a tree and yelled out for us to come around and listen to something that he wanted to read to us. It appeared that he had two leaves taken out of some book. And he said: "We have all heard about the so-called Mormon prophet Joseph Smith and here is something remarkable that he said some twenty-five years ago." And then he read from those leaves he held in his hand that the Prophet Joseph Smith had predicted about the war which should break out between the North and South. [D&C 87.]

"Just think, boys," he said, "he died many years ago somewhere in Nauvoo, if I remember correctly, and here he said not only that a war should break out but the very place where the first gun should be fired, and whether true or false we are witnesses of this fact, are we not?" (Charles M. Nielsen, "Witness Tells Oliver Cowdery's Testimony On Book of Mormon," *The Deseret News* [October 17, 1931]: 3).

Philadelphia Mercury Newspaper

(On May 5, 1861, the Mercury *printed an article citing D&C 87.)*

We have in our possession a pamphlet, published at Liverpool, in 1851, containing a selection from the "revelations, translations and narrations" of Joseph Smith, the founder of Mormonism. The following prophesy is here said to have been made by Smith, on the 25th [of] December, 1832. In view of our present troubles, this prediction seems to be in progress of fulfillment, whether Joe Smith was a humbug or not:

> —"A Revelation and Prophesy by the Prophet, Seer, and Revelator, Joseph Smith. Verily thus saith the Lord, concerning the wars that will shortly come to pass, beginning at the rebellion of South Carolina, which will eventually terminate in the death and misery of many souls. The days will come that war will be poured out upon all

nations, beginning at that place; for behold, the Southern States shall be divided against the Northern States, and the Southern States will call on other nations, even the nation of Great Britain, as it is called, and they shall also call upon other nations, in order to defend themselves against other nations; and thus the war shall be poured out upon all nations. And it shall come to pass, after many days, slaves shall rise up against their masters, who shall be marshaled and disciplined for war; and it shall come to pass, also, that the remnants who are left of the land will marshal themselves, and shall become exceedingly angry, and shall vex the Gentiles with a sore vexation; and thus, with the sword, and by bloodshed, the inhabitants of the earth shall mourn; and with famine, and plague, and earthquakes, and the thunder of Heaven, and the fierce and vivid lightning also, shall the inhabitants of the earth be made to feel the wrath, and indignation, and chastening hand of an Almighty God, until the consumption decreed hath made a full end of all nations; that the cry of the Saints, and of the blood of the Saints, shall cease to come up into the ears of the Lord of Sabbath, from the earth, to be avenged of their enemies. Wherefore, stand ye in holy places, and be not moved, until the day of the Lord come; for behold it cometh quickly, saith the Lord. Amen." The war began in South Carolina. Insurrections of slaves are already dreaded. Famine will certainly afflict some Southern communities. The interferences of Great Britain, on account of the want of cotton, is not improbable, if the war is protracted. In the meantime, a general war in Europe appears to be imminent. Have we not had a prophet among us? ("A Mormon Prophecy," *Sunday Philadelphia Mercury* [May 5, 1861]: n.p.; spelling standardized).

Abraham Lincoln

(President Lincoln recognized that God's justice would be fully satisfied before the Civil War would end. In his Second Inaugural Address, he made the following statement.)

Fondly do we hope, fervently do we pray, that this mighty scourge of war may speedily pass away.

Yet if God will that it continue until all the wealth piled by the bondsmen's two hundred and fifty years of unrequited toil shall be sunk, and until every drop of blood drawn with the lash shall be paid by another drawn with the sword, as was said three thousand years ago, so still it must be said, "The judgments of the Lord are true and righteous altogether" (Abraham Lincoln, *Addresses Delivered at the Presentation of the Portrait of Abraham Lincoln by the Committee of the House of Assembly February 12 1867* [Trenton, New Jersey: Office of the State Gazette, 1867], 36).

John Taylor

*(As the conflict deepened, the Saints viewed the Civil War with mixed emotions. They considered the bloodshed and devastation in the states a judgment upon the nation for the murders of Joseph and Hyrum Smith, for not keeping the commandments of God, and for the injustices inflicted upon the Saints in Missouri and Illinois. Despite this, members of the Church followed Joseph Smith's lead in firmly supporting the American Constitution [*Church History in the Fulness of Times *(Salt Lake City: The Church of Jesus Christ of Latter-day Saints, 1989), 381].)*

We have been driven from city to city, from state to state for no just cause or complaint. We have been banished from the pale of what is termed civilization, and forced to make a home in the desert wastes. . . . Shall we join the North to fight against the South? No! . . . Why? They have both, as before shown, brought it upon themselves, and we have had no hand in the matter. . . . We know no North, no South, no East, no West; we abide strictly and positively by the Constitution (John Taylor, "Ceremonies at the Bowery," *Deseret News* [July 10, 1861]: 149–52).

Brigham Young

(After the Civil War had raged for nearly a year, President Young acknowledged that the Saints were much better off in the West.)

Had we not been persecuted, we would now be in the midst of the wars and bloodshed that are desolating the nation, instead of where we are, comfortably located in our peaceful dwellings in these silent, far off mountains and valleys. Instead of seeing my brethren comfortably seated around me to-day, many of them would be found in the front ranks on the battle field. I realize the blessings of God in our present safety. We are greatly blessed, greatly favored and greatly exalted, while our enemies, who sought to destroy us, are being humbled (in *Journal of Discourses*, 26 vols. [London: Latter-day Saints' Book Depot, 1854–86], 10:38–39).

The School of the Elders and the School of the Prophets

The Encyclopedia of Mormonism

(The encyclopedia gives this description of the School of the Elders and the School of the Prophets.)

Between 1833 and 1884, Church leaders from time to time organized schools for instructing members in Church doctrine and secular subjects and for discussing political and social issues relevant to the Church's mission. Although they varied greatly in form and purpose, these schools were called Schools of the Prophets, or sometimes Schools of the Elders.

The first such school met on January 23, 1833, in Kirtland, Ohio, in response to a revelation (D&C 88:119–33) instructing the Church to prepare priesthood members to carry the gospel to the world.

The School of the Prophets met in Kirtland through the winter and early spring of 1833, usually in a room above Newel K. Whitney's store. Joseph Smith presided, and Orson Hyde was the instructor. Enrollment was limited to selected priesthood holders and probably never exceeded twenty-five. In accordance with the revelation about the school, members were initiated through the washing of feet, then reaffirmed their commitment and mutual goodwill by exchanging a formal salutation at the commencement of each class. School usually convened at sunrise and dismissed in late afternoon. Instruction focused on scripture and doctrine, though some time was devoted to secular topics such as grammar. During the February 27, 1833, meeting, Joseph Smith received the revelation known as the Word of Wisdom (D&C 89), which thereafter was binding upon members of the school.

The school ended in April 1833, when spring weather permitted active missionary work to begin, and never reconvened. Instead, a series of educational efforts expanded on the original idea and took on added responsibilities. Two of these later schools, known as the School of the Elders or School of the Prophets, convened in Jackson County, Missouri, during the summer of 1833 and in Kirtland, Ohio, from late fall to early spring in 1834–1835 and 1835–1836. These had larger enrollments than the first School of the Prophets and, in addition to the spiritual preparation of priesthood members, taught students an expanded secular curriculum, including penmanship, English, Hebrew, grammar, arithmetic, philosophy, literature, government, geography, and history. These later schools did not observe the earlier initiation rite and formalized salutation. Parley P. Pratt led the Missouri school, and Joseph Smith, Sidney Rigdon, Frederick G. Williams, and William E. McLellan taught in Kirtland. During the 1834–1835 school year, students in Kirtland heard the lectures later published in the Doctrine and Covenants as the Lectures on Faith.

Following the closure of the School of the Elders in 1836, the School of the Prophets did not meet again until the Church moved west (Steven R. Sorensen, "Schools of the Prophets," *Encyclopedia of Mormonism,* 4 vols., ed. Daniel H. Ludlow [New York: Macmillan Publishing Co., 1992], 1269–70).

Parley P. Pratt

(Describing the School of the Elders in Missouri.)

Parley P. Pratt
(Courtesy of the Church Archives, The Church of Jesus Christ of Latter-day Saints)

I devoted almost my entire time in ministering among the churches; holding meetings; visiting the sick; comforting the afflicted, and giving counsel. A school of Elders was also organized, over which I was called to preside. This class, to the number of about sixty, met for instruction once a week. The place of meeting was in the open air, under some tall trees, in a retired place in the wilderness, where we prayed, preached and prophesied, and exercised ourselves in the gifts of the Holy Spirit. Here great blessings were poured out, and many great and marvelous things were manifested and taught. The Lord gave me great wisdom, and enabled me to teach and edify the Elders, and comfort and encourage them in their preparations for the great work which lay before us. I was also much edified and strengthened. To attend this school I had to travel on foot, and sometimes with bare feet at that, about six miles. This I did once a week, besides visiting and preaching in five or six branches a week (Parley P. Pratt, *Autobiography of Parley P. Pratt*, ed. Scot Facer Proctor and Maurine Jensen Proctor [Salt Lake City: Deseret Book, 2000], 112–14).

Doctrine & Covenants 88:117–18, 122–37

(Giving instructions for organizing the School of the Prophets in Kirtland.)

Therefore, verily I say unto you, my friends, call your solemn assembly, as I have commanded you.

And as all have not faith, seek ye diligently and teach one another words of wisdom; yea, seek ye out of the best books words of wisdom; seek learning, even by study and also by faith. . . .

Appoint among yourselves a teacher, and let not all be spokesmen at once; but let one speak at a time and let all listen unto his sayings, that when all have spoken that all may be edified of all, and that every man may have an equal privilege.

See that ye love one another; cease to be covetous; learn to impart one to another as the gospel requires.

Cease to be idle; cease to be unclean; cease to find fault one with another; cease to sleep longer than is needful; retire to thy bed early, that ye may not be weary; arise early, that your bodies and your minds may be invigorated.

And above all things, clothe yourselves with the bond of charity, as with a mantle, which is the bond of perfectness and peace.

Pray always, that ye may not faint, until I come. Behold, and lo, I will come quickly, and receive you unto myself. Amen.

And again, the order of the house prepared for the presidency of the school of the prophets, established for their instruction in all things that are expedient for them, even for all the officers of the church, or in other words, those who are called to the ministry in the church, beginning at the high priests, even down to the deacons—

And this shall be the order of the house of the presidency of the school: He that is appointed to be president, or teacher, shall be found standing in his place, in the house which shall be prepared for him.

Therefore, he shall be first in the house of God, in a place that the congregation in the house may hear his words carefully and distinctly, not with loud speech.

And when he cometh into the house of God, for he should be first in the house—behold, this is beautiful, that he may be an example—

Let him offer himself in prayer upon his knees before God, in token or remembrance of the everlasting covenant.

And when any shall come in after him, let the teacher arise, and, with uplifted hands to heaven, yea, even directly, salute his brother or brethren with these words:

Art thou a brother or brethren? I salute you in the name of the Lord Jesus Christ, in token or remembrance of the everlasting covenant, in which covenant I receive you to fellowship, in a determination that is fixed, immovable, and unchangeable, to be your friend and brother through the grace of God in the bonds of love, to walk in all the commandments of God blameless, in thanksgiving, forever and ever. Amen.

And he that is found unworthy of this salutation shall not have place among you; for ye shall not suffer that mine house shall be polluted by him.

And he that cometh in and is faithful before me, and is a brother, or if they be brethren, they shall salute the president or teacher with uplifted hands to heaven, with this same prayer and covenant, or by saying Amen, in token of the same.

Behold, verily, I say unto you, this is an ensample unto you for a salutation to one another in the house of God, in the school of the prophets.

And ye are called to do this by prayer and thanksgiving, as the Spirit shall give utterance in all your doings in the house of the Lord, in the school of the prophets, that it may become a sanctuary, a tabernacle of the Holy Spirit to your edification.

Joseph Smith Jr.

You will see that the Lord commanded us, in Kirtland, to . . . establish a school for the Prophets, this is the word of the Lord to us and we must, yea, the Lord helping us, we will obey; as on conditions of our obedience He has promised us great things; yea, even a visit from the heavens to honor us with His own presence (Joseph Smith, *History of The Church of Jesus Christ of Latter-day Saints*, 7 vols., ed. B. H. Roberts [Salt Lake City: Deseret Book, 1978], 1:316).

Brigham Young

The first school of the prophets was held in a small room situated over the Prophet Joseph's kitchen . . . In the rear of this building [the Whitney store] was a kitchen, probably ten by fourteen feet, containing rooms and pantries. Over this kitchen was situated the room in which the Prophet received revelations and in which he instructed his brethren. The brethren came to that place for hundreds of miles to attend school in a little room probably no larger than eleven by fourteen (in *Journal of Discourses*, 12:158).

Joseph Smith Jr.

On the 23rd of January, we [the School of the Prophets] again assembled in conference; when, after much speaking, singing, praying, and praising God, all in tongues, we proceeded to the washing of feet (according to the practice recorded in the 13th chapter of John's Gospel), as commanded of the Lord. Each Elder washed his own feet first, after which I girded myself with a towel and washed the feet of all of them, wiping them with the towel with which I was girded. Among the number, my father presented himself, but before I washed his feet, I asked of him a father's blessing, which he granted by laying his hands upon my head, in the name of Jesus Christ, and declaring that I should continue in the Priest's office until Christ comes. At the close of the scene, Brother Frederick G. Williams, being moved upon by the Holy Ghost, washed my feet in token of his fixed determination to be with me in suffering, or in journeying, in life or in death, and to be continually on my right hand; in which I accepted him in the name of the Lord (*History of the Church*, 1:323).

Zebedee Coltrin

The School of the Prophets commenced on the 24th day of January, 1833, agreeable to the commandment of the Lord which said the first elders should be called in and receive learning by study and by faith and prepare themselves to go forth for the last time to bind up the law and seal up the testimony . . .

And during the time of the school there [were] many powerful manifestations of the holy spirit and many councils held, at which times much useful instruction was obtained by the gift and power of the holy spirit and also the gift of tongues and the interpretation thereof. The science we engaged in for the winter was English grammar during which time we obtained a general knowledge of that science (Zebedee Coltrin, *Journal of Zebedee Coltrin* [LDS Church Archives, The Church of Jesus Christ of Latter-day Saints, Salt Lake City, Utah], n.p.).

Joseph Smith Jr.

(Significant spiritual manifestations blessed the meetings of the School of the Prophets. The following occurred when the First Presidency was organized during the school's session held March 18, 1833.)

Great joy and satisfaction continually beamed in the countenances of the School of the Prophets, and the Saints, on account of the things revealed, and our progress in the knowledge of God. The High Priests assembled in the school room of the Prophets, and were organized according to revelation . . .

Elder Rigdon expressed a desire that himself and Brother Frederick G. Williams should be ordained to the offices to which they had been called, viz., those of Presidents of the High Priesthood, and to be equal in holding the keys of the kingdom with Brother Joseph Smith, Jun., according to the revelation given on the 8th of March, 1833. Accordingly I laid my hands on Brothers Sidney and Frederick, and ordained them to take part with me in holding the keys of this last kingdom, and to assist in the Presidency of the High Priesthood, as my Counselors; after which I exhorted the brethren to faithfulness and diligence in keeping the commandments of God, and gave much instruction for the benefit of the Saints, with a promise that the pure in heart should see a heavenly vision; and after remaining a short time in secret prayer, the promise was verified; for many present had the eyes of their understanding opened by the Spirit of God, so as to behold many things. I then blessed the bread and wine, and distributed a portion to each. Many of the brethren saw a heavenly vision of the Savior, and concourses of angels, and many other things, of which each one has a record of what he saw (*History of the Church*, 1:334–35).

Zebedee Coltrin

(Conversing with President John Taylor, as recorded by Truman Coe.)

I believe I am the only living man now in the church who was connected with the School of the Prophets when it was organized in 1833, the year before we went up in Zion's Camp . . .

Brother Coltrin: When the Word of Wisdom was first presented by the Prophet Joseph (as he came out of the translating room) and was read to the School, there were twenty out of the twenty-one who used tobacco and they all immediately threw their tobacco and [pipes] into the fire (Truman Coe, "Mormonism," *Cincinnati Journal and Western Luminary* [August 25, 1835]: n.p.; as cited in *Writings of Early Latter-day Saints and Their Contemporaries, a Database Collection*, comp. Milton V. Backman [Provo, Utah: BYU Religious Studies Center, 1996], 55–58).

Zebedee Coltrin

(Zebedee was present at the School of the Prophets. In 1878 he related a visionary experience at the school to a group of high priests in Spanish Fork, Utah.)

I saw a personage passing through the room as plainly as I see you now. Joseph asked us if we knew who it was and answered himself, 'That is Jesus our Elder Brother, the Son of God!'" After the vision closed, Joseph then told those present to resume their former position of prayer. "Again I saw passing through the same room, a personage whose glory and brightness was so great, that I can liken it to nothing but the burning bush that Moses saw, and its power was so great that had it continued much longer I believe it would have consumed us." After this personage had disappeared from the room, Joseph announced that the men had seen the father of the Lord Jesus Christ. Zebedee Coltrin concluded his testimony by saying, "I saw him" (Keith W. Perkins, "The Prophet Joseph Smith in 'the Ohio,'" *The Prophet Joseph: Essays on the Life and Mission of Joseph Smith*, ed. Larry C. Porter and Susan Easton Black [Salt Lake City: Deseret Book, 1988], 110–11; see also *High Priests Records of Spanish Fork, Feb. 5, 1878* [LDS Church Archives, The Church of Jesus Christ of Latter-day Saints, Salt Lake City, Utah]; n.p.).

John Murdock

(Describing the same experience.)

In one of those [prayer] meetings the prophet told us, if we could humble ourselves before God, and exercise strong faith, we should see the face of the Lord. And about mid-day, the visions of my mind were opened, and the eyes of my understanding were enlightened, and I saw the form of a man, most lovely! The visage of his face was sound and fair as the sun. His hair, a bright silver grey, curled in most majestic form, His eyes, a keen penetrating blue, and the skin of his neck a most beautiful white, and He was covered from the neck to the feet with a loose garment, pure white, whiter than any garment I have ever before seen. His countenance was most penetrating, and yet most lovely! And while I was endeavoring to comprehend the whole personage, from head to feet, it slipped from me, and the vision was closed up. But it left on my mind the impression of love, for months, that I never before felt, to that degree! (John Murdock, *A Brief Synopsis of the Life of John Murdock*, ed. Reva Baker Holt [L. Tom Perry Special Collections, Harold B. Lee Library, Brigham Young University, Provo, Utah], 8; capitalization standardized).

John Whitmer

The spirit of the Lord fell upon Joseph in an unusual manner. . . . After he had prophesied, he laid his hands upon Lyman Wight [and ordained him] to the High Priesthood . . . And the Spirit . . . fell upon Lyman, and he prophesied, concerning the coming of Christ . . . He saw the heavens opened, and the Son of Man sitting on the right hand of the Father, making intercession for his brethren, the Saints. He said that God would work a work in these last days that tongue cannot express, and the mind is not capable to conceive. The glory of the Lord shone around (*From Historian to Dissident: The Book of John Whitmer,* 69–70; punctuation and capitalization standardized).

Joseph Smith Jr.

(Relating a vision experienced in the Kirtland Temple, January 21, 1836.)

The heavens were opened upon us, and I beheld the celestial kingdom of God, and the glory thereof, whether in the body or out I cannot tell. I saw the transcendent beauty of the gate through which the heirs of that kingdom will enter, which was like unto circling flames of fire; also the blazing throne of God, whereon was seated the Father and the Son. I saw the beautiful streets of that kingdom, which had the appearance of being paved with gold. . . .

Many of my brethren . . . saw glorious visions also. Angels ministered unto them as well as to myself, and the power of the Highest rested upon us, the house was filled with the glory of God, and we shouted Hosanna to God and the Lamb (*History of the Church,* 2:380–81. The vision was added to the Doctrine and Covenants in 1981 as section 137; see also Karl Ricks Anderson, *Joseph Smith's Kirtland* [Salt Lake City: Deseret Book, 1989], 110).

Lucy Mack Smith

(Recounting another experience in which those in the school enjoyed an outpouring of the Spirit.)

Joseph took all the male portion of the family into the room where the School of the Prophets was kept and, girding himself, administered to them the ordinance of washing of feet according to the directions of the Savior, who said, "If I then, your Lord and Master, have washed your feet; ye also ought to wash one another's feet." When the ceremony was over, the Spirit of the Lord fell upon them and they spoke in other tongues and prophesied as on the day of Pentecost. The brethren gathered together to witness the manifestation of the power of God.

At that time, I was on the farm a short distance from the place where the meeting was held, but those of my children who could not bear that Mother should miss anything dispatched a messenger in great haste for me. I was putting some loaves of bread into the oven, but the brother who ran for me would not wait till I had set my bread to baking. I went and shared with the rest one of the most glorious outpourings of the Spirit of God that had ever been witnessed in the Church at that time (Lucy Mack Smith, *The Revised and Enhanced History of Joseph Smith by His Mother,* ed. Scot Facer Proctor and Maurine Jensen Proctor [Salt Lake City: Bookcraft, 1996], 307–8).

Word of Wisdom
(February 27, 1833)

Joseph and Emma Smith lived in the Newel K. Whitney store and home where the School of the Prophets was held. Their kitchen was directly below the room where the brethren would meet. The brethren were used to entering the room and immediately lighting up their pipes or chewing tobacco. These habits created a terrible mess in the room, leaving Emma to clean up after them day after day. When she brought this to Joseph's attention, he inquired of the Lord, and on February 27, 1833, Joseph received what is now Doctrine and Covenants Section 89, commonly known as the Word of Wisdom.

Brigham Young

When the school of the prophets was inaugurated one of the first revelations given by the Lord to His servant Joseph was the Word of Wisdom. The members of that school were but a few at first, and the prophet commenced to teach them in doctrine to prepare them to go out into the world to preach the gospel unto all people, and gather the elect from the four quarters of the earth, as the prophets anciently have spoken. While this instruction prepared the Elders to administer in word and doctrine, it did not supply the teachings necessary to govern their private or temporal lives; it did not say whether they should be merchants, farmers, mechanics, or money changers. The prophet began to instruct them how to live that they might be the better prepared to perform the great work they were called to accomplish.

I think I am as well acquainted with the circumstances which led to the giving of the Word of Wisdom as any man in the Church, although

I was not present at the time to witness them. . . . When they assembled together in this room after breakfast, the first [thing] they did was to light their pipes, and, while smoking, talk about the great things of the kingdom, and spit all over the room, and as soon as the pipe was out of their mouths a large chew of tobacco would then be taken. Often when the Prophet entered the room to give the school instructions he would find himself in a cloud of tobacco smoke. This, and the complaints of his wife at having to clean so filthy a floor, made the Prophet think upon the matter, and he inquired of the Lord relating to the conduct of the Elders in using tobacco, and the revelation known as the Word of Wisdom was the result of his inquiry (in *Journal of Discourses*, 12:157–58).

Doctrine and Covenants 89:4–17

(Excerpts from the Word of Wisdom.)

Behold, verily, thus saith the Lord unto you: In consequence of evils and designs which do and will exist in the hearts of conspiring men in the last days, I have warned you, and forewarn you, by giving unto you this word of wisdom by revelation—

That inasmuch as any man drinketh wine or strong drink among you, behold it is not good, neither meet in the sight of your Father, only in assembling yourselves together to offer up your sacraments before him.

And, behold, this should be wine, yea, pure wine of the grape of the vine, of your own make.

And, again, strong drinks are not for the belly, but for the washing of your bodies.

And again, tobacco is not for the body, neither for the belly, and is not good for man, but is an herb for bruises and all sick cattle, to be used with judgment and skill.

And again, hot drinks are not for the body or belly.

And again, verily I say unto you, all wholesome herbs God hath ordained for the constitution, nature, and use of man—

Every herb in the season thereof, and every fruit in the season thereof; all these to be used with prudence and thanksgiving.

Yea, flesh also of beasts and of the fowls of the air, I, the Lord, have ordained for the use of man with thanksgiving; nevertheless they are to be used sparingly;

And it is pleasing unto me that they should not be used, only in times of winter, or of cold, or famine.

All grain is ordained for the use of man and of beasts, to be the staff of life, not only for man but for the beasts of the field, and the fowls of heaven, and all wild animals that run or creep on the earth;

And these hath God made for the use of man only in times of famine and excess of hunger.

All grain is good for the food of man; as also the fruit of the vine; that which yieldeth fruit, whether in the ground or above the ground—

Nevertheless, wheat for man, and corn for the ox, and oats for the horse, and rye for the fowls and for swine, and for all beasts of the field, and barley for all useful animals, and for mild drinks, as also other grain.

Joseph Smith Jr.

No official member in this Church is worthy to hold an office, after having the Word of Wisdom properly taught him, and he, the official member, neglecting to comply with or obey it (*History of the Church*, 2:35).

Joel H. Johnson

(Relating something he heard the Prophet say during a Sunday meeting.)

I understand that some of the people are excusing themselves using tea and coffee, because the Lord only said, "hot drinks" in the revelation of the Word of Wisdom. . . . Tea and coffee . . . are what the Lord meant when he said, "hot drinks" (Joel H. Johnson, *A Voice From the Mountains* [Mesa, Arizona: Joel Hills Johnson Arizona Committee, 1982], 12).

Marlin K. Jensen

In 1997 Elder W. Eugene Hansen and I were asked to host the Honorable Michael Moore, attorney general of Mississippi, during a brief visit he made to Utah and Church headquarters. In a wide-ranging conversation with Mr. Moore, Elder Hansen and I raised questions about the lawsuit he had filed against the large American tobacco companies on behalf of the state of Mississippi. We knew Mississippi had recovered a sizeable judgment and that other states, including Utah, were then undertaking similar action. We asked him specifically upon what legal theory the state of Mississippi's claim had been based.

Much to our surprise, Mr. Moore informed us that the state's cause of action had been based on a theory of "conspiracy," which the evidence eventually conclusively showed existed among the tobacco companies and even among their lawyers. As Mr. Moore talked of his conspiracy theory and the efforts made by the tobacco companies to hide from the public the addictive and harmful effects of tobacco, my mind almost instinctively turned to section 89 of the Doctrine and Covenants. A copy of that book of scripture was quickly located, and after briefly explaining the background and import of section 89, I asked Mr. Moore to read verse 4.

We listened attentively as he slowly and deliberately read that verse out loud in his appealing southern accent: "Behold, verily, thus saith the Lord unto you: In consequence of evils and designs which do and will exist in the hearts of *conspiring* men in the last days, I have warned you, and forewarn you, by giving unto you this word of wisdom by revelation" (italics added).

The scriptural reference to "conspiring men" was not lost on Mr. Moore. As he finished reading verse 4, a broad smile came across his face, and with a twinkle in his eyes he said, "I never dreamed in visiting Utah I might find 10 million people who would agree with my conspiracy theories!"

My heart burned within me that day and has many times since as I have though about Joseph Smith's gifts as a prophet and seer. There is really no other explanation for the origin of that 1833 revelation (Marlin K. Jensen, "May the Kingdom of God Go Forth," *Out of Obscurity: The LDS Church in the Twentieth Century* [Salt Lake City: Deseret Book, 2000], 9).

Seek Learning—By Study and Also by Faith

Besides the School of the Prophets, the Lord encouraged the Saints to seek learning of every kind.

Doctrine and Covenants 88:78–80, 118

Teach ye diligently and my grace shall attend you, that you may be instructed more perfectly in theory, in principle, in doctrine, in the law of the gospel, in all things that pertain unto the kingdom of God, that are expedient for you to understand;

Of things both in heaven and in the earth, and under the earth; things which have been, things which are, things which must shortly come to pass; things which are at home, things which are abroad; the wars and the perplexities of the nations, and the judgments which are on the land; and a knowledge also of countries and of kingdoms—

That ye may be prepared in all things when I shall send you again to magnify the calling whereunto I have called you, and the mission with which I have commissioned you. . . .

And as all have not faith, seek ye diligently and teach one another words of wisdom; yea, seek ye out of the best books words of wisdom; seek learning, even by study and also by faith.

Joseph Smith Jr.

Spent the day at school. The Lord has blessed us in our studies. This day we commenced reading in our Hebrew Bibles with much success. It seems as if the Lord opens our minds in a marvelous manner, to understand His word in the original language; and my prayer is that God will speedily endow us with a knowledge of all languages and tongues, that His servants may go forth for the last time the better prepared to bind up the law, and seal up the testimony (*History of the Church*, 2:376–77).

2

Zion's Camp

During the construction of the Kirtland Temple, in May and June of 1834, the Lord called a large group of men to help the Missouri militia restore the Saints' property that had been unlawfully taken by mobs in Jackson County, Missouri (D&C 101, 103, and 105). The group was named Zion's Camp and consisted of two hundred and one men, eleven women and seven children, ranging from ages sixteen to seventy-nine. The camp was organized in order "to carry money, clothing, and provisions to the Saints in Clay County [and] to join the state militia of Missouri and assist the Mormons to recover their property in Jackson County" (Carter Eldredge Grant, *The Kingdom of God Restored* [Salt Lake City: Deseret Book, 1955], 182). Although Zion's Camp was not successful in restoring the land to the Missouri Saints, it proved to be a great testing ground for the future leaders of the Church. Many participants in Zion's Camp also testified to the importance of the camp in preparing men to later lead the pioneer trek to the Salt Lake Valley.

The Call to Serve in Zion's Camp

Doctrine and Covenants 103:30–34

(This revelation was received when Parley P. Pratt and Lyman Wight came from Missouri to Kirtland, Ohio, to counsel with the Prophet Joseph Smith about helping restore the Saints to their homes in Jackson County, Missouri. The Lord indicated

that Zion's Camp was to enlist one hundred to five hundred men.)

It is my will that my servant Parley P. Pratt and my servant Lyman Wight should not return to the land of their brethren, until they have obtained companies to go up unto the land of Zion, by tens, or by twenties, or by fifties, or by an hundred, until they have obtained to the number of five hundred of the strength of my house.

Behold this is my will; ask and ye shall receive; but men do not always do my will. Therefore, if you cannot obtain five hundred, seek diligently that peradventure you may obtain three hundred. And if ye cannot obtain three hundred, seek diligently that peradventure ye may obtain one hundred.

But verily I say unto you, a commandment I give unto you, that ye shall not go up unto the land of Zion until you have obtained a hundred of the strength of my house, to go up with you unto the land of Zion.

Parley P. Pratt

(Explaining an experience wherein he learned that an angel went before Zion's Camp.)

I had traveled all night to overtake the camp with some men and means, and having breakfasted with them and changed horses, I again started ahead on express to visit other branches, and do business to again overtake them. At noon I had turned my horse loose from the carriage to feed on the grass in the midst of a broad, level plain. No habitation was near; stillness and repose reigned around me; I sank down overpowered with a deep sleep, and might have lain in a state of oblivion till the shades of night had gathered about me, so completely was I exhausted for want of sleep and rest; but I had only slept a few moments till the horse had grazed sufficiently, when a voice, more loud and shrill than I have ever before heard, fell on my ear, and thrilled through every part of my system; it said: *"Parley, it is time to be up and on your journey."* In the twinkling of an eye I was perfectly aroused; I sprang to my feet so suddenly that I could not at first recollect where I was, or what was before me to perform. I related the circumstance afterwards to brother Joseph Smith, and he bore testimony that it was the angel of the Lord who went before the camp, who found me overpowered with sleep, and thus awoke me (Parley P. Pratt, *Autobiography of Parley P. Pratt,* ed.

Parley P. Pratt Jr. [Salt Lake City: Deseret Book, 1985], 93–94).

Hosea Stout

(Describing his feelings on hearing the call to join Zion's Camp.)

The effect of their preaching was powerful on me, and when I considered that they were going up to Zion to fight for their lost inheritances under the special directions of God it was all that I could do to refrain from going (Hosea Stout, "Autobiography of Hosea Stout, 1810 to 1835," *Utah Historical Quarterly* [Summer 1962]: 259–60; spelling and punctuation standardized).

Joseph Smith Jr.

(As recorded by Brigham Young.)

Brother Brigham [Young] and brother Joseph [Young], if you will go with me in the camp to Missouri and keep my counsel, I promise you, in the name of the Almighty, that I will lead you there and back again, and not a hair of your heads shall be harmed (Brigham Young, *The Journal of Brigham: Brigham Young's Own Story in His Own Words,* comp. Leland R. Nelson [Provo, Utah: Council Press, 1980], 6).

William Farrington Cahoon

The last part of August I returned home and labored with my hands until May 5, 1834. I then enlisted to go to the land of Zion in Jackson County and started with the Volunteer Company under the Prophet Joseph Smith for the delivery of the brethren who had been driven from their homes by a ruthless band of mobocrats.

On May 5, 1834 the Camp left Missouri. It was truly a solemn morning, we left our wives, children and friends, not knowing whether we would see them again as we were threatened by enemies that would destroy and exterminate us from the land. We were facing the "lion in his den."

Joseph Smith had made this pledge to us, "If you will go with me to Missouri and keep my counsel, I pledge that I will lead you there and back and not a hair of your head shall be hurt." This camp . . . marched through a population of tens of thousands of people like lambs among wolves, but no man among them opened his mouth to say, "Why do you do so?" On we marched singing our favorite song, "Hark listen to the Trumpeters" (As cited in *Reynolds Cahoon and His Stalwart Sons*, ed. Stella Cahoon Shurtleff and Brent Farrington Cahoon [Salt Lake City: Paragon Press, 1960] 81–82).

Nathan Bennett Baldwin

It was the will of God that five hundred of the strength of his house should go to the redemption of Zion. But he says, men do not always do his will, therefore, if that number could not be obtained, his servants were to seek diligently to obtain one hundred, but gave commandment not to go with less than that number. Some over that number being collected, Joseph considered himself justified in starting to relieve the brethren in Missouri, and on the 5th of May [1834] that company began to move. Two days travel brought us to New Portage, about fifty miles distance, where the company was enlarged by being joined by a small company that had gone before. During these two days travel each individual provided for himself, but on the 7th, a consecration of money was called for, and the whole company organized into smaller companies, consisting generally of twelve in each (Nathan Bennett Baldwin, *Autobiography of Nathan Bennett Baldwin* [LDS Church Archives, The Church of Jesus Christ of Latter-day Saints, Salt Lake City, Utah], n.p.; punctuation and grammar standardized).

Joseph Smith Jr.

(May 7, 1834, New Portage, Ohio)

I continued to organize the company, appoint such other officers as were required, and gave such instructions as were necessary for the discipline, order, comfort and safety of all concerned. I also divided the whole band into companies of twelve, leaving each company to elect its own captain, who assigned each man in his respective company his post and duty, generally in the following order: Two cooks, two firemen; two tent men, two watermen, one runner, two wagoners and horsemen, and one commissary. We purchased flour and meal, baked our own bread, and cooked our own food, generally, which was good, though sometimes scanty; and sometimes we had johnny-cake, or corn-dodger, instead of flour bread. Every night before retiring to rest, at the sound of the trumpet, we bowed before the Lord in the several tents, and presented our thank-offerings with prayer and supplication; and at the sound of the morning trumpet, about four o'clock, every man was again on his knees before the Lord, imploring His blessing for the day (Joseph Smith, *History of The Church of Jesus Christ of Latter-day Saints,* 7 vols., ed. B. H. Roberts [Salt Lake City: Deseret Book, 1978], 2:64–65).

Experiences During the March of Zion's Camp

Joseph Smith Jr.

(The Prophet relates an incident when his inspired counsel was rejected by some brethren while Zion's Camp was stationed on the Mississippi River.)

Some of the brethren went on to the sand bar and got a quantity of turtles' eggs, as they supposed. I told them they were snakes' eggs, and they must not eat them; but some of them thought they knew more about it than I did, and still persisted they were turtles' eggs. I said they were snakes' eggs—eat snakes' eggs, will you? The man that eats them will be sorry for it; you will be sick. Notwithstanding all I said, several brethren ate them, and were sick all the day after it (*History of the Church,* 2:82–83).

William Farrington Cahoon

While traveling across the vast prairie, treeless and waterless, they camped at night after a long and wearisome day's march. They had been without water since early morning, and men and animals suffered greatly from thirst, for it had been one of the hottest days of June. Joseph sat at his tent looking out upon the scene. All at once he called for a spade. When it was brought, he looked about him and selected a spot, the most convenient in the Camp for men and teams to get water. Then he dug a shallow well, and immediately the water came bubbling up into it and filled it, so that the horses and mules could stand and drink from it. While the camp stayed there, the well remained full, despite the fact that about two hundred men and scores of horses and mules were supplied from it (*Reynolds Cahoon and His Stalwart Sons,* 82).

Joseph Smith Jr.

(Commenting on an incident that occurred while Zion's Camp marched through Indiana.)

During our travels we visited several of the mounds which had been thrown up by the ancient inhabitants of this country—Nephites, Lamanites, etc., and this morning I went up on a high mound, near the river, accompanied by the brethren. From this mound we could overlook the tops of the trees and view the prairie on each side of the river as far as our vision could extend, and the scenery was truly delightful.

On the top of the mound were stones which presented the appearance of three altars having been erected one above the other, according to the ancient order; and the remains of bones were strewn over the surface of the ground. The brethren procured a shovel and a hoe, and removing the earth to the depth of about one foot, discovered the skeleton of a man, almost entire, and between his ribs the stone point of a Lamanitish arrow, which evidently produced his death. Elder Burr Riggs retained the arrow. The contemplation of the scenery around us produced peculiar sensations in our bosoms; and subsequently the visions of the past being opened to my understanding by the Spirit of the Almighty, I discovered that the person whose skeleton was before us was a white Lamanite, a large, thick-set man, and a man of God. His name was Zelph. He was a warrior and chieftain under the great prophet Onandagus, who was known from the Hill Cumorah, or eastern sea to the Rocky mountains. The curse was taken from Zelph, or, at least, in part—one of his thigh bones was broken by a stone flung from a sling, while in battle, years before his death. He was killed in battle by the arrow found among his ribs, during the last great struggle of the Lamanites and Nephites (*History of the Church,* 2:79–80).

Joseph Smith Jr.

In pitching my tent we found three massasaugas or prairie rattlesnakes, which the brethren were about to kill, but I said, "Let them alone—don't hurt them! How will the serpent ever lose his venom, while the servants of God possess the same disposition, and continue to make war upon it? Men must become harmless, before the brute creation; and when men lose their vicious dispositions and cease to destroy the animal race, the lion and the lamb can dwell together, and the sucking child can play with the serpent in safety." The brethren took the serpents carefully on sticks and carried them across the creek. I exhorted the brethren not to kill a serpent, bird, or an animal of any kind during our journey unless it became necessary in order to preserve ourselves from hunger.

I had frequently spoken on this subject, when on a certain occasion I came up to the brethren who were watching a squirrel on a tree, and to prove them and to know if they would heed my counsel, I took one of their guns, shot the squirrel and passed on, leaving the squirrel on the ground. Brother Orson Hyde, who was just behind, picked up the squirrel, and said, "We will cook this, that nothing may be lost." I perceived that the brethren understood what I did it for, and in their practice gave more heed to my precept than to my example, which was right (*History of the Church*, 2:71–72).

Miracle at the Fork of Big and Little Fishing Rivers

While the company was stopped to repair their wagons on a hill between the two main branches of Fishing River, between Richmond and Liberty, Missouri, a mob of over three hundred men gathered on the bank opposite the camp. Five men representing the mob rode into camp and swore terrible oaths against the brethren, threatening to kill them. The company was hemmed in on two sides by the steep banks of Fishing River which formed a natural trap.

Nathan Bennett Baldwin

As we neared our place of destination, the excitement of the people in the surrounding country increased. Many threats were thrown out against us but none were consummated. At an early hour at evening, on the 19th of June [1834] we encamped on an eminence between two forks of Fishing River, near a Baptist meeting house, built of hewn logs. While we busied ourselves preparing for the night, several armed men rode by (as we were camped on one side of the road) and swore that we should see hell before morning, and they told us of companies that were coming from various places, report said sixteen hundred sworn to our destruction. Soon after these men left, a small black cloud appeared in the west and increased in size until shortly the whole blue arch was draped in black, presenting a vengeful appearance, while the rain descended in torrents, the winds bellowed and such vivid flashes of lightning and such peals of thunder are seldom seen and heard.

The Lord had previously said he would fight the battles of his saints, and it seemed as though the mandate had gone forth from his presence, to ply the artillery of heaven in defense of his servants. Some small hail fell in the camp but from half a mile to a mile around, we were told by the inhabitants that the hailstones were as big as tumblers; and the appearance of their destructiveness showed that their size was not over-estimated. Limbs of trees were broken off, fence rails were marred and splintered and the growing corn was cut into shreds. But the casualties were all on the side of our enemies. While their gathering hosts were hastening to our destruction, the wrathful elements met them in a manner they had not been accustomed to in their previous deeds of darkness, while persecuting the Saints. Thus brought to a sudden stand, they crept under trees, wagons and anything that afforded shelter and they held their horses as long as they could stand the pelting of these chunks of ice on their arms and gunstocks, the maddened steeds broke loose from the grasp and left them to face danger on foot, while their would-be victims were secure from harm, with the exception of some few tents which were blown down and a few men were rained on, but others were safely housed in the meeting house before mentioned. All were conscious that God was engaged in the conflict, and thankful that they were under his special care and kind protection.

Next morning the streams before and behind us were wonderfully swollen so that we could not advance, neither could our enemies reach us if they had had a mind so to do, but it appears from the sequel that they were so dumbfounded by this singular defeat that their anxiety and determination to kill Jo Smith and his army was considerably abated, so much so that they were hardly willing to hazard another battle when Jehovah fights.

We moved our camp four or five miles north to a more convenient location and halted for a few days. On Saturday the 21st [June 1834], Colonel Sconce with two other leading men from Ray County came to see us, desiring to know what our intentions were, for, said he, "I see that there is an Almighty power that protects this people, for I started from Richmond, Ray County, with a company of armed men, having a full determination to destroy you, but was kept back by the storm and was not able to reach you." When he entered our camp he was seized with such a trembling that he was obliged to sit down to compose himself before he made known the object of their visit. But when a proper explanation was made by Joseph the Prophet in a lengthy speech, they were melted into compassion and cordially took Joseph by the hand and promised to use their influence to allay the excitement of the people in the surrounding country, which they afterwards fulfilled by riding amongst the people and made unwearied exertions to that effect (*Autobiography of Nathan Bennett Baldwin*, n.p.; as cited in Milton V. Backman Jr. and Richard O. Cowan, *Joseph Smith and the Doctrine and Covenants* [Salt Lake City: Deseret Book, 1992], 99–100).

Philo Dibble

In Clay County I enjoyed some rest from persecution, and had two children born to me, Emma and Philo, Jun. I was there when Zion's Camp came up. I met them on Fishing River. There the power of the Lord was manifested by His sending a thunder storm, which raised Fishing River ten feet higher than it was ever known to rise before. I saw the cloud coming up in the west when I was ten miles from Fishing River in the middle of the afternoon. As it moved on eastwardly it increased in size and in blackness, and when it got over the camp it stopped, and in the night the rain and hail poured down in torrents, and the lightning flashed from the cloud continuously for three hours.

Philo Dibble and his wife, Hannah Dubois

(Courtesy of the Church Archives, The Church of Jesus Christ of Latter-day Saints)

Just before night, two men came into camp and asked where Mr. Smith was. Joseph said, "I am the man." They then advised him to disband his camp, "for," said they, "the mob are gathering, and there won't be one of you left to-morrow morning!"

Joseph smiled, and said: "I guess not." Seeing that Joseph did not believe what they came to tell him, they went off vexed.

We learned afterwards that the hail was so heavy on the mob, that they were forced to seek shelter, and the leader of them swore he would never go against the "Mormons" again (Philo Dibble, "Early Scenes in Church History," *Four Faith Promoting Classics* [Salt Lake City: Bookcraft, 1968], 85–86; capitalization standardized).

Joseph Smith Jr.

During this day, the Jackson county mob, to the number of about two hundred, made arrangements to cross the Missouri river, above the mouth of Fishing river, at Williams' ferry, into Clay county, and be ready to meet the Richmond mob near Fishing river ford, for our utter destruction; but after the first scow load of about forty had been set over the river, the scow in returning was met by a squall, and had great difficulty in reaching the Jackson side by dark.

When these five men were in our camp, swearing vengeance, the wind, thunder, and rising cloud indicated an approaching storm, and in a short time after they left the rain and hail began to fall. The storm was tremendous; wind and rain, hail and thunder met them in great wrath, and soon softened their direful courage, and frustrated all their designs to "kill Joe Smith and his army." Instead of continuing a cannonading which they commenced when the sun was about one hour high, they crawled under wagons, into hollow trees, and filled one old shanty, till the storm was over, when their ammunition was soaked, and the forty in Clay county were extremely anxious in the morning to return to Jackson, having experienced the pitiless pelting of the storm all night; and as soon as arrangements could be made, this "forlorn hope" took the "back track" for Independence, to join the main body of the mob, fully satisfied, as were those survivors of the company who were drowned, that when Jehovah fights they would rather be absent. The gratification is too terrible (*History of the Church,* 2:103–4).

Heber C. Kimball

Soon after these men left us we discovered a small black cloud rising in the west, and not more than twenty minutes passed away before it began to rain and hail; but we had very little hail in our camp. All around us the hail was heavy; some of the hailstones, or rather lumps of ice, were as large as hens' eggs. The thunder rolled with awful majesty, and the red lightnings flashed through the horizon, making it so light that I could see to pick up a pin almost any time all through the night. The earth quaked and trembled, and there being no cessation it seemed as though the Almighty had issued forth His mandate of vengeance. The wind was so terrible that many of our tents were blown down. We were not able to hold them up; but there being an old meeting house close at hand, many of us fled there to secure ourselves from the storm. Many trees were blown down, and others were twisted and wrung like a withe. The mob came to the river two miles from us, but the river had risen to that height that they were obliged to stop without crossing over. The hail fell so heavily upon them that it beat holes in their hats, and in some instances even broke the stocks off their guns; their horses, being frightened, fled, leaving the riders on the ground. Their powder was wet, and it was evident that the Almighty fought in our defense. This night the river raised forty feet (Orson F. Whitney, *Life of Heber C. Kimball, an Apostle: the Father and Founder of the British Mission* [Salt Lake City: Bookcraft, 1974], 52–53; this location was also the site where the revelation known as Doctrine and Covenants 105 was received).

Heber C. Kimball
(Courtesy of the Church Archives, The Church of Jesus Christ of Latter-day Saints)

Wilford Woodruff

When the five men entered the camp there was not a cloud to be seen in the whole heavens, but as the men left the camp there was a small cloud like a black spot appeared in the north west, and it began to unroll itself like a scroll, and in a few minutes the whole heavens were covered with a pall as black as ink. This indicated a sudden storm which soon broke upon us with wind, rain, thunder and lightning and hail. Our beds were soon afloat and our tents blown down over our heads. We all fled into a Baptist meetinghouse. As the Prophet Joseph came in shaking the water from his hat and clothing he said, "Boys, there is some meaning to this. God is in this storm." We sang praises to God, and lay all night on benches under cover while our enemies were in the pelting storm. It was reported that the mob cavalry who fled into the schoolhouse had to hold their horses by the bridles between the logs, but when the heavy hail storm struck them they broke away, skinning the fingers of those who were holding them. The horses fled before the storm and were not found for several days. It was reported that the captain of the company in the schoolhouse said it was a strange thing that they could do nothing against the Mormons but what there must be some hail storm or some other thing to hinder their doing anything, but they did not feel disposed to acknowledge that God was fighting our battles (*History of the Church*, 2:104).

Joseph Smith Jr.

Although threatened by our enemies that we should not pass through Indianapolis, we passed through that city on the 21st unmolested. All the inhabitants were quiet. At night we encamped a few miles west of Indianapolis. There had previously been so many reports that we should never be permitted to pass through this place, and that the governor would have us dispersed, that some of the brethren were afraid that we might have difficulty there. But I had told them, in the name of the Lord, we should not be disturbed and that we would pass through Indianapolis without the people knowing it. When near the place many got into the wagons, and, separating some little distance, passed through the city, while others walked down different streets, leaving the inhabitants wondering "when that big company would come along" (*History of the Church*, 2:70).

Arriving at Jackson County

George A. Smith

(Recounting what happened to one group that threatened the Prophet when Zion's Camp reached Jackson County.)

In the history of our persecutions there have arisen a great many anecdotes; but one will perhaps serve to illustrate the condition in which I wish to see every man that raises in these mountains the hand of oppression upon the innocent. I wish to see such men rigged out with the same honors and comforts as was the honorable Samuel C. Owen,

Commander-in-Chief of the Jackson County mob. He, with eleven men, was engaged at a mass meeting, to raise a mob to drive the Saints from Clay County. This was in the year 1834, in the month of June. They had made speeches, and done everything to raise the indignation of the people against the Saints. In the evening, himself, James Campbell, and nine others, commenced to cross the Missouri river on their way home again; and the Lord, or some accident, knocked a hole in the bottom of the boat. When they discovered it, says Commander Owen to the company on the ferry boat, "We must strip to the bone, or we shall all perish." Mr. Campbell replied, "I will go to hell before I will land naked." He had his choice, and went to the bottom. Owen stripped himself of every article of clothing, and commenced floating down the river. After making several attempts he finally landed on the Jackson side of the river, after a swim of about fourteen miles. He rested some time, being perfectly exhausted, and then started into the nettles, which grow very thick and to a great height, in the Missouri bottoms, and which was his only possible chance in making from the river to the settlements. He had to walk four miles through the nettles, which took him the remainder of the night, and when he got through the nettles, he came to a road, and saw a young lady approaching on horseback, who was the belle of Jackson County. In this miserable condition he laid himself behind a log, so that she could not see him. When she arrived opposite the log, he says, "Madam, I am Samuel C. Owen, the Commander-in-Chief of the mob against the Mormons; I wish you to send some men from the next house with clothing, for I am naked." The lady in her philanthropy dismounted, and left him a light shawl and a certain unmentionable under garment, and passed on. So His Excellency Samuel C. Owen, who was afterwards killed in Mexico by foolishly exposing himself, contrary to orders, took up his line of march for the town, in the shawl and petticoat uniform, after his expedition against the "Mormons."

My young friends, have the goodness to use every man so, who comes into your country to mob and oppress the innocent; and LADIES, DON'T LEND HIM ANY CLOTHING (in *Journal of Discourses*, 26 vols. [London: Latter-day Saints' Book Depot, 1854–86], 2:24).

Joseph Smith Jr.

The tempest of an immediate conflict seemed to be checked, and the Jackson mob to the number of about fifteen, with Samuel C. Owens and James Campbell at their head, started for Independence, Jackson county, to raise an army sufficient to meet me, before I could get into Clay county. Campbell swore, as he adjusted his pistols in his holsters, "The eagles and turkey buzzards shall eat my flesh if I do not fix Joe Smith and his army so that their skins will not hold shucks, before two days are passed." They went to the ferry and undertook to cross the Missouri river after dusk, and the angel of God saw fit to sink the boat about the middle of the river, and seven out of twelve that attempted to cross, were drowned. Thus, suddenly and justly, went they to their own place. Campbell was among the missing. He floated down the river some four or five miles, and lodged upon a pile of drift wood, where the eagles, buzzards, ravens, crows, and wild animals ate his flesh from his bones, to fulfill his own words, and left him a horrible example of God's vengeance. He was discovered about three weeks after by one Mr. Purtle. Owens saved his life only, after floating four miles down the stream, where he lodged upon an island, "swam off naked about day light, borrowed a mantle to hide his shame, and slipped home rather shy of the vengeance of God" (*History of the Church,* 2:99–100).

A Scourge of Cholera Attacks the Camp

Joseph Smith

While we were refreshing ourselves and teams about the middle of the day [June 3], I got up on a wagon wheel, called the people together, and said that I would deliver a prophecy. . . . I said the Lord had revealed to me that a scourge would come upon the camp in consequence of the factious and unruly spirits that appeared among them, and they should die like sheep with the rot; still, if they would repent and humble themselves before the Lord, the scourge, in a great measure, might be turned away; but, as the Lord lives, the members of this camp will suffer for giving way to their unruly temper. . . .

This night [June 24] the cholera burst forth among us, and about midnight it was manifested in its most virulent form. Our ears were saluted with cries and moanings and lamentations on every hand; even those on guard fell to the earth with their guns in their hands, so sudden and powerful was the attack of this terrible disease. At the commencement, I attempted to lay on hands for their recovery, but I quickly learned by painful experience that when the great Jehovah decrees destruction upon any people and makes known His determination, man must not attempt to stay His hand. The moment I attempted to rebuke the disease I was attacked, and had I not desisted in my attempt to save the life of a brother, I would have sacrificed my own. The disease seized upon me like the talons of a hawk, and I said to the brethren: "If my work were done, you would have [had] to put me in the ground without a coffin" (*History of the Church*, 2:80, 114; punctuation standardized).

Heber C. Kimball

When the Cholera first broke out in the camp, Brother John S. Carter was the first who went forth to rebuke it, but he himself, was immediately seized by it, and . . . was the first who was slain. . . . At this scene my feelings were beyond expression. Those only who witnessed it, can realize anything of the nature of our sufferings, and I felt to weep, and pray to the Lord that He would spare my life that I might behold my dear family again. I felt to covenant with my brethren, and I felt in my heart never to commit another sin while I lived. We felt to sit and weep over our brethren, and so great was our sorrow that we could have washed them with our tears, to realize that they had traveled one thousand miles through so much fatigue to lay down their lives for our brethren—and who hath greater love than he who is willing to lay down his life for his brethren? This increased our love to them (*History of the Church*, 2:116).

Joseph Smith Jr.

(Indicating that those who were smitten with cholera were not wicked men. Trials fall on the just as well as on the unjust.)

Brethren, I have seen those men who died of the cholera in our camp; and the Lord knows, if I get a mansion as bright as theirs, I ask no more (*History of the Church*, 2:181).

Harrison Burgess

Brother Joseph received the word of the Lord by revelation, relative to the camp, informing us that we were not to fight at that time; that Zion could not be redeemed then [D&C 105]; and that he had required us to come thus far, as a trial of our faith; that He had accepted of our offering, etc. Some individuals of the camp felt to murmur at this decree, and wanted to fight the enemies of God. Brother Joseph said the Lord would send a scourge upon us in consequence of this unrighteous feeling. The cholera was upon us in a few hours after this prediction, and some eighteen of our brethren fell victims to its grasp. Among the number I attended upon and helped to bury was Brother John S. Carter. My feelings on this occasion can never be described. At length I was violently seized myself, but through faith in God and the kind assistance of Brother Zera H. Cole, I was rescued from the grasp of death. When the camp broke up I received an honorable discharge from Lyman Wight, our commander-in-chief (Harrison Burgess, "Sketch of a Well-spent Life," *Twelfth Book of the Faith Promoting Series* [Salt Lake City: Juvenile Instructor Office, 1884], 66–67).

Observations about Zion's Camp

Lyman Wight
(Courtesy of the Church Archives, The Church of Jesus Christ of Latter-day Saints)

Lyman Wight

[The Prophet] said that he was now willing to return home, that he was fully satisfied that he had done the will of God, and that the Lord had accepted our sacrifice and offering, even as he had Abraham's when he offered his son Isaac; and in his benediction asked the heavenly Father to bless us with eternal life and salvation (*The History of the Reorganized Church of Jesus Christ of Latter Day Saints,* 8 vols. [Independence, Missouri: Herald Publishing House, 1896], 1:515–16).

Wilford Woodruff

(Describing the blessings and leadership training that resulted from Zion's Camp.)

We gained an experience that we never could have gained in any other way. We had the privilege of beholding the face of the prophet, and we had the privilege of traveling a thousand miles with him, and seeing the workings of the Spirit of God with him, and the revelations of Jesus Christ unto him and the fulfillment of those revelations. And he gathered some two hundred elders from throughout the nation in that early day and sent us broadcast into the world to preach the gospel of Jesus Christ. Had I not gone up with Zion's Camp I should not have been here to-day, and I presume that would have been the case with many others in this territory. By going there we were thrust into the vineyard to preach the gospel, and the Lord accepted our labors. And in all our labors and persecutions, with lives often at stake, we have had to work and live by faith (in *Journal of Discourses,* 13:158; capitalization standardized).

Joseph Smith Jr.

Notwithstanding our enemies were continually breathing threats of violence, we did not fear, neither did we hesitate to prosecute our journey, for God was with us, and His angels went before us, and the faith of our little band was unwavering. We know that angels were our companions, for we saw them (*History of the Church,* 2:73).

George A. Smith

The Prophet Joseph took a full share of the fatigues of the entire journey. In addition to the care of providing for the camp and presiding over it, he walked most of the time and had a full proportion of blistered, bloody, and sore feet, which was the natural result of walking from 25 to 40 miles a day in the hot season of the year. But during the entire trip he never uttered a murmur or complaint, while most of the men in the camp complained to him of sore toes, blistered feet, long drives, scanty supply of provisions, poor quality of bread, bad corn dodger, frowzy butter, strong honey, maggoty bacon and cheese, and etc., even a dog could not bark at some men without their murmuring at Joseph. If they had to camp with bad water it would nearly cause rebellion, yet we were the Camp of Zion, and many of us were prayerless, thoughtless, careless, heedless, foolish or devilish, and yet we did not know it. Joseph had to bear with us and tutor us, like children. There were many, however, in the camp who never murmured and who were always ready and willing to do as our leader desired (George A. Smith, "My Journal," *Writings of Early Latter-day Saints and Their Contemporaries, a Database Collection,* comp. Milton V. Backman [Provo, Utah: BYU Religious Studies Center, 1996], 217).

Brigham Young

When I returned from that mission to Kirtland, a brother said to me, "Brother Brigham, what have you gained by this journey?" I replied, "Just what we went for; but I would not exchange the knowledge I have received this season for the whole of Geauga County; for property and mines of wealth are not to be compared to the worth of knowledge" (in *Journal of Discourses,* 2:10).

Joseph Smith Jr.

Brethren, some of you are angry with me, because you did not fight in Missouri; but let me tell you, God did not want you to fight. He could not organize His Kingdom with twelve men to open the Gospel door to the nations of the earth, and with seventy men under their direction to follow in their tracks, unless He took them from a body of men who had offered their lives, and who had made as great a sacrifice as did Abraham. Now the Lord has got His Twelve and His Seventy, and there will be other quorums of Seventies called, who will make the sacrifice, and those who have not made their sacrifices and their offerings now, will make them hereafter (*History of the Church,* 2:182).

3

Priesthood Quorums Organized

In every gospel dispensation God has revealed his priesthood authority. The keys of the priesthood are the rights of presidency, or the power given by God to man to direct and govern God's kingdom on earth. The president of the Church holds all the priesthood keys that have been revealed (D&C 107:65–67, 91–92; 132:7). The calling of president is held by only one man at a time, and he is the only person on earth authorized to exercise all the keys of the priesthood (D&C 107:64–67).

The higher or greater priesthood was initially called the Holy Priesthood, After the Order of the Son of God. However, out of respect for the sacred name of the Son of God, it was later known as the Melchizedek Priesthood (D&C 107:1–4).

President Spencer W. Kimball taught:

> It is a great privilege and blessing to hold the priesthood of God. Priesthood is divine authority bestowed upon worthy men that they might officiate in the ordinances of the gospel. The keys that have been given to those who hold the priesthood have come from heaven, for the priesthood is an everlasting principle that has existed with God from the beginning, and it will exist throughout all eternity. (Spencer W. Kimball, "The Privilege of Holding the Priesthood," in *Priesthood* [Salt Lake City: Deseret Book, 1981], 1)

The priesthood is "a perfect system of government, of laws and ordinances, by which we can be prepared to pass from one gate to another; and from one sentinel to another, until we go into the presence of our

Father and God" (in *Journal of Discourses*, 26 vols. [London: Latter-day Saints' Book Depot, 1854–86], 2:139).

The restoration of priesthood keys, authority and offices is the primary distinguishing feature of The Church of Jesus Christ of Latter-day Saints.

Important Events in the Restoration of the Priesthood and the Organization of the Kingdom of God on Earth

May 15, 1829 (*Harmony, Pennsylvania*): John the Baptist conferred the Aaronic Priesthood on Joseph Smith and Oliver Cowdery by the laying on of hands (D&C 13).

Late May or Early June 1829 (*Fayette, New York*): Peter, James, and John conferred the Melchizedek Priesthood on Joseph Smith and Oliver Cowdery by the laying on of hands (D&C 27:12–13; 128:20; Joseph Smith, *History of The Church of Jesus Christ of Latter-day Saints*, 7 vols., ed. B. H. Roberts [Salt Lake City: Deseret Book, 1980], 1:40–42).

April 6, 1830 (*Fayette, New York*): The Church of Jesus Christ of Latter-day Saints was organized (D&C 20 and 21).

February 4, 1831 (*Kirtland, Ohio*): The first presiding bishop, Edward Partridge, was called and ordained (D&C 41:9).

March 18, 1833: The First Presidency was organized; Joseph Smith Jr., Sidney Rigdon, and Frederick G. Williams were called as Presidents of the High Priesthood (*History of the Church*, 1:334; see also D&C 81:1–3).

December 18, 1833: Joseph Smith Sr. was ordained as the first Patriarch of the church. Prior to this time, the Prophet, Joseph Smith Jr., was serving as Patriarch (Joseph Fielding Smith, *Essentials in Church History* [Salt Lake City: Deseret Book, 1979], 141–42).

February 17, 1834 (*Kirtland, Ohio*): The Church's first stake was organized; Joseph Smith, Sidney Rigdon and Frederick G. Williams were called as the stake presidency (*History of the Church*, 2:28; see also *Essentials in Church History*, 711).

February 14, 1835: The Council of the Twelve Apostles was organized.

February 28, 1835: The first Quorum of the Seventy was organized. They are to be traveling ministers, ready to preach the gospel in all the world, under direction of the Twelve (D&C 107: 25–26, 34).

April 3, 1836: The Savior appeared in the Kirtland Temple. Additional keys of the priesthood were restored by Moses, Elias, and Elijah to Joseph Smith and Oliver Cowdery, by the laying on of hands (D&C 110). Bruce R. McConkie stated of the event:

> Moses committed unto them "the keys of the gathering of Israel from the four parts of the earth, and the leading of the ten tribes from the land of the north." Thus the priesthood was to be used for those purposes.
>
> Elias "committed the dispensation of the gospel of Abraham, saying that in us and our seed all generations after us should be blessed." That is, he brought back the authorization to use the priesthood to perfect eternal family units, even as this commission and covenant was had by Abraham and those who followed after him.
>
> Then Elijah came and restored the sealing power, the power that binds on earth and seals in heaven, the power by which all ordinances have efficacy beyond the grave, the power that turns the hearts of children to their fathers and fathers to their children. It is a power that operates for the living and the dead. (D&C 110:11–16) (Bruce R. McConkie, *The Millennial Messiah* [Salt Lake City: Deseret Book, 1982], 119)

October 1839: The first three wards were organized in Nauvoo, Illinois (*History of the Church*, 4:12).

April 1997: The first Area Authority Seventy Quorum is organized by President Gordon B. Hinckley (D&C 107:98).

Calling of the Twelve and the Seventy

In February 1835, five months after Zion's Camp was disbanded, the Quorum of the Twelve Apostles and the First Quorum of the Seventy were organized. Nine of the Twelve Apostles and all members of the Seventy had served in Zion's Camp.

Some of the Responsibilities of the Twelve

Special Witnesses: "The Twelve traveling councilors are called to be the Twelve Apostles, or special witnesses of the name of Christ in all the world" (D&C 107:23).

Build and Regulate All Affairs of the Church: "The Twelve are . . . under the direction of the Presidency of the Church . . . to build up the church, and regulate all the affairs of the same in all nations" (D&C 107:33).

Proclaim the Gospel: "The Twelve being sent out, holding the keys, to open the door by the proclamation of the gospel of Jesus Christ, and first unto the Gentiles and then unto the Jews" (D&C 107:35).

Direct the Seventy: The Twelve "call upon the Seventy, when they need assistance, to fill the several calls for preaching and administering the gospel" (D&C 107:38).

Ordain and Supervise Church Officers: "It is the duty of the Twelve, also, to ordain and set in order all the other officers of the church" (D&C 107:58).

Joseph Smith Jr.

(Speaking to Brigham Young.)

"I wish you to notify all the brethren living in the branches, within a reasonable distance from this place, to meet at a general conference on Saturday next. I shall then and there appoint twelve Special Witnesses, to open the door of the Gospel to foreign nations, and you . . . will be one of them." . . . Agreeable to his request to Elder Brigham Young, the branches were all notified, and a meeting of the brethren in general conference was held in Kirtland, in the new school house under the printing office, on the following Saturday, February 14th (*History of the Church*, 2:181).

Orson Hyde

Joseph said to me, although I was young, weak, inexperienced, especially in public speaking, and ignorant of many important things which we now all understand, that I should be one of this Twelve. It seemed to me a very great saying. I looked upon the Twelve Apostles who lived in ancient days with a great deal of reverence—as being almost superhuman. They were, indeed, great men—not by virtue of the flesh, nor their own natural capacities, but they were great because God called them. When Joseph told me that I would be one of the Twelve, I knew all things were possible with God, but it seemed to me that I would have to be altogether changed to occupy such a great position in the Church and Kingdom of our God (in *Journal of Discourses,* 12:86).

Nathan Bennett Baldwin

(On being called as a member of the Seventy.)

On the 14th of February [1835], all the members of Zion's Camp that were in that region, were at a meeting called for that purpose, and out of which the Twelve Apostles of the Latter-day work were mostly chosen, and ordained by the three witnesses to the Book of Mormon on that day and the next, which was Sunday, excepting Thomas B. Marsh, Parley P. Pratt and Orson Pratt, who were ordained afterward. These meetings were continued on Saturday and Sunday for some time and after the twelve were ordained, all that were present, seventy others were wholly chosen out of that company and ordained by the presidency of the Church. On the 28th of February [1835], I was (and many more were) ordained into that quorum, one year and ten months from the day I was baptized (Nathan Bennett Baldwin, *Autobiography of Nathan Bennett Baldwin* [LDS Church Archives, The Church of Jesus Christ of Latter-day Saints, Salt Lake City, Utah], n.p.; grammar standardized).

Caroline Crosby

(On the organization of the First Quorum of the Seventy, February 1835.)

I will recollect the sensations with which my mind was actuated when I learned the fact that my husband had been called and ordained to the Melchisedek priesthood and would undoubtedly be required to travel and preach the gospel to the nations of the earth. I realized in some degree the immense responsibility of the office, and besought the Lord for grace and wisdom to be given him that he might be able to magnify his high and holy calling (Caroline Crosby, *Memoirs* [Utah State Historical Society, Salt Lake City, Utah] n.p.; as cited in Kenneth W. Godfrey, Audrey M. Godfrey, and Jill Mulvay Derr, *Women's Voices* [Salt Lake City: Deseret Book, 1982], 48).

William Farrington Cahoon

(The command to priesthood brethren to watch over the Church was further extended in 1830 with the call to visit each family in their homes. William Cahoon humbly accepted the duty to visit the Prophet Joseph and his family.)

I was called and ordained to act as a teacher to visit the families of the Saints. I got along very well till I found that I was obliged to call and pay a visit to the Prophet. Being young, only about seventeen years of age, I felt my weakness in visiting the Prophet and his family in the capacity of a teacher. I almost felt like shrinking from duty. Finally I went to his door and knocked, and in a minute the Prophet came to the door. I stood there trembling, and said to him:

"Brother Joseph, I have come to visit you in the capacity of a teacher, if it is convenient for you."

He said, "Brother William, come right in, I am glad to see you; sit down in that chair there and I will go and call my family in."

They soon came in and took seats. He then said, "Brother William, I submit myself and family into your hands," and then took his seat. "Now Brother William," said he, "ask all the questions you feel like."

By this time all my fears and trembling had ceased, and I said, "Brother Joseph, are you trying to live your religion?"

He answered, "Yes."

I then said, "Do you pray in your family?"

He said, "Yes."

"Do you teach your family the principles of the gospel?"

He replied, "Yes, I am trying to do it."

"Do you ask a blessing on your food?"

He answered, "Yes."

"Are you trying to live in peace and harmony with all your family?"

He said that he was.

I then turned to Sister Emma, his wife, and said, "Sister Emma, are you trying to live your religion? Do you teach your children to obey their parents? Do you try to teach them to pray?"

To all these questions she answered, "Yes, I am trying to do so."

I then turned to Joseph and said, "I am now through with my questions as a teacher; and now if you have any instructions to give, I shall be happy to receive them."

He said, "God bless you, Brother William; and if you are humble and faithful, you shall have power to settle all difficulties that may come before you in the capacity of a teacher."

I then left my parting blessing upon him and his family, as a teacher, and took my departure (William Farrington Cahoon, "Recollection of William Farrington Cahoon," *The Juvenile Instructor* [July 1892]: 492–93; punctuation standardized).

4

The Kirtland Temple

Throughout various gospel dispensations, the Lord has commanded His children to build temples. The children of Israel were commanded to build a tabernacle (Exodus 26:1), King Solomon of old constructed a temple in his day (1 Kings 7:51), and even Nephi's people were directed to raise up a house to the Lord (2 Nephi 5:16), as were the people living at the time of the resurrected Savior's visit in ancient America (3 Nephi 11:1). This commandment was renewed in our dispensation, beginning with the building of the Kirtland temple. While the Saints were in New York, the Lord commanded them to move to Ohio where they would "be endowed with power from on high" (D&C 38:32). Once in Kirtland, the Lord commanded that a lot be dedicated for the work of the ministry "in all things pertaining to the church and kingdom" (D&C 94:3). The design of the Kirtland Temple was shown in vision to Joseph Smith, Sidney Rigdon, and Frederick G. Williams in May 1833. Even though the members of the Church were extremely poor and lacked sufficient laborers and funds, these faithful Saints sacrificed practically everything they owned to build a house to the Lord.

Lucy Mack Smith

Preceding Joseph's return from Missouri, the brethren called a council with the view of investigating the subject of building a meeting-house, to accommodate the increased congregation.

In this council, Joseph requested that each of the brethren should give his views with regard to the house; and when they had all got through, he would give his opinion concerning the matter. They all complied with his request. Some were in favor of building a frame house, but others were of a mind to put up a log house. Joseph reminded them

Lucy Mack Smith
(Courtesy of the Church Archives, The Church of Jesus Christ of Latter-day Saints)

that they were not building a house for a man, but for God; "and shall we, brethren," said he, "build a house for our God, of logs? No, I have a better plan than that. I have a plan of the house of the Lord, given by himself; and you will soon see by this, the difference between our calculations and his idea of things."

He then gave them a full pattern of the house of the Lord at Kirtland, with which the brethren were highly delighted, particularly Hyrum, who was much more animated than if it were designed for himself.

After the close of the meeting, Joseph took the brethren with him, for the purpose of selecting a spot for the building to stand upon. The place which they made choice of was situated in the north-west corner of a field of wheat, which was sown by my sons the fall previous, on the farm upon which we were then living. In a few minutes the fence was removed, and the standing grain was leveled, in order to prepare a place for the building and Hyrum commenced digging a trench for the wall, he having declared that he would strike the first blow upon the house.

On the following Monday, the brethren went to work at the house with great ambition; and although not thirty families of Saints now remained in Kirtland, they never suffered the work to stop until it was accomplished. They had to endure great fatigue and privation, in consequence of the opposition they met with from their enemies, and which was so great, that they were compelled to keep a guard around the walls much of the time until they were completed. They "gave no sleep to their eyes, nor slumber to their eyelids, until they found a place for the Lord, a habitation for the mighty God of Jacob." . . .

There was but one mainspring to all our thoughts and actions, and that was, the building of the Lord's house (Lucy Mack Smith, *History of Joseph Smith by His Mother* [Salt Lake City: Bookcraft, 1958], 230–31; spelling standardized).

Brief History of the Kirtland Temple

December 28, 1832: A revelation is given to Joseph Smith commanding the Saints to "establish . . . a house of God" (D&C 88:119).

May 1832: The Saints are chastised for their delay.

June 3–4, 1833: Joseph Smith, Sidney Rigdon, and Frederick G. Williams see the temple in vision. Later, leading mechanic John Carl, a carriage builder, wants to arrange seats in the temple contrary to Joseph's proposal. Joseph insists on arranging seating according to the vision.

June 5–6, 1833: Construction on the temple begins. George A. Smith hauls the first load of stone; Hyrum Smith and Reynolds Cahoon dig a trench for the walls.

July 23, 1833: Temple cornerstones are laid.

July–August 1833: Joel Hills Johnson begins making bricks for the temple.

September 4, 1833: Temple work makes great progress. Joseph Smith labors with his own hands. Joseph Smith hopes to be finished by spring 1834 so "we can have a place to worship where we shall not be molested" (Joseph Smith, *Personal Writings of Joseph Smith,* ed. Dean C. Jessee [Salt Lake City: Deseret Book, 2002], 319).

September 25, 1833: Members are so poor that "there was not a scraper and hardly a plow that could be obtained among the Saints" to dig the temple's foundation (Benjamin Johnson, *My Life's Review* [Mesa, Arizona: Lofgreen Printing Co., 1979], 16).

October 10, 1833: Temple construction is discontinued for the winter due to lack of materials. Workers plan to recommence in early spring.

Summer 1834: Zion's Camp interrupts temple construction. The departure of Zion's Camp leaves a small number of men in Kirtland, including a few to work on the temple. Those who remain in Kirtland are required to work on the temple one day of each week.

Fall 1834: The temple walls reach four feet high.

Fall–Winter 1833–34: Men stand guard at night to protect temple walls from the threats of mob violence. The temple walls are still under construction.

January 21, 1835: John Tanner arrives in Kirtland on January 20 in answer to Joseph Smith's prayer. The next day, Tanner loans Joseph Smith $2,000 to keep the mortgage from foreclosing and later loans $13,000 to the temple committee.

November 1835: The exterior plastering begins.

November 9, 1835: The interior plastering is begun by Jacob Bump. Artemus Millet and Lorenzo Young are engaged in exterior plastering and finishing. They endure extremely cold weather, and Young contracts consumption.

December 10–13, 1835: The kiln that prepares wood for the temple catches fire on these days; considerable lumber is lost.

February 1836: The temple's interior is finished.

January 21–May 1, 1836: The Saints experience great spiritual outpouring in Kirtland, similar to the day of Pentecost.

January 21–22, 1836: Revelations, the ministering of angels and visions, including one of the face of Christ, occur. Joseph Smith receives a vision of the celestial kingdom (D&C 137).

February 6, 1836: Priesthood meeting is held in the temple; some participants see visions (*Personal Writings of Joseph Smith*, 185–87).

March 27, 1836: The Kirtland temple is dedicated (D&C 109).

March 29–30, 1836: All-day, all-night fast meetings are held. Some see the Savior, while others are ministered to by angels.

March 31, 1836: Another dedicatory ceremony is held for those who, due to space constraints in the temple, were unable to attend the first dedication.

April 3, 1836: The Savior Jesus Christ, Moses, Elias, and Elijah appear and restore priesthood keys to Joseph Smith and Oliver Cowdery (D&C 110).

December 1, 1836: Joseph Smith Sr. gives patriarchal blessings in the temple.

April 7, 1837: Night meeting is held, in which the gift of prophecy is present. Holy Ghost "was like fire . . . shut up in our bones" (Dean

C. Jessee, "The Kirtland Diary of Wilford Woodruff," *BYU Studies* [Summer 1972]: 392–93; punctuation and capitalization standardized).

April 20, 1837: During temple service, members receive the gift of tongues and the interpretation of tongues.

June 1837: Heber C. Kimball prays daily in attic of temple in preparation for his mission to England.

September 18, 1837: Before leaving Kirtland, Joseph Smith and Sidney Rigdon hold a farewell meeting in the temple.

September 1845: Apostates led by Jacob Bump break into the temple and take possession of it.

1846–48: Brigham Young decides to sell the temple in order to save it from vandalism and attack, but Almon Babbitt is unable to carry out this assignment. A title to the temple is filed in the names of several trustees-in-trust for the Church and recorded in Painesville, Ohio.

About 1850: The temple is used as a community hall.

1862: Russell Huntley buys the temple for $150.

1866: By this date, much of the interior woodwork and ornamentation has been broken up and stripped by curiosity hunters.

1869: Martin Harris serves as a temple custodian and spends his days on temple grounds, bearing testimony to the truthfulness of the Book of Mormon to those who visit the site. The temple keys are held by a Mr. Bond.

August 1870: The temple is in poor condition. Martin Harris leaves Kirtland.

1873: Russell Huntley sells the temple to Joseph Smith III and Mark Forscutt for $150.

September 1874: A civic meeting is held in the lower court of the temple and a banquet in the upper court.

August 13, 1904: Lightning strikes the temple tower, damaging the belfry and roof.

1955: A new cement finish is applied to the exterior walls.

1977: The temple is designated a National Historic Landmark by the U.S. Department of the Interior and U.S. Park Service.

November 6, 1993: The first LDS meeting is held in the Kirtland Temple since the Saints departed Kirtland in 1837.

The Commandment to Build the Temple

Joseph Smith Jr.

(In a letter to William W. Phelps, January 11, 1833.)

You will see that the Lord commanded us, in Kirtland, to build a house of God, . . . this is the word of the Lord to us, and we must, yea, the Lord helping us, we will obey . . . He has promised us great things; yea, even a visit from the heavens to honor us with His own presence (Joseph Smith, *History of The Church of Jesus Christ of Latter-day Saints,* 7 vols., ed. B. H. Roberts [Salt Lake City: Deseret Book, 1964], 1:316).

Brigham Young

The Church, through our beloved Prophet Joseph, was commanded to build a Temple to the Most High, in Kirtland, Ohio, and this was the next House of the Lord we hear of on the earth, since the days of Solomon's Temple. Joseph not only received revelation and commandment to build a Temple, but he received a *pattern* also, as did Moses for the Tabernacle, and Solomon for his Temple; for without a pattern, he could not know what was wanting, having never seen one, and not having experienced its use (in *Journal of Discourses,* 26 vols. [London: Latter-day Saints' Book Depot, 1854–86], 2:31).

Truman O. Angell

I here desire to mention a few more items in connection with the [Kirtland] Temple. The work on the lower hall went on to the finishing of the stands and pews or slips, plastering and painting complete.

About this time Frederick G. Williams, one of President Smith's counselors, came into the temple when the following dialogue took place in my presence: Carpenter Rolph said, "Doctor, what do you think of the House?" He answered, "It looks to me like the pattern precisely." He then related the following:

"Joseph received the word of the Lord for him to take his two counselors, [Frederick G.] Williams and [Sidney] Rigdon, and come before the Lord and He would show them the plan or model of the house to be built. We went upon our knees, called on the Lord, and the building [the Kirtland Temple] appeared within viewing distance. I being the first to discover it. Then all of us viewed it together. After we had taken a good look at the exterior, the building seemed to come right over us, and the makeup of this hall seemed to coincide with what I there saw to a minutia."

Joseph was accordingly enabled to dictate to the mechanics and his counselors stood as witnesses, and this was strictly necessary in order to satisfy the spirit of unbelief in consequence of the weakness or childishness of the brethren of those days. The following are a few items which transpired about this time. One I will note:

Joseph came into the hall. The leading mechanic, John Carl, by profession a carriage builder, wanted to seat the house contrary to what Joseph had proposed. Joseph answered him that he had seen the inside of every building that had been built unto the Lord upon this earth and he hated to have to say so. Under such childlike feeling, they prepared to dedicate the lower hall. The hall was filled at an early hour in the afternoon, I being present among the rest. The dedicatory prayer was offered, Sidney Rigdon being mouth.

When about midway during the prayer, there was a glorious sensation passed through the house; and we, having our heads bowed in prayer, felt a sensation very elevating to the soul. At the close of the prayer, F. [Frederick] G. Williams being in the upper east stand—Joseph being in the speaking stand next below—rose and testified that midway during the prayer an holy angel came and seated himself in the stand. When the afternoon meeting assembled, Joseph, feeling very much elated, arose the first thing and said the personage who had appeared in the morning was the Angel Peter come to accept the dedication (Truman O. Angell, "Autobiography, Our Pioneer Heritage," *Writings of Early Latter-day Saints and Their Contemporaries, a Database Collection,* comp. Milton V. Backman [Provo, Utah: BYU Religious Studies Center, 1996], 197–98).

Sacrifices Made to Build the Kirtland Temple

Eliza R. Snow

At that time . . . the Saints were few in number, and most of them very poor; and, had it not been for the assurance that God had spoken, and had commanded that a house should be built to his name, of which he not only revealed the form, but also designated the dimensions, an attempt towards building that Temple, under the then existing circumstances, would have been, by all concerned, pronounced preposterous (Eliza R. Snow, *Eliza R. Snow, An Immortal: Selected Writings of Eliza R. Snow* [Salt Lake City: Nicholas G. Morgan Sr., Foundation, 1957], 54).

Brigham Young

Without commandment, the Church were too few in numbers, too weak in faith, and too poor in purse, to attempt such a mighty enterprise. But by means of all these stimulants, a mere handful of men, living on air, and a little hominy [dried corn] and milk, and often salt or no salt when milk could not be had; the great Prophet Joseph, in the stone quarry, quarrying rock with his own hands; and the few then in the Church, following his example of obedience and diligence wherever most needed; with laborers on the walls, holding the sword in one hand to protect themselves from the mob, while they placed the stone and moved the trowel with the other, the Kirtland Temple . . . was so far completed as to be dedicated (in *Journal of Discourses,* 2:31).

Heber C. Kimball

Joseph said, "Come, brethren, let us go into the stone-quarry and work for the Lord." And the Prophet went himself, in his tow frock and tow breeches, and worked at quarrying stone like the rest of us. Then, every Saturday we brought out every team to draw stone to the Temple, and so we continued until that house was finished (in *Journal of Discourses,* 10:165).

Heber C. Kimball

After we returned from our journey to the west, the whole church united in this undertaking and every man lent a helping hand. Those who had no teams went to work in the stone quarry and prepared the stones for drawing to the house. President Joseph Smith Jr. being our foreman in the quarry. The Presidency, High Priests, and Elders all alike assisting.—Those who had teams assisted in drawing the stone to the house. These all laboring one day in the week, brought as many stones to the house as supplied the masons through the whole week. We continued in this manner until the walls of the house were reared (Heber C. Kimball, "History of Joseph Smith," *Times and Seasons* [April 15, 1845]: 867–68).

Daniel Tyler

How often have I seen those humble, faithful servants of the Lord, after toiling all day in the quarry, or on the building, when the walls were in course of erection, weary and faint, yet with cheerful countenances, retiring to their homes with a few pounds of corn meal that had been donated. And in the case of those who lacked a cow to give a little milk, the corn meal was sometimes for days together, all that they and their families had to subsist upon. When a little flour, butter, or meat came in, they were luxuries (as cited in Levi Edgar Young, "Joseph Smith—Prophet," *Improvement Era* [December 1947]: 799).

Lorenzo Young

(Winter 1835–36)

It was then the last of November, and the weather daily grew colder. A Brother Stillman assisted me a day or two, but said that he could not stand the cold, and quit the work. I continued, day after day, determined, if possible, to complete the job. When I got badly chilled I went into my house, warmed myself and returned again to the work.

I completed the task in the fore part of December, but was sick the last two days. I had caught a bad cold, had a very severe cough, and, in a few days was confined to my bed.

My disease was pronounced to be the quick consumption. I sank rapidly for six or seven weeks. For two weeks I was unable to talk (Lorenzo

Young, "Removal to Kirtland," *Fragments of Experience: Faith-Promoting Series*, 6 vols. [Salt Lake City: Juvenile Instructor Office, 1882], 6:43).

Erastus Snow

Joseph Smith and Brigham Young worked on that building day after day; also, many others did so. They did not have molasses to eat with their johnny cake. Sometimes they had shoes, and sometimes not; sometimes they would have tolerable pants, and, sometimes, very ragged ones (Andrew Karl Larson, *Erastus Snow* [Salt Lake City: The University of Utah Press, 1971], 466).

Erastus Snow
(Courtesy of the Church Archives, The Church of Jesus Christ of Latter-day Saints)

Heber C. Kimball

(Speaking of Sidney Rigdon.)

Looking at the sufferings and poverty of the church, he frequently used to go upon the walls of the building both by night and day and frequently wetting the walls with his tears, crying aloud to the Almighty to send means whereby we might accomplish the building ("History of Joseph Smith," 867).

Artemus Millet and the Kirtland Temple

Brigham Young was given a special mission [by the Prophet Joseph Smith] to go to Canada and baptize Bro. Artemus Millet, . . . which call resulted from a consultation held at Kirtland respecting the building of the Temple there, and as to who they could get that was capable of taking charge of the work. When Elder Lorenzo Young exclaimed to the Prophet "I know the very man who is capable of doing this work," "Who is he?" asked the Prophet. Lorenzo replied ["It] is Artemus Millet." The Prophet turned to Brigham and said "I give you a mission to go to Canada and baptize Brother Artemus Millet, and bring him here. Tell him to bring a thousand dollars with him." Artemus was much surprised when Brigham announced his mission to him and [he] asked "What kind of a church is that?" Then Brigham explained the principles of the Gospel to him and he accepted and was baptized ("A Brief

History of Artemus Millet," *Millet Family History* [LDS Church Archives, The Church of Jesus Christ of Latter-day Saints, Salt Lake City, Utah], 70–71; as cited in Karl Ricks Anderson, *Joseph Smith's Kirtland* [Salt Lake City: Deseret Book, 1989], 15–16; spelling standardized).

Heber C. Kimball

While we were building the Temple, in Kirtland . . . we were persecuted and were under the necessity of laying upon the floor with our firelocks by our sides to sustain ourselves, as there were mobs gathering all around us to destroy us, and prevent us from building the Temple. And when they were driven, every man that was in the church, arose, and we took our firelocks, to reinstate our brethren, and in the night we laid upon the floor; we laid upon Brother Joseph's floor, and upon Sidney Rigdon's floor, so as to be ready to keep our enemies at bay ("History of Joseph Smith," 972).

Joseph Smith Jr.

(January 1836)

Elder Roger Orton saw a mighty angel riding upon a horse of fire, with a flaming sword in his hand, followed by five others, encircle the house, and protect the Saints, even the Lord's anointed, from the power of Satan and a host of evil spirits, which were striving to disturb the Saints (*History of the Church*, 2:386–87).

Oliver B. Huntington

(The Saints who gathered to Kirtland after the temple was built were struck with awe at the sight.)

O, what joy again came over every one of us as we came in sight of the temple. "The Lord's House," solemnly exclaimed every one, as we were trudging along in a confused flock. It makes me think of tribes going up to Jerusalem to worship, [as] anciently (Oliver B. Huntington, *Diary of Oliver B. Huntington Part I (1842–47)* [L. Tom Perry Special Collections, Harold B. Lee Library, Brigham Young University, Provo, Utah], 27; punctuation and capitalization standardized).

THE SISTERS' SACRIFICES TO HELP BUILD THE KIRTLAND TEMPLE

Heber C. Kimball

Our women were engaged in spinning and knitting in order to clothe those who were laboring at the building, and the Lord only knows the scenes of poverty, tribulation, and distress which we passed through in order to accomplish this thing. My wife toiled all summer in lending her aid towards its accomplishment. She had a hundred pounds of wool, which, with the assistance of a girl, she spun in order to furnish clothing for those engaged in the building of the Temple, and although she had the privilege of keeping half the quantity of wool for herself, as a recompense for her labor, she did not reserve even so much as would make her a pair of stockings; but gave it for those who were laboring at the house of the Lord. She spun and wove and got the cloth dressed, and cut and made up into garments, and gave them to those men who labored on the Temple; almost all the sisters in Kirtland labored in knitting, sewing, spinning, &c., for the purpose of forwarding the work of the Lord ("History of Joseph Smith," 867).

Aroet Hale

The Prophet required all the Church to work on the temple. All that was not on missions did work all most constant from the time it was commenced till it was completed. Some women and children labored and tended mason. One sister I have forgot the name [of] drove two yoke of cattle and hauled rock (Aroet Hale, "Reminiscences," *First Book or Journal of the Life and Travels of Aroet L. Hale* [LDS Church Archives, The Church of Jesus Christ of Latter-day Saints, Salt Lake City, Utah], 4; as cited in Elwin C. Robison, *The First Mormon Temple: Design, Construction, and Historic Context of the Kirtland Temple* [Provo, Utah: Brigham Young University Press, 1997], 47; spelling, punctuation and capitalization standardized).

Joseph Smith

This afternoon the sisters met again at the Temple to work on the veil.

Towards the close of the day I met with the Presidency and many of the brethren in the house of the Lord, and made some remarks from the pulpit upon the rise and progress of the Church of Christ of Latter-day Saints, and pronounced a blessing upon the sisters, for their liberality in giving their services so cheerfully, to make the veil for the Lord's House (*History of the Church*, 2:399).

Joseph Smith Jr.

(As quoted by Polly Angell.)

Well, sisters, . . . you are always on hand. The sisters are always first and foremost in all good works. Mary was first at the resurrection; and the sisters now are the first to work on the inside of the temple (Edward W. Tullidge, *The Women of Mormondom* [New York: n.p., 1877], 76).

Artemus Millet

When the wall of the Temple was finished, [Artemus] sent men and boys to the different towns and places to gather old crockery and glass to put in the cement which [he] had invented. Not that glass and crockery had any adhesive property but it had its use. . . . Many ladies would smooth their hands over the plaster, which looked so smooth, then look at their hands and tell where the fine glass had cut them and made them bleed (as cited in *Joseph Smith's Kirtland*, 163).

Elizabeth Ann Whitney

(Like many sisters, Elizabeth was separated from her husband for short periods of time while he was called away on missions or to serve in other priesthood callings.)

Elizabeth Ann Whitney
(Courtesy of the Church Archives, The Church of Jesus Christ of Latter-day Saints)

During all these absences and separations from my husband I never felt to murmur or complain in the least . . . I was more than satisfied to have him give all, time, talents and ability into the service of the Kingdom of God; and the change in our circumstances and associations which were consequent upon our embracing the Gospel, never caused me a moment's sorrow. I looked upon it as a real pleasure to give all for the sake of my faith in the religion of Jesus, considering all as naught in comparison with the example of our blessed Savior (Elizabeth Ann Whitney, "A Leaf From an Autobiography," *Women's Exponent* [October 1, 1878]: 71).

Spiritual Manifestations in the Kirtland Temple

Before the temple was formally dedicated, the Saints began holding meetings in the unfinished building. Beginning in January 1836, continuing through the dedication of the Kirtland Temple in March and for several weeks following, there came a season of spiritual manifestations to the Saints at Kirtland. Numerous Saints recounted miraculous events and visions that occurred, including incidents of beholding the Savior and angels.

Wilford Woodruff

[I] repaired to the house of the Lord where Father Smith met a number of Saints to pronounce upon them a patriarchal blessing. This was the first meeting of the kind that I ever attended and I found it to be highly edifying and interesting as there was great and glorious things pronounced upon their heads by the spirit of prophesy and revelation (Wilford Woodruff, *Wilford Woodruff's Journal,* 9 vols., ed. Scott G. Kenney [Midvale, Utah: Signature Books, 1983], 1:110; spelling and capitalization standardized).

Lorenzo Snow

(Recalling how he was impressed with the patriarchal blessings being given, even though he was not yet a member of the Church.)

I listened with astonishment to him telling the brethren and sisters their parentage, their lineage, and other things which I could not help but believe he knew nothing about, save as the Spirit manifested them unto him. After listening to several patriarchal blessings pronounced upon the heads of different individuals with whose history I was acquainted, and of whom I knew the Patriarch was entirely ignorant, I was struck with astonishment to hear the peculiarities of those persons positively and plainly referred to in their blessings. I was convinced that an influence, superior to human prescience, dictated his words (LeRoi C. Snow, "How Lorenzo Snow Found God," *Improvement Era* [January 1937]: 84).

History of the Church

Another series of remarkable visions occurred in the Kirtland Temple on 6 February while Joseph Smith was again instructing the priesthood concerning sealing. On this occasion, the high priests and elders met again in the west room of the temple's top floor, the seventies and the twelve in the second room, and bishops in the east room. On that night the Prophet told the priesthood members the precise order God had shown him concerning the sealing of their blessings. First, he said, the men should engage in solemn prayer. President Sidney Rigdon was to offer the sealing prayer, after which "all the quorums were to shout with one accord a solemn hosanna to God and the Lamb," followed by three amens. Then all were to "take seats and lift up their hearts in silent prayer to God." If anyone beheld a vision or received a prophecy, that individual, he advised, should "rise and speak" so that all might rejoice and be edified. Some of the elders did not comply with these specific instructions, evidently believing that the precise order and wording were not essential. Consequently, the Prophet observed, "this caused the Spirit of the Lord to withdraw," depriving the quorum members of blessings they otherwise might have received. Members of other quorums followed the instructions and enjoyed a great flow of the Holy Spirit. "Many arose and spoke, testifying that they were filled with the Holy Ghost, which was like fire in their bones, so that they could not hold their peace, but were constrained to cry hosanna to God and the Lamb, and glory in the highest," the Prophet declared. He also affirmed that William Smith saw in vision the Twelve Apostles laboring in England; Zebedee Coltrin saw a vision of the Lord's host; and others, filled with the Spirit of God, spoke in tongues and prophesied. "This was a time of rejoicing," he concluded, "long to be remembered" (*History of the Church*, 2:391–92).

Eliza R. Snow

On [fast] days, Father Smith (the Prophet's father) was in the habit of entering the Temple very early in the morning, and there offering up his prayers to God, in that holy place, before the rising of the sun, after having told the Saints, publicly, that they were welcome to come as early as they pleased. The result was that many assembled before the hour of 10 A.M., and did not leave till after 4 P.M. . . .

The Saints were humble, and through our united faith, the Spirit of God was poured out in copious effusion, and, for one hour, we enjoyed Pentecostal refreshings from on high. On these occasions the gifts of the Gospel were powerfully manifest—speaking and singing in tongues, the interpretation of tongues, the gift of healing and of prophecy, were freely exercised. . . .

Father Smith presided over the meeting in the northwest section of the Temple, and after the meeting was opened by singing, he was mouth in prayer, and in course of supplication he very earnestly prayed that the Spirit of God might be poured out as on the day of Pentecost—that it might come "as a rushing mighty wind." Some time after, in the midst of the exercises of the forenoon, it did come; and whether Father Smith had forgotten what he had prayed for, or whether in the fervency of his heart, when praying he did not realize what he prayed for, I never ascertained; but when the sound came and filled the house, with an expression of great astonishment he raised his eyes, exclaiming, "What! Is the house on fire?" (Eliza R. Snow Smith, *Biography and Family Record of Lorenzo Snow* [Salt Lake City: Deseret News Company, 1884], 12–14; capitalization standardized).

Prescindia Huntington

I was in the temple with my sister Zina. The whole of the congregation were on their knees, praying vocally, for such was the custom at the close of these meetings when Father Smith presided; yet there was no confusion; the voices of the congregation mingled softly together. While the congregation was thus praying, we both heard, from one corner of the room above our heads, a choir of angels singing most beautifully. They were invisible to us, but myriads of angelic voices seemed to be united in singing some song of Zion, and their sweet harmony filled the temple of God.

We were also in the temple at the pentecost. In the morning Father Smith prayed for a pentecost, in opening the meeting. That day the power of God rested mightily upon the saints. There was poured out upon us abundantly the spirit of revelation, prophecy and tongues. The Holy Ghost filled the house; and along in the afternoon a noise was heard. It was the sound of a mighty rushing wind (*The Women of Mormondom,* 207–8; spelling standardized).

Prescindia Huntington

A little girl came to my door and in wonder called me out, exclaiming, "The meeting is on the top of the meetinghouse!" I went to the door, and there I saw on the temple angels clothed in white covering the roof from end to end. They seemed to be walking to and fro; they appeared and disappeared. The third time they appeared and disappeared before I realized that they were not mortal men. Each time in a moment they vanished, and their reappearance was the same. This was in broad daylight, in the afternoon. A number of the children in Kirtland saw the same.

When the brethren and sisters came home in the evening, they told of the power of God manifested in the temple that day, and of the prophesying and speaking in tongues. It was also said, in the interpretation of tongues, "That the angels were resting down upon the house" (*The Women of Mormondom,* 207).

Joseph Smith Jr.

I left the meeting in the charge of the Twelve, and retired about nine o'clock in the evening. The brethren continued exhorting, prophesying, and speaking in tongues until five o'clock in the morning. The Savior made His appearance to some, while angels ministered to others, and it was a Pentecost and an endowment indeed, long to be remembered, for the sound shall go forth from this place into all the world, and the occurrences of this day shall be handed down upon the pages of sacred history, to all generations; as the day of Pentecost, so shall this day be numbered and celebrated as a year of jubilee, and time of rejoicing to the Saints of the Most High God (*History of the Church,* 2:432–33; March 30, 1836).

Prescindia Huntington

A cousin of ours came to visit us at Kirtland. She wanted to go to one of the saints' fast meetings to hear some one sing or speak in tongues, but she said she expected to have a hearty laugh.

Accordingly we went with our cousin to the meeting, during which a Brother McCarter rose and sang a song of Zion in tongues; I arose and sang simultaneously with him the same tune and words, beginning and ending each verse in perfect unison, without varying a word. It was just as though we had sung it together a thousand times. After we came out of meeting, our cousin observed, "Instead of laughing, I never felt so solemn in my life" (*Women in Mormondom*, 208–9).

Joseph Smith Jr.

The visions of heaven were opened to them [those in attendance] also. Some of them saw the face of the Savior, and others were ministered unto by holy angels, and the spirit of prophecy and revelation was poured out in mighty power; and loud hosannas, and glory to God in the highest, saluted the heavens, for we all communed with the heavenly host. And I saw in my vision all of the Presidency in the celestial kingdom of God, and many others that were present. Our meeting was opened by singing, and prayer was offered up by the head of each quorum; and closed by singing, and invoking the benediction of heaven, with uplifted hands. Retired between one and two o'clock in the morning (*History of the Church*, 2:382; January 28, 1836).

KIRTLAND TEMPLE DEDICATION

After years of anxious anticipation and sacrifice, the first Latter-day Saint temple was completed in Kirtland, Ohio, in 1836. The spiritual manifestations that had begun in the days just prior to the completion of the temple continued throughout the dedication on March 27th.

Karl Ricks Anderson

The dedicatory services began at nine o'clock with Sidney Rigdon, a counselor in the First Presidency, reading Psalms 96 and 24. A choir then sang the hymn "Ere Long the Veil Will Rend in Twain," after which President Rigdon offered the invocation. This was followed by a song by the congregation, "O Happy Souls, Who Pray Where God Appoints to Hear." Then President Rigdon spoke for two and a half hours, using as his text Matthew, chapter 8, verses 18–20. He emphasized the Savior's comment that "the foxes have holes, and the birds of the air have nests, but the Son of man hath not where to lay his head." According to Eliza R. Snow, although it was a lengthy sermon, it was eloquent and moving. "At one point," she said, "as he reviewed the toils and privations of those who had labored in rearing the walls of that sacred edifice, he drew tears from many eyes, saying, there were those who had wet those walls with their tears, when, in the silent shades of the night, they were praying to the God of heaven to protect them, and stay the unhallowed hands of ruthless spoilers, who had uttered a prophecy, when the foundation was laid, that the walls should never be erected."

Following President Rigdon's talk, Joseph Smith was sustained as a prophet and seer, first by the priesthood quorums and then by the congregation. This part of the service concluded with the choir and congregation standing to sing "Now Let Us Rejoice in the Day of Salvation." An intermission of about fifteen or twenty minutes followed, during which most people remained in the building. The service then continued with another song, "This Earth Was Once a Garden Place," also known as "Adam-ondi-Ahman." After a few brief remarks by Joseph Smith, the congregation sustained various officers of the Church and then sang another song, "How Pleased and Blessed Was I."

Joseph Smith then read the dedicatory prayer, which had been revealed to him. This prayer [is] recorded in section 109 of the Doctrine and Covenants . . . Following the dedicatory prayer, the choir sang a hymn written by William W. Phelps.

After the song, the quorums accepted the dedicatory prayer and the sacrament was passed to members of the Church. Then Joseph Smith, Don Carlos Smith, Oliver Cowdery, Frederick G. Williams, and David Whitmer bore their testimonies. After some remarks by Hyrum Smith and Sidney Rigdon and a short prayer by Sidney Rigdon, the congregation gave the Hosanna Shout, shouting three times, "Hosanna, hosanna,

hosanna to God and the Lamb." Each series of hosannas ended with three amens. Brigham Young then arose and spoke briefly in tongues while David W. Patten interpreted, and David W. Patten delivered a short exhortation in tongues. At about four o'clock, the Prophet concluded the seven-hour dedicatory service by blessing the congregation (*Joseph Smith's Kirtland*, 179–82; punctuation standardized).

Eliza R. Snow

The ceremonies of that dedication may be rehearsed, but no mortal language can describe the heavenly manifestations of that memorable day. Angels appeared to some, while a sense of divine presence was realized by all present, and each heart was filled with "joy inexpressible and full of glory" (*Women of Mormondom*, 95).

Joseph Smith Jr.

All the congregation simultaneously arose, being moved upon by an invisible power; many began to speak in tongues and prophesy; others saw glorious visions; and I beheld the Temple was filled with angels, which fact I declared to the congregation. The people of the neighborhood came running together (hearing an unusual sound within, and seeing a bright light like a pillar of fire resting upon the Temple), and were astonished at what was taking place (*History of the Church*, 2:428).

Heber C. Kimball

During the ceremonies of the dedication, an angel appeared and sat near President Joseph Smith, Sen., and Frederick G. Williams, so that they had a fair view of his person. He was a very tall personage, black eyes, white hair, and stoop shouldered; his garment was whole, extending to near his ankles; on his feet he had sandals. He was sent as a messenger to accept of the dedication. [This messenger was identified by Joseph as Peter, the apostle] (Orson F. Whitney, *The Life of Heber C. Kimball* [Salt Lake City: Deseret Book, 2001], 90–91; see also Truman O. Angell, *Journal* [L. Tom Perry Special Collections, Harold B. Lee Library, Brigham Young University, Provo, Utah], 5).

Joseph Smith Jr.

(January 28, 1836)

Elder Roger Orton saw a mighty angel riding upon a horse of fire . . .

President William Smith, one of the Twelve, saw the heavens opened, and the Lord's host protecting the Lord's anointed. . . .

I retired to my home, filled with the Spirit, and my soul cried hosanna to God and the Lamb, through the silent watches of the night; and while my eyes were closed in sleep, the visions of the Lord were sweet unto me, and His glory was round about me (*History of the Church*, 2:386–87).

Harrison Burgess

(January 28, 1836)

The Lord blessed His people abundantly in that Temple with the Spirit of prophecy, the ministering of angels, visions, etc. I will here relate a vision which was shown to me. It was near the close of the endowments. I was in a meeting for instruction in the upper part of the Temple, with about a hundred of the High Priests, Seventies and Elders. The Saints felt to shout "Hosanna!" and the Spirit of God rested upon me in mighty power and I beheld the room lighted up with a peculiar light such as I had never seen before. It was soft and clear and the room looked to me as though it had neither roof nor floor to the building and I beheld the Prophet Joseph and Hyrum Smith and Roger Orton enveloped in the light: Joseph exclaimed aloud, "I behold the Savior, the Son of God." Hyrum said, "I behold the angels of heaven." Brother Orton exclaimed, "I behold the chariots of Israel." All who were in the room felt the power of God to that degree that many prophesied, and the power of God was made manifest, the remembrance of which will remain with me while I live upon the earth (Harrison Burgess, *Sketch of a Well-Spent Life* [Salt Lake City: Juvenile Instructor Office, 1883], 67).

Nancy Tracy

(She wrote the following concerning her experience at the dedication of the temple.)

Nancy Tracy
(Courtesy of the Church Archives, The Church of Jesus Christ of Latter-day Saints)

They were two of the happiest days of my life . . . It was verily true that the Heavenly Influence rested down upon that house . . . Heavenly beings appeared to many. Solemn assemblies were called. Endowments were given. The Elders went from house to house, blessing the Saints and administering the sacrament. Feasts were given. Three families joined together and held one at our house. We baked a lot of bread and had the best of wine (Nancy Naomi Alexander Tracy, *Diary. Incidents, Travels, and Life of Nancy Naomi Alexander Tracy, Including Many Important Events in Church History* [Provo, Utah: Brigham Young University, 1960], n.p.).

Oliver Cowdery

Sunday, the 27th attended on the dedication of the Lord's house . . . In the evening, I met with the officers of the church in the Lord's House. The Spirit was poured out—I saw the glory of God, like a great cloud, come down and rest upon the house, and fill the same like a mighty rushing wind. I also saw cloven tongues, like as of fire, rest upon many (for there were 316 present), while they spake with other tongues and prophesied (Leonard J. Arrington, "Oliver Cowdery's Sketch Book," *BYU Studies* [Summer 1972]: 426; punctuation standardized).

Sylvia Cutler Webb

One of my earliest recollections was the dedication of the Temple. My father took us up on his lap and told us why we were going and what it meant to dedicate a house to God. And although so very young at that time, I clearly remember the occasion. I can look back through the lapse of years and see as I saw then Joseph the Prophet, standing with his hands raised towards heaven, his face ashy pale, the tears running down his cheeks as he spoke on that memorable day. Almost all seemed to be in tears. The house was so crowded the children were mostly sitting on older people's laps; my sister sat on father's, I on my mother's lap. I can even remember the dresses we wore. My mind was too young at that time to grasp the full significance of it all, but as time passed it dawned more and more upon me, and I am very grateful that I was privileged to be there (*Saints' Herald* [March 24, 1915]: 289; as cited in *Joseph Smith's Kirtland,* 182–83).

George A. Smith

There were great manifestations of power, such as speaking in tongues, seeing visions, administration of angels. Many individuals bore testimony that they saw angels, and David Whitmer bore testimony that he saw three angels passing up the south aisle, and there came a shock on the house like the sound of a mighty rushing wind, and almost every man in the house arose, and hundreds of them were speaking in tongues, prophesying or declaring visions, almost with one voice (in *Journal of Discourses,* 11:10).

Lorenzo Snow

There we had the gift of prophecy—the gift of tongues—the interpretation of tongues—visions and marvelous dreams were related—the singing of heavenly choirs was heard, and wonderful manifestations of the healing power, through the administrations of the Elders, were witnessed. The sick were healed—the deaf made to hear—the blind to see and the lame to walk, in very many instances. It was plainly manifest that a sacred and divine influence—a spiritual atmosphere pervaded that holy edifice (*Biography and Family Record of Lorenzo Snow,* 11).

Zebedee Coltrin

(Courtesy of the Church Archives, The Church of Jesus Christ of Latter-day Saints)

Zebedee Coltrin

In [the] Kirtland Temple, I have seen the power of God as it was in the day of Pentecost! And cloven tongues as of fire have rested on the brethren and they have spoken with other tongues as the spirit gave them utterance. I saw the Lord, high and lifted up, and frequently throng the solemn assemblies; the angels of God rested on the temple, and we heard their voices singing heavenly music (Zebedee Coltrin, "Address, Spanish Fork High Priest Quorum, February 5, 1870," *Writings of Early Latter-day Saints*, 103; capitalization and punctuation standardized).

Orson Pratt

God was there, his angels were there, the Holy Ghost was in the midst of the people, the visions of the Almighty were opened to the minds of the servants of the living God; the veil was taken off from the minds of many; they saw the heavens opened; they beheld the angels of God; they heard the voice of the Lord; and they were filled from the crown of their heads to the soles of their feet with the power and inspiration of the Holy Ghost, and uttered forth prophecies in the midst of that congregation, which have been fulfilling from that day to the present time (in *Journal of Discourses*, 18:132).

George A. Smith

(Some Church members became offended by the actions of other members and allowed an offense to fester until they were led into apostasy. The following is a summarization of one such incident, related by George A. Smith.)

When the Kirtland Temple was completed, many Saints gathered for the dedication. The seats in the temple filled quickly, and many people were allowed to stand, but still not everyone could be accommodated inside the building. Elder Frazier Eaton, who had given seven hundred dollars for the building of the temple, arrived after it had been filled, so he was not allowed inside for the dedication. The dedication was repeated the next day for those who could not be accommodated the first day, but this did not satisfy Frazier Eaton, and he apostatized (in *Journal of Discourses*, 11:9).

William Draper

(Commenting on what happened in one particular meeting.)

After giving instructions on the spirit of prophecy to those assembled, Joseph called upon them to prophesy good concerning the Saints;

he promised that the first one to speak would be filled with the spirit of prophecy. George A. Smith stood upon his feet and began to prophesy. Immediately the room was filled with the sound of a violent motion of wind, and the vibration seemed to lift the men simultaneously to their feet. Men old and young began to speak in tongues and to prophesy and to see visions. The Prophet beheld the temple filled with angels and informed the brethren of what he saw. William Draper, a counselor in one of the Aaronic Priesthood quorums, affirmed that the outpouring of the Spirit of the Lord was so immense "that my pen is inadequate to write it in full or my tongue to express it. But I will here say that the spirit was poured out and came like a mighty rushing wind and filled the house, that many that were present spoke in tongues and had visions and saw angels and prophesied, and had a general time of rejoicing such as had not been known in this generation" (William Draper, "Autobiography," *Writings of Early Latter-day Saints*, 2).

Benjamin Brown

The succeeding winter, I again went up to Kirtland, to attend the dedication of the Temple, and to meet with the solemn assembly that was there convened. There the Spirit of the Lord, as on the day of Pentecost, was profusely poured out. Hundreds of Elders spoke in tongues, but many of them being young in the Church, and never having witnessed the manifestation of this gift before, felt a little alarmed. This caused the Prophet Joseph Smith to pray the Lord to withhold the Spirit. Joseph [Smith Jr.] then instructed them on the nature of the gift of tongues, and the operation of the Spirit generally.

We had a most glorious and never-to-be-forgotten time. Angels were seen by numbers present, and the first endowments were received. It was during this assembly that the Saints' favorite hymn was given by inspiration, commencing—

"The Spirit of God, like a fire, is burning!
The latter-day glory begins to come forth;
The visions and blessings of old are returning,
The angels are coming to visit the Earth."

The beauty and applicability of this hymn will be seen by the Saints, on reading the third and fourth verses, when it is recollected that this was a solemn assembly, and that the ordinance of washing of feet, etc., was just then being attended to.

It was also at this time that Elijah the Prophet appeared, and conferred upon Joseph the keys of turning the hearts of the fathers to the children, previous to the reinstitution of the ordinance of baptism for the dead (Benjamin Brown, *Testimonies for the Truth: A Record of Manifestations of the Power of God, Miraculous and Providential, Witnessed in the Travels and Experience of Benjamin Brown, High Priest in The Church of Jesus Christ of Latter-day Saints, Pastor of the London, Reading, Kent, and Essex Conferences* [London: S. W. Richards, 1853], 6; spelling standardized).

Restoration of Priesthood Keys by Moses, Elias, and Elijah

Although the keys of the Aaronic and Melchizedek Priesthoods were restored to Joseph and Oliver in 1829 prior to the organization of the Church, the keys held by the Old Testament prophets Moses, Elias, and Elijah were restored on Passover, one week following the dedication of the temple, on April 3, 1836.

Joseph Smith Jr.

In the afternoon, I assisted the other Presidents in distributing the Lord's Supper to the Church, receiving it from the Twelve, whose privilege it was to officiate at the sacred desk this day. After having performed this service to my brethren, I retired to the pulpit, the veils being dropped, and bowed myself, with Oliver Cowdery, in solemn and silent prayer. After rising from prayer, the following vision was opened to both of us—

Vision Manifested to Joseph the Seer and Oliver Cowdery

The veil was taken from our minds, and the eyes of our understanding were opened. We saw the Lord standing upon the breastwork of the pulpit, before us, and under His feet was a paved work of pure gold in color like amber.

His eyes were as a flame of fire, the hair of His head was white like the pure snow, His countenance shone above the brightness of the sun, and His voice was as the sound of the rushing of great waters, even the voice of Jehovah, saying—

I am the first and the last, I am He who liveth, I am He who was slain, I am your advocate with the Father.

Behold, your sins are forgiven you, you are clean before me, therefore lift up your heads and rejoice.

Let the hearts of your brethren rejoice, and let the hearts of all my people rejoice, who have, with their might, built this house to my name.

For behold, I have accepted this house, and my name shall be here, and I will manifest myself to my people in mercy in this House.

Yea, I will appear unto my servants, and speak unto them with mine own voice, if my people will keep my commandments, and do not pollute this holy house.

Yea the hearts of thousands and tens of thousands shall greatly rejoice in consequence of the blessings which shall be poured out, and the endowment with which my servants have been endowed in this house;

And the fame of this house shall spread to foreign lands, and this is the beginning of the blessing which shall be poured out upon the heads of my people. Even so. Amen (*History of the Church*, 2:435; see also D&C 110:1–10).

Charles W. Penrose

Jesus Christ of the New Testament, is Jehovah of the Old Testament; and he so proclaimed it when he came to the Prophet Joseph and Oliver Cowdery in the temple of the Lord (Charles W. Penrose, in Conference Report, April 1920, 30).

Joseph Fielding Smith

Elias came, after Moses had conferred his keys, and brought the gospel of the dispensation in which Abraham lived. Everything that pertains to that dispensation, the blessings that were conferred upon Abraham, the promises that were given to his posterity, all had to be restored [Abraham 2:8–11], and Elias, who held the keys of that dispensation, came (Joseph Fielding Smith, *Doctrines of Salvation,* 3 vols., ed. Bruce R. McConkie [Salt Lake City: Bookcraft, 1956], 3:142).

It was, I am informed, on the third day of April, 1836, that the Jews, in their homes at the Paschal feast, opened their doors for Elijah to enter. On that very day Elijah did enter—not in the home of the Jews to partake of the Passover with them, but he appeared in the House of the Lord . . . in Kirtland, and there bestowed his keys (Joseph Fielding Smith, in Conference Report, April 1936, 75).

What was the nature of this restoration? It was the conferring upon men in this dispensation of *the sealing power of the priesthood* . . . It gave the authority to Joseph Smith to perform in the temple of God *all the ordinances essential to salvation for both the living and the dead* (*Doctrines of Salvation,* 2:118; italics added).

5

The Book of Commandments

On November 1, 1831, a council of elders held a conference in Hiram, Ohio, to consider plans for publishing the revelations received to that point in a book, to be called the Book of Commandments. The Lord approved the publication of these revelations and gave a revelation to be used as the preface (D&C 1) and another to be used as an appendix (D&C 133).

Joseph Smith Jr.

The book of revelations . . . being the foundation of the Church in these last days, and a benefit to the world, . . . therefore the conference voted that they prize the revelations to be worth to the Church the riches of the whole earth, speaking temporally (Joseph Smith, *History of The Church of Jesus Christ of Latter-day Saints,* 7 vols., ed. B. H. Roberts [Salt Lake City: Deseret Book, 1978], 1:235).

Historical Note to D&C 67

Some of the ten elders present at the Hiram Conference (Joseph Smith, Oliver Cowdery, David Whitmer, John Whitmer, Peter Whitmer Jr., Sidney Rigdon, William E. McLellan, Luke Johnson, Lyman Johnson, and Orson Hyde) expressed concern over the seemingly uneducated language found in the revelations then ready for printing. In response, Joseph Smith received section 67, which challenged the wisest of those present to duplicate any revelation, "even the least that is among them." William E. McLellan, a newly baptized school teacher from Paris, Tennessee, accepted the challenge but failed.

Care should be taken not to condemn McLellan unduly for his

participation in this matter. McLellan had met Joseph Smith for the first time only seven days before this meeting. Because he later became a bitter enemy of the Prophet, it is easy to adopt a retroactive interpretation of this circumstance. Consider section 68, which refers to him as one of "the faithful elders of my church."

After McLellan's attempt to write a revelation, Joseph Smith concluded:

> The Elders and all present that witnessed this vain attempt of a man to imitate the language of Jesus Christ, renewed their faith in the fulness of the Gospel, and in the truth of the commandments and revelations which the Lord had given to the Church through my instrumentality (*Times and* Seasons 5, April 15, 1844, 496). (Lyndon W. Cook, *The Revelations of the Prophet Joseph Smith: A Historical and Biographical Commentary of the Doctrine and Covenants* [Provo, Utah: Seventy's Mission Bookstore, 1981], 107–8)

Warnings about the Tribulations in Jackson County

While the Prophet was visiting Jackson County, Missouri, for the first time, in August 1831, a revelation and warning was given to the Saints:

> Hearken, O ye elders of my church, and give ear to my word, and learn of me what I will concerning you, and also concerning this land unto which I have sent you.
>
> For verily I say unto you, blessed is he that keepeth my commandments, whether in life or in death; and he that is faithful in tribulation, the reward of the same is greater in the kingdom of heaven.
>
> Ye cannot behold with your natural eyes, for the present time, the design of your God concerning those things which shall come hereafter, and the glory which shall follow after much tribulation.
>
> For after much tribulation come the blessings. Wherefore the day cometh that ye shall be crowned with much glory; the hour is not yet, but is nigh at hand.

> Remember this, which I tell you before, that you may lay it to heart, and receive that which is to follow. (D&C 58:1–5)

Zion was to be built according to the faith and righteousness of the Saints. Again, in September 1831, a revelation declared that "the rebellious shall be cut off out of the land of Zion, and shall be sent away, and shall not inherit the land" (D&C 64:35).

Despite the repeated warnings, dissension arose among the Saints in Jackson County. The building of the temple was delayed; and in January 1833, the Prophet Joseph Smith wrote from Kirtland, Ohio, stating that if Zion would not purify herself, God would "seek another people" (*History of the Church*, 1:316). An accompanying letter, written by Hyrum Smith and Orson Hyde, pled with the Saints to repent lest they be "cut off"(*History of the Church*, 1:320).

In July 1833, the printing press and the Book of Commandments were destroyed and the Saints were driven out of Jackson County. The printing of the Book of Commandments was interrupted so suddenly by this devastation that the book ends mid-sentence. It is interesting to note that the very verses that were being printed at the time of this destruction read:

> Behold the Lord requireth the heart and a willing mind;
>
> And the willing and obedient shall eat the good of the land of Zion in these last days;
>
> And the rebellious shall be cut off out of the land of Zion, and shall be sent away and shall not inherit the land:
>
> For verily I say that the rebellious are not of the blood of Ephraim. (*A Book of Commandments, for the Government of the Church of Christ* [Zion: W. W. Phelps & co., 1833], 160)

After the July 1833 mobbings in Independence, when the Saints were driven from Jackson County, the Prophet Joseph Smith observed:

> I have always expected that Zion would suffer some affliction, from what I could learn from the commandments which have been given. But I would remind you of a certain clause in one which says, that after *much* tribulation cometh

> the blessings. . . . But how many will be the days of her purification, tribulation, and affliction, the Lord has kept from my eyes. (*History of the Church*, 1:453–54)

A few months later, the Prophet further admonished the Saints to obey Zion's laws; otherwise, they "would be driven from state to state, from city to city, from one abiding place to another" (as cited in Hyrum L. Andrus, *Anticipations of the Civil War in Mormon Thought* [Provo, Utah: Extension Publications, 1966], 13). He continued:

> You say I am a Prophet. Well, then, I will prophesy, and when you go home write it down and remember it. You think you have been badly treated by your enemies; but if you don't do better than you are doing, I prophesy that the state of Missouri will not hold you. Your sufferings have hardly commenced. ("Historical Address by President George A. Smith," *The Juvenile Instructor*, reported by David W. Evans [March 15, 1892]: 173)

Mary Elizabeth Rollins Lightner

(In July 1833, when a mob was in the act of destroying William W. Phelps's home and the printing press in Independence, where the Book of Commandments was being printed, Mary and her sister Caroline risked their lives to save copies of the Book of Commandments.)

Mary Lightner

(Courtesy of the Church Archives, The Church of Jesus Christ of Latter-day Saints)

When the mob was tearing down the printing office, a two story building, driving Brother [William W.] Phelps' family out of the lower part of the house, they (the mob) brought out some large sheets of paper, saying, "Here are the Mormon commandments." My sister [Caroline], 12 years old (I was then 14) and myself were in a corner of a fence watching them.

When they spoke about them being the commandments, I was determined to have some of them. So while their backs were turned, prying out the gable end of the house, we ran and gathered up all we could carry in our arms. As we turned away, two of the mob got down off the house and called for us to stop, but we ran as fast as we could through a gap in the fence into a large corn field, and the two men after us. We ran a long way in the field, laid the papers on the ground, then laid down on top of them. The corn was very high and thick. They hunted all around us, but did not see us. After we were satisfied they had given up the search, we tried to find our way out of the field. The corn was so tall we thought we were lost. On looking up we saw some trees that had been girdled to kill them. We followed them and came to an old log stable, which looked like it had not been used for years. Sister Phelps and family were there, carrying in brush and piling it up on one side of the stable to make their beds on. She asked us what we had. We told her and also how we came by them. She took them and placed them between her beds. Subsequently Oliver Cowdery bound them in small books and gave me one (Mary E. Rollins Lightner, "Ran From the Mob," *Deseret Evening News* [February 20, 1904]: 24).

6

The Book of Abraham

During the summer of 1835, Michael Chandler arrived in Kirtland with a display of four Egyptian mummies and papyri. The Prophet Joseph was intrigued by the papyri, and it was soon revealed to him that they contained portions of the record of Abraham. He offered to buy them from Chandler, however, Chandler would not sell the papyri apart from the mummies. Therefore, the entire collection was purchased by the Church for $2,400, and the translation of the papyri became part of the Pearl of Great Price.

> These Mummies, with seven others, were taken from the Catacombs of Egypt, near where the ancient, and we may say, almost unparalleled city of Thebes once stood, by the celebrated French traveler Antonio Lebolo; at a great expense, under the protection of the French Consul, by the consent of Mehemt Ali, the Viceroy of Egypt. It is to be noticed that several hundred Mummies, differently embalmed were found in the same catacomb, but only the eleven in a state to be removed. The seven have been sold to gentlemen for private museums, and in consequence are kept from the eye of the public. . . . These strangers illustrious from their antiquity, may have lived in the days of Jacob, Moses, or David, and of course some thousand years have elapsed since these bodies were animated with the breath of life! History records the fact, that the higher class concealed their knowledge from the lower, in figures and hieroglyphic characters—A few of those, upon papyrus, used by the Egyptians for writing, will be exhibited with the Mummies. ("Egyptian Antiquities," *Times and Seasons* [May 2, 1842]: 774)

Chronology of the Book of Abraham Papyri

1818–21: Antonio Lebolo, an archaeologist/treasure hunter, discovers a collection of mummies in upper Egypt. He takes them to Italy in 1822.

1833: Michael Chandler, an Irishman living in America, obtains eleven mummies (in coffins) with some papyrus documents.

1833–35: Chandler tours the U.S. with mummies, coffins, and papyri, selling some as he travels from place to place.

July 1835: Chandler arrives in Kirtland. Joseph Smith, with financial help from the Saints, purchases four mummies, two rolls of papyrus, and other fragments for $2,400.

1835–36: Joseph Smith studies and translates from the papyri.

1842: The current text of the Book of Abraham is published in the *Times and Seasons* in three installments.

1844–56: Lucy Mack Smith keeps the mummies and papyrus until her death.

1856: Emma Smith sells all four mummies and presumably all the records to a Mr. Abel Combs, for an unknown price.

1856 : Combs sells two of the mummies and the papyri to the St. Louis Museum.

1863: The St. Louis Museum sells the mummies and papyri to the Wood's Museum, in Chicago.

1871: The Great Chicago Fire seizes the city, and the papyri and mummies are assumed to be destroyed.

1946: Comb's housekeeper's son-in-law sells eleven papyrus fragments to the Metropolitan Museum of Art, in New York.

1966: The fragments are discovered there and brought to the attention of the Church by Dr. Aziz Atiya.

1967: The Church buys the eleven fragments from the Metropolitan Museum of Art.

Descriptions of the Papyrus

Oliver Cowdery

Oliver Cowdery
(Courtesy of the Church Archives, The Church of Jesus Christ of Latter-day Saints)

Upon the subject of the Egyptian records, or rather the writings of Abraham and Joseph . . . , may I say a few words. This record is beautifully written in papyrus with black, and a small part, red ink or paint, in perfect preservation. The characters are such as you find upon the coffins of mummies, hieroglyphics and etc. with many characters or letters exactly like the present, though perhaps not quite so square form of the Hebrew without points (Oliver Cowdery, "Oliver Cowdery to Mr. Wm. Frye, Esq., 22 Dec. 1835," *Letters, Oliver Cowdery* [LDS Church Archives, The Church of Jesus Christ of Latter-day Saints, Salt Lake City, Utah]; as cited in Stanley R. Gunn, *Oliver Cowdery. Second Elder and Scribe* [Salt Lake City: Bookcraft, 1962], 235–36).

Wilford Woodruff

We . . . viewed four Egyptian mummies and also the Book of Abraham written by his own hand and not only the hieroglyphics but also many figures that this precious treasure contains are calculated to make a lasting impression upon the mind which is not to be erased (as cited in Dean C. Jessee, "The Kirtland Diary of Wilford Woodruff," *BYU Studies* [Summer 1972]: 371; spelling and capitalization standardized).

Hugh Nibley

In 1906, while visiting Nauvoo, President Joseph F. Smith related . . . seeing his Uncle Joseph in the front rooms of the Mansion House working on the Egyptian manuscripts. According to President Smith, one of the rolls of papyri, "when unrolled on the floor extended through two rooms of the Mansion House" (Hugh Nibley, "The Joseph Smith Egyptian Papyri," *Dialogue: A Journal of Mormon Thought* [Summer 1968]: 101).

Translating the Papyrus

Orson Pratt

The Prophet took them and repaired to his room and inquired of the Lord concerning them. The Lord told him they were sacred records (in *Journal of Discourses,* 26 vols. [London: Latter-day Saints' Book Depot, 1854–86], 20:65; see also Joseph Smith, *History of The Church of Jesus Christ of Latter-day Saints,* 7 vols., ed. B. H. Roberts [Salt Lake City: Deseret Book, 1965], 2:235).

Orson Pratt

(On witnessing the translation of the papyri, January 1836.)

I saw his [Joseph Smith's] countenance lighted up as the inspiration of the Holy Ghost rested upon him, dictating the great and most precious revelations now printed for our guide. I saw him translating, by inspiration, the Old and New Testaments, and the inspired book of Abraham from Egyptian Papyrus (in *Journal of Discourses,* 7:176).

Orson Pratt
(Courtesy of the Church Archives, The Church of Jesus Christ of Latter-day Saints)

Joseph Smith Jr.

Soon after this [between July 5 and July 9], some of the Saints at Kirtland purchased the mummies and papyrus, a description of which will appear hereafter, and with W. W. Phelps and Oliver Cowdery as scribes, I commenced the translation of some of the characters or hieroglyphics, and much to our joy found that one of the rolls contained the writings of Abraham, another the writings of Joseph of Egypt, etc.,—a more full account of which will appear in its place, as I proceed to examine or unfold them. Truly we can say, the Lord is beginning to reveal the abundance of peace and truth (*History of the Church,* 2:236).

Recovering Portions of the Papyrus

Dr. Aziz Atiya

(In 1967, Dr. Aziz Atiya, former director of the University of Utah's Middle East Center, discovered portions of the Joseph Smith Papyri in the Metropolitan Museum of Art. He also found a letter signed by Emma Smith Bidamon, widow of the Prophet Joseph, and their son Joseph Smith III, attesting that the papyri had been the property of the Prophet.)

I was writing a book at the time . . . and I went to the Metropolitan Museum of Art looking for documents, papyri, pictures, and illustrations to serve the book. It must have been in the early spring of 1966.

While I was in one of the dim rooms where everything was brought to me, something caught my eye, and I asked one of the assistants to take me behind the bars into the storehouse of documents so that I could look some more. While there I found a file with these documents. I at once recognized the picture part of it. When I saw this picture, I knew that it had appeared in the Pearl of Great Price. I knew the general format of the picture. This kind of picture one can find generally on other papyri, but this particular one has special peculiarities. For instance, the head had fallen off, and I could see that the papyrus was stuck on paper, nineteenth century paper. The head was completed in pencil, apparently by Joseph Smith, who must have had it when that part fell off. He apparently drew the head in his own hand on the supplementary paper. . . .

When I saw these documents, I really was taken back. I know the Mormon community, what it stands for, its scripture, etc., and I said at once that these documents don't belong here. They belong to the Mormon Church (Jay M. Todd, "Egyptian Papyri Rediscovered," *The Improvement Era* [January 1968]: 13–14).

7

Missouri Persecutions (Part I)

From 1831 to 1837, the anti-Mormon feelings continued to rise in Missouri until the entire state was in an uproar. This persecution reached a climax in 1838, when Governor Lilburn W. Boggs issued an extermination order that resulted in the Saints being driven from the state.

Orange L. Wight

(He gave the following overview of the Missouri persecutions.)

Now we were driven—I call it—or requested to make our place of gathering further north in the unsettled counties of Caldwell and Daviess Counties, Missouri. . . . I was an eyewitness to nearly all that happened. It was different from the happenings in Jackson County. Here the mob commenced the trouble without cause or provocation by trying to prevent the Saints voting [in the Gallatin elections]. By the aid of some hickory clubs and canes, cut from the crabapple trees, the brethren succeeded in polling their votes. This exasperated the mob so that, by the aid of plenty of bad whiskey, they commenced destroying property—not right there, but away and out of danger of the crabapple and hickory weapons that were welded in the hands of such men as John Buller, Jake Killian, and others of like strength. They succeeded in driving several families to Diahman [Adam-ondi-Ahman], and spread reports throughout the county that the Mormons were destroying property, and doing all they could to raise an excitement both in Daviess and Caldwell Counties, and also in Ray County.

They succeeded to such an extent that caused many to leave their homes, and also caused the Haun's Mill Massacre, beside abusing men and women wherever they could find them unprotected. Now when it came to my father, Colonel Lyman Wight, [he] called on the militia to quell the disturbance and restore order; he did not call out the troops for one party or the other, but to quiet the disturbance generally. But Colonel Wight being a Mormon, the mob took it for granted that he was on the Mormon's side and tried to organize a party to oppose him. Now that was an illegal step, for the Colonel was regular by elected and held a commission from the governor of the state.

The mob organized a company a few miles from Diahman and procured a cannon somewhere—I never knew where—and [an] old iron piece, about a six pounder. Father [Lyman Wight] sent one of the captains with a company to disperse them. When they found they were about to be attacked by the militia, they buried the big gun and scattered corn over the ground so that the hogs would root over the ground and annihilate the scene. But one of the hogs rutted the ground off the muzzle of the gun. Some of the militia discovered it, and in a short time, exhumed the gun and appropriated a wagon and brought it to Diahman [Adam-ondi-Ahman] during the night; and the next day the gun was mounted and placed on the hill near the temple lot and fired three times as a salute and to let the enemy know we had the gun and were ready for them.

Now, the foregoing I have written simply to give my own version of the affair, although it is quite correctly written in history; but, being an eyewitness, I thought you would likely like to have my version of the proceedings which led to general hostility and bad feelings between parties. Hence it went on from one thing to another, until, like all wars both civil and otherwise, the soldiers became exasperated and began to appropriate and destroy property on both sides. And, about this time, Captain David Patten was sent with a company to disperse a company of mob that had gathered on Crook River, by one Captain Bogart. Captain David Patten and Simeon Carter were killed; also several others were wounded, among which were Brother Hendricks and Arthur Millikin (Orange L. Wright, "Notebook of Orange L. Wright," *Writings of Early Latter-day Saints and Their Contemporaries, a Database Collection,* comp. Milton V. Backman [Provo, Utah: BYU Religious Studies Center, 1996], 12–14; punctuation standardized).

Apostasy of Thomas B. Marsh *(1838)*

During the difficult persecutions in Missouri, several lost their faith and apostatized from the Church. One of these was Thomas B. Marsh, president of the Quorum of the Twelve Apostles. President Marsh was living in Far West at the time the following incident occurred.

George A. Smith

George A. Smith
(Courtesy of the Church Archives, The Church of Jesus Christ of Latter-day Saints)

Some members are deceived because of their pride. The following story illustrates how pride led Thomas B. Marsh and his wife, Elizabeth, into apostasy.

While living in Far West, Missouri, Sister Marsh and Sister Harris decided to exchange milk so they could each make a larger cheese than they otherwise could. They agreed to send each other both the milk and the cream from their cows. But Sister Marsh saved a pint of cream from each cow and sent Sister Harris the milk without the cream.

A quarrel arose, and the matter was referred to the bishop. When he determined that Sister Marsh had violated her agreement, she and her husband were upset and appealed the matter to the High Council, and then to the First Presidency. Each council approved the original decision: that Sister Marsh had been in error.

Thomas B. Marsh declared that he would sustain the character of his wife. Soon afterward, he turned against the Church and went before a government official to declare that the Latter-day Saints were hostile toward the state of Missouri (See *Journal of Discourses,* 26 vols. [London: Latter-day Saints' Book Depot, 1854–86], 3:283–84).

President Gordon B. Hinckley

(Describing this incident.)

What a very small and trivial thing—a little cream over which two women quarreled. But it led to, or at least was a factor in, Governor

Boggs' cruel exterminating order which drove the Saints from the state of Missouri, with all of the terrible suffering and consequent death that followed. The man who should have settled this little quarrel, but who, rather, pursued it . . . lost his standing in the Church. He lost his testimony of the gospel (Gordon B. Hinckley, "Small Acts Lead to Great Consequences," *Ensign*, May 1984, 83).

Gordon B. Hinckley
(Courtesy of the Church Archives, The Church of Jesus Christ of Latter-day Saints)

Thomas B. Marsh

(After nineteen years of darkness and painful bitterness, Marsh eventually made his way to the Salt Lake Valley and asked Brigham Young to forgive him and permit his rebaptism into the Church. In a letter to Heber C. Kimball, first counselor in the First Presidency, he wrote the following.)

Thomas B. Marsh
(Courtesy of the Church Archives, The Church of Jesus Christ of Latter-day Saints)

I began to awake to a sense of my situation. . . . I know that I have sinned against Heaven and in thy sight. . . . . The Lord could get along very well without me and He has lost nothing by my falling out of the ranks; But O what have I lost?! Riches, greater riches than all this world or many planets like this could afford (Thomas B. Marsh, "Thomas B. Marsh to Heber C. Kimball, 5 May 1857," *Brigham Young Collection* [LDS Church Archives, The Church of Jesus Christ of Latter-day Saints, Salt Lake City, Utah]; as cited in James E. Faust, "The Prophetic Voice," *Ensign*, May 1996, 7).

Election Day Battle at Gallatin
(August 6, 1838)

William E. Berrett

Among the new towns laid out in northern Missouri [were] Adam-ondi-Ahman, Gallatin and Millport in Daviess County, Haun's Mill in Caldwell County and De Witt in Carroll County. . . .

The population of the Church in Daviess, Caldwell, Ray, and Carroll Counties was swelled rapidly by the steady stream of immigrants from the East. The long caravans of covered wagons cut deep ruts across the Missouri prairies. Twelve hundred had been driven out of Jackson County. By the summer of 1838, the numbers in northern Missouri totaled fifteen thousand.

It was inevitable that persecution would follow. All the old causes of disquiet were there intensified by numbers. One county would not hold the Mormons. They were overflowing into all northwestern Missouri. In a few years they might conceivably dominate the state. Even the finest citizens became alarmed, and in that alarm all the wild and lawless element of the frontier found an opportunity to plunder and ravage.

The renewed persecution began at Gallatin, Daviess County. It was election day, August 6, 1838. A group of Latter-day Saint men appeared at the polls to vote. A much larger group led by Colonel William P. Peniston, a candidate for the state legislature, sought to prevent the casting of ballots (William E. Berrett, *The Restored Church* [Salt Lake City: Deseret Book, 1965], 137–38).

Joseph Smith Jr.

Some two weeks previous to this, Judge Morin, who lived at Mill Port, informed John D. Lee and Levi Stewart that it was determined by the mob to prevent the "Mormons" from voting at the election on the sixth day of August, and thereby elect Colonel William P. Peniston, who led the mob in Clay county. He also advised them to go prepared for an attack, to stand their ground, and have their rights.

The brethren, hoping better things, gave little heed to Judge Morin's friendly counsel, and repaired to the polls at Gallatin, the shire town of Daviess county, without weapons.

About eleven o'clock a. m., William P. Peniston mounted a barrel and harangued the electors for the purpose of exciting them against the "Mormons," saying, "The Mormon leaders are a set of horse thieves, liars, counterfeiters, and you know they profess to heal the sick, and cast out devils, and you all know that is a lie." He further said that the members of the Church were dupes, and not too good to take a false oath on any common occasion; that they would steal, and he did not consider property safe where they were; that he was opposed to their settling in Daviess county; and if they suffered the "Mormons" to vote, the people would soon lose their suffrage; "and," said he, addressing the Saints, "I headed a mob to drive you out of Clay county, and would not prevent your being mobbed now."

Richard (called Dick) Welding, the mob bully, just drunk enough for the occasion, began a discussion with Brother Samuel Brown, by saying, "The Mormons were not allowed to vote in Clay county no more than the negroes," and attempted to strike Brown, who gradually retreated, parrying the blow with his umbrella, while Welding continued to press upon him, calling him a liar, etc., and meanwhile trying to repeat the blow on Brown. Perry Durphy sought to suppress the difficulty by holding Welding's arm, when five or six of the mobbers seized Durphy and commenced beating him with clubs, [and] boards, and crying, "*Kill him, kill him,*" when a general scuffle commenced with fists and clubs, the mobbers being about ten to one of the brethren. Abraham Nelson was knocked down and had his clothes torn off, and, while trying to get up, was attacked again, when his brother, Hyrum Nelson, ran in amongst them, and knocked the mobbers down with the butt of his whip. Riley Stewart struck Welding on the head, which brought him to the ground. The mob cried out, "Dick Weldin's dead; who killed Dick?" And they fell upon Riley, knocked him down, kicked him, crying, "Kill him, kill him; shoot him," and they would have killed him, had not John L. Butler sprung in amongst them and knocked them down. During about five minutes it was one succession of knock downs, when the mob dispersed to get fire arms.

Very few of the brethren voted. Riley, escaping across the river, had his wounds dressed, and returned home.

John L. Butler called the brethren together and made a speech, saying, "We are American citizens; our fathers fought for their liberty, and we will maintain the same principles." The authorities of the county finally came to the brethren and requested them to withdraw, stating that it was a premeditated thing to prevent the "Mormons" from voting.

The brethren held a council about one-fourth of a mile out of town, where they saw mob recruits coming in, in small parties, from five and ten, to twenty-five in number cursing and swearing, and armed with clubs, pistols, dirks, and some guns. The brethren not having arms, thought it wisdom to return to their farms, collect their families, and hide them in a thicket of hazel bush, which they did, and stood guard around them through the night, while the women and children lay on the ground in the rain (Joseph Smith, *History of The Church of Jesus Christ of Latter-day Saints,* 7 vols., ed. B. H. Roberts [Salt Lake City: Deseret Book, 1978], 3:56–58; punctuation standardized).

Battle at Crooked River
(October 1838)

William Draper

I will here say that after we arrived in the city there was quite a stir among the people for reports were daily and almost hourly that the mob was gathering on every side, so it kept us on the look out all the time, day and night until on or about the 22nd day of October there came a report that the mob was ruining houses, destroying property and killing our brethren that had not gathered into Far West, but lived about . . . 14 miles out from Far West. On hearing the report there was a company of about seventy-five men raised and dispatched to see what the trouble might be, they traveled on until they came to the place of trouble near Crooked River as it was called.

There they came in contact [Battle of Crooked River], with the mob which opened fire on our brethren and quite a skirmish issued which resulted in the death of David W. Patten one of the twelve apostles, also Simeon Carter and a young man by the name of [Patrick] O'Banion and some more of the brethren badly wounded (William Draper, "Autobiography of William Draper," *Writings of Early Latter-day Saints,* 8; spelling standardized).

George Washington Gill Averett

One bloody fight took place before at Crooked River where a number of the mob was killed and wounded and several of the Saints was wounded and one noble man of the Saints was killed, David Patten, and one of the twelve apostles, a noble spirit much lamented by all the Saints. One of the Madge family and one of the Henricks family was also shot and badly wounded at that encounter at Crooked River but both recovered after a long time suffering (George Washington Gill Averett, "Autobiography of George Washington Gill Averett," *Writings of Early Latter-day Saints,* 6).

Charles Henry Hales

I arrived just a few hours before the Crooked River Battle. I was one of the company engaged in that affair, although I was lame and tired. I borrowed a horse and a gun, (for I had neither) and went to defend my brethren. I saw Brother [Patrick] O'Banion when he fell. Soon after the battle, the governor's troops came to Far West, and demanded every man that was engaged in the Crooked River Battle. At this time, we were under the necessity of having our houses and grain burnt and our cattle driven off, or else if we stood up for our rights and defended ourselves like men and saints of the Most High we must be hunted by an authorized mob and be driven from our homes and families, or be killed, just as they pleased.

As soon as we learned their intentions were to take every man that was in the Crooked River Battle we all started for Illinois, going by the way of Diahman [Adam-ondi-Ahman], since we were surrounded on every other side. Before we arrived at Diahman my horse gave out, so the brethren counseled me to stay in Diahman as I was not known by any of the mob in that county. Accordingly, I stayed till the arms were given up and the brethren returned again to Far West (Charles Hales, "Autobiography, Kenneth Hales," *Writings of Early Latter-day Saints,* 35–36; punctuation standardized).

The Extermination Order of Governor Boggs
(October 27, 1838)

While the persecution in Missouri up to this point had been merely a civil conflict, on October 27, 1838, Gov. Lilburn W. Boggs issued an extermination order, calling for an armed march against the Saints in Far West. This was the result of various false and exaggerated reports of a conflict that had taken place in Jefferson County, where it was said the Saints had attacked the Ray County militia. This shameful order was not rescinded until 1976.

David R. Atchison and Samuel D. Lucas

(In communication addressed to Governor Boggs.)

SIR—From late outrages committed by the "Mormons," civil war is inevitable. They have set the laws of the country at defiance and are in open rebellion. We have about two thousand men under arms to keep them in check. The presence of the commander in chief is deemed absolutely necessary, and we most regretfully urge that your excellency be at the seat of *war* as soon as possible.

Your most obedient, ect.

David R. Atchison, M. G. 3rd Div.

Samuel D. Lucas, M.G. 4th Div. (B. H. Roberts, *The Missouri Persecution* [Salt Lake City: Bookcraft, 1965], 230).

Lilburn W. Boggs

SIR:—Since the order of the morning to you, directing you to cause four hundred mounted men to be raised within your division, I have received by Amos Rees, Esq., and Wiley C. Williams, Esq., one of my aids, information of the most appalling character, which changes the whole face of things, and places the Mormons in the attitude of open and avowed defiance of the laws, and of having made open war upon the people of this state. Your orders are, therefore, to hasten your operations and endeavor to reach Richmond, in Ray county, with all possible speed. The Mormons must be treated as enemies and *must be exterminated* or driven from the state, if necessary for the public good.

Their outrages are beyond all description. If you can increase your force, you are authorized to do so, to any extent you many think necessary. I have just issued orders to Major-General Wallock, of Marion county, to raise five hundred men, and to march them to the northern part of Daviess and there to unite with General Doniphan, of Clay, who has been ordered with five hundred men to proceed to the same point for the purpose of intercepting the retreat of the Mormons to the north. They have been directed to communicate with you by express; and you can also communicate with them if you find it necessary. Instead, therefore, of proceeding as at first directed, to reinstate the citizens of Daviess in their homes, you will proceed immediately to Richmond, and there operate against the Mormons. Brigadier-General Parks, of Ray, has been ordered to have four hundred men of his brigade in readiness to join you at Richmond. The whole force will be placed under your command.

L. W. BOGGS,

Governor and Commander-in-Chief (*History of the Church*, 3:175).

Horace S. Eldredge

Difficulties and jealousies, both in political and religious questions, soon arose between some of our people and other settlers, and the Mormons in some settlements in upper Missouri were forbidden to vote or to come to the polls to exercise their franchise. This finally resulted in a very serious quarrel on an election day in an adjoining county. Thus started, the difficulty was not easily quelled, as the feud was encouraged and the spark thus ignited fanned by hireling priests and political demagogues until it became very serious, and finally culminated in the extermination order of L. [Lilburn] W. Boggs, then governor of the state of Missouri. Scores of our people were then ruthlessly murdered, women ravished and helpless women and children turned out of doors in the bleakness of a severe winter, and added to all, our prophet and several other leading men were incarcerated in prison.

But these atrocities have been published to the world and it is not a pleasant theme for me to write about; but I would mention that about twelve thousand of our people were banished from the state to seek refuge in a more congenial clime. . . .

There was no law for Mormons in that state, and no one that professed to be a Mormon was allowed to remain unless he would renounce his religion. I therefore left in the month of December [1838], and returned to my friends in the state of Indiana. I will here state that I still hold the titles to my land in Missouri, having never received the first dollar for them (Horace S. Eldredge, "Autobiography," *Writings of Early Latter-day Saints*, 406; punctuation standardized).

Governor Christopher S. Bond Rescinds the Extermination Order *(June 25, 1976)*

WHEREAS, on October 27, 1838, the Governor of the State of Missouri, Lilburn W. Boggs, issued an order calling for the extermination or expulsion of Mormons from the State of Missouri; and

WHEREAS, Governor Boggs' order clearly contravened the rights to life, liberty, property and religious freedom as guaranteed by the Constitution of the United States, as well as the Constitution of the State of Missouri; and

WHEREAS, in this Bicentennial year as we reflect on our nation's heritage, the exercise of religious freedom is without question one of the basic tenets of our free democratic republic;

NOW, THEREFORE, I, CHRISTOPHER S. BOND, Governor of the State of Missouri, by virtue of the authority vested in me by the Constitution and the laws of the State of Missouri, do hereby order as follows:

Expressing on behalf of all Missourians our deep regret for the injustice and undue suffering which was caused by this 1838 order, I hereby rescind Executive Order Number 44 dated October 27, 1838, issued by Governor Lilburn W. Boggs.

IN WITNESS WHEREOF: I have hereunto set my hand and caused to be affixed the great seal of the State of Missouri in the City of Jefferson on this 25th day of June, 1976.

Christopher S. Bond GOVERNOR (Christopher S. Bond, *Executive Orders, 1838–1976* [L. Tom Perry Special Collections, Harold B. Lee Library, Brigham Young University, Provo, Utah], n.p.).

8

Missouri Persecutions (Part II)

Haun's Mill Massacre
(October 30, 1838)

Beginning in 1833, many Latter-day Saints formed settlements throughout Caldwell County surrounding the area known as Far West. Jacob Haun settled one of the first of these, at Shoal Creek, and named it Haun's Mill. The Missourians were not pleased with their new

Illustration of Haun's Mill
(Courtesy of the Church Archives, The Church of Jesus Christ of Latter-day Saints)

neighbors. As disdain for the Mormons increased, violence erupted throughout the county. The tranquil silence of the Haun's Mill settlement was suddenly shattered on October 30, 1838. Joseph Young, one of the victims of that fateful day, wrote: "No one expressed any apprehension of the awful crisis that was near us—even at our doors" (as cited in Parley P. Pratt, *Autobiography of Parley P. Pratt*, ed. Parley P. Pratt Jr. [Salt Lake City: Deseret Book, 1985], 172).

John D. Lee

(Describing how Joseph Smith warned the Saints at Haun's Mill to gather to Far West for safety and protection.)

John D. Lee
(Courtesy of the Church Archives, The Church of Jesus Christ of Latter-day Saints)

The morning after the Battle of Crooked River, Haughn [sic] came to Far West to consult with the Prophet concerning the policy of the removal of the settlers on Log Creek to the fortified camps. Col. White [i.e., Wight] and myself were standing by when the Prophet said to him: "Move in, by all means, if you wish to save your lives." Haughn [sic] replied that if the settlers left their homes, all of their property would be lost and the Gentiles would burn their houses and other buildings. The Prophet said: "You had better lose your property than your lives one can be replaced, the other cannot be restored; but there is no need of your losing either if you will only do as you are commanded." Haughn [sic] said that he considered the best plan was for all the settlers to move in and around the mill, and use the blacksmith's shop and other buildings as a fort in case of attack; in this way he thought they would be perfectly safe. "You are at liberty to do so if you think best," said the Prophet. Haughn [sic] then departed, well satisfied that he had carried his point.

The Prophet turned to Col. White [sic] and said: "That man did not come for counsel, but to induce me to tell him to do as he pleased; which I did. Had I commanded them to move in here and leave their property, they would have called me a tyrant. I wish they were here for their own safety. I am confident that we will soon learn that they have been butchered in a fearful manner" (Leland Homer Gentry, *A History of the Latter-day Saints in Northern Missouri from 1836 to 1839* [Provo, Utah: Joseph Fielding Smith Institute for Latter-day Saint History and BYU Studies, 2000], 153–54).

Joseph Smith Jr.

None had ever been killed who abode by my counsel. At Haun's Mill the brethren went contrary to my counsel; if they had not, their lives would have been spared (Joseph Smith, *History of The Church of Jesus Christ of Latter-day Saints*, 7 vols., ed. B. H. Roberts [Salt Lake City: Deseret Book, 1978], 5:137).

Benjamin Brown

The Saints that I gathered at Portland, and that met at my house, were richly blessed with the various gifts of the Spirit—tongues, interpretations, prophecy, etc. I will relate an instance or two. One Sunday morning, while opening the meeting with prayer, the gift of tongues came upon me, but thinking of Paul's words, that it is sometimes wisdom not to speak in tongues, unless one is present who can interpret, and forgetting that a sister, possessing the gift of interpretation, was present, I quenched the Spirit, and it left me. Immediately, another brother broke out in tongues, the interpretation of which was, that, "the Lord knew we were anxious to learn of the affairs of our brethren in Missouri, and that if we would humble ourselves before Him, and ask, He would reveal unto us the desires of our hearts." Missouri was some thousand miles from Portland. We accordingly bowed again in supplication before the Lord, and, after rising from our knees, and reseating ourselves, the same brother broke out singing in tongues, in a low, mournful strain. But judge our feelings when the interpretation was given, and was found to be some thirteen or fourteen verses of poetry, descriptive of affairs in Missouri, the murder of our brethren there, and telling us that just at that time—

"Our brethren lay bleeding on the ground,
With their wives and children weeping around."

We had so often proved the truth of similar communications, that we felt as assured of the truth of this shocking news, as though our eyes actually beheld the horrid sight. Our hearts were filled with sorrow. In a fortnight afterwards, we received a letter from John P. Green, a faithful Elder of the Church in Missouri, who was, at the time he managed to write, secreted in the woods. The letter detailed and confirmed all the events previously revealed in tongues, proving that on the very day we had been informed of the transactions occurring a thousand miles off, the bleeding corpses of our brethren lay stretched on the ground after the slaughter. It was either at or about this time, that the massacre at Haun's Mill took place (Benjamin Brown, *Testimonies for the Truth. A Record of Manifestations of the Power of God, Miraculous and Providential, Witnessed in The Travels and Experience of Benjamin Brown, High Priest in The Church of Jesus Christ of Latter-day Saints, Pastor of the London, Reading, Kent, and Essex Conferences* [Liverpool: S. W. Richards, 1853], 7; spelling standardized).

Amanda Smith

We sold our beautiful home in Kirtland for a song, and traveled all summer to Missouri—our teams poor, and with hardly enough to keep body and soul together.

We arrived in Caldwell county, near Haun's Mill, nine wagons of us in company. Two days before we arrived we were taken prisoners by an armed mob that had demanded every bit of ammunition and every weapon we had. We surrendered all. They knew it, for they searched our wagons.

Amanda Smith

(Courtesy of the Church Archives, The Church of Jesus Christ of Latter-day Saints)

A few miles more brought us to Haun's Mill, where that awful scene of murder was enacted. My husband pitched his tent by a blacksmith's shop.

Brother David Evans made a treaty with the mob that they would not molest us. He came just before the massacre and called the company together and they knelt in prayer.

I sat in my tent. Looking up I suddenly saw the mob coming—the same that took away our weapons. They came like so many demons or wild Indians.

Before I could get to the blacksmith's shop door to alarm the brethren, who were at prayers, the bullets were whistling amongst them.

I seized my two little girls and escaped across the mill-pond on a slab-walk. Another sister fled with me. Yet though we were women, with tender children, in flight for our lives, the demons poured volley after volley to kill us.

A number of bullets entered my clothes, but I was not wounded. The sister, however, who was with me, cried out that she was hit. We had just reached the trunk of a fallen tree, over which I urged her, bidding her to shelter there where the bullets could not reach her, while I continued my flight to some bottom land.

When the firing had ceased I went back to the scene of the massacre, for there were my husband and three sons, of whose fate I as yet knew nothing.

As I returned I found the sister in a pool of blood where she had fainted, but she was only shot through the hand. Farther on was lying dead Brother McBride, an aged white-haired revolutionary soldier. His murderer had literally cut him to pieces with an old corn-cutter. His hands had been split down when he raised them in supplication for mercy. Then the monster cleft open his head with the same weapon, and the veteran who had fought for his country, in the glorious days of the past, was numbered with the martyrs.

Passing on I came to a scene more terrible still to the mother and wife. Emerging from the blacksmith shop was my eldest son, bearing on his shoulders his little brother Alma.

"Oh! my Alma is dead!" I cried, in anguish.

"No, mother; I think Alma is not dead. But father and brother Sardius are killed!"

What an answer was this to appall me! My husband and son murdered; another little son seemingly mortally wounded; and perhaps before the dreadful night should pass the murderers would return and complete their work!

But I could not weep then. The fountain of tears was dry; the heart overburdened with its calamity, and all the mother's sense absorbed in its anxiety for the precious boy which God alone could save by his miraculous aid.

The entire hip joint of my wounded boy had been shot away. Flesh, hip bone, joint and all had been ploughed out from the muzzle of the gun which the ruffian placed to the child's hip through the logs of the shop and deliberately fired.

We laid little Alma on a bed in our tent and I examined the wound. It was a ghastly sight. I knew not what to do. It was night now.

There were none left from that terrible scene, throughout that long, dark night, but about half a dozen bereaved and lamenting women, and the children. Eighteen or nineteen, all grown men excepting my murdered boy and another about the same age, were dead or dying; several more of the men were wounded, hiding away, whose groans through the night too well disclosed their hiding places, while the rest of the men had fled, at the moment of the massacre, to save their lives.

The women were sobbing, in the greatest anguish of spirit; the children were crying loudly with fear and grief at the loss of fathers and brothers; the dogs howled over their dead masters and the cattle were terrified with the scent of the blood of the murdered.

Yet was I there, all that long, dreadful night, with my dead and my wounded, and none but God as our physician and help.

"Oh my Heavenly Father," I cried, "what shall I do? Thou seest my poor wounded boy and knowest my inexperience. Oh Heavenly Father direct me what to do!"

And then I was directed as by a voice speaking to me.

The ashes of our fire was still smoldering. We had been burning the bark of the shag-bark hickory. I was directed to take those ashes and make a lye and put a cloth saturated with it right into the wound. It hurt, but little Alma was too near dead to heed it much. Again and again I saturated the cloth and put it into the hole from which the hip-joint had been ploughed, and each time mashed flesh and splinters of bone came away with the cloth; and the wound became as white as chicken's flesh.

Having done as directed I again prayed to the Lord and was again instructed as distinctly as though a physician had been standing by speaking to me.

Nearby was a slippery-elm tree. From this I was told to make a slippery-elm poultice and fill the wound with it.

My eldest boy was sent to get the slippery-elm from the roots, the poultice was made, and the wound, which took fully a quarter of a yard of linen to cover, so large was it, was properly dressed.

It was then I found vent to my feelings in tears, and resigned myself to the anguish of the hour.

And all that night we, a few poor, stricken women, were thus left there with our dead and wounded. All through the night we heard the groans of the dying. Once in the dark we crawled over the heap of dead in the blacksmith's shop to try to help or soothe the sufferers' wants; once we followed the cries of a wounded brother who hid in some bushes from the murderers, and relieved him all we could.

It has passed from my memory whether he was dead in the morning or whether he recovered.

Next morning brother Joseph Young came to the scene of the massacre.

"What shall be done with the dead?" he inquired, in horror and deep trouble.

There was not time to bury them, for the mob was coming on us. Neither were there left men to dig the graves. All the men excepting the two or three who had so narrowly escaped were dead or wounded. It had been no battle, but a massacre indeed.

"Do anything, Brother Joseph," I said, "rather than leave their bodies to the fiends who have killed them."

There was a deep dry well close by. Into this the bodies had to be hurried, eighteen or nineteen in number.

No funeral service could be performed, nor could they be buried with customary decency. The lives of those who in terror performed the last duty to the dead were in jeopardy. Every moment we expected to be fired upon by the fiends who we supposed were lying in ambush waiting the first opportunity to dispatch the remaining few who had escaped the slaughter of the preceding day. So in the hurry and terror of the moment some were thrown into the well head downwards and some feet downwards.

But when it came to the burial of my murdered boy Sardius, Brother Joseph Young, who was assisting to carry him on a board to the well, laid down the corpse and declared that he could not throw that boy into this horrible grave.

All the way on the journey, that summer, Joseph had played with the interesting lad who had been so cruelly murdered. It was too much for one whose nature was so tender as Uncle Joseph's, and whose sympathies by this time were quite overwrought. He could not perform that last office. My murdered son was left unburied.

"Oh! they have left my Sardius unburied in the sun," I cried, and ran and got a sheet and covered his body.

There he lay until the next day, and then I, his mother, assisted by his elder brother, had to throw him into the well. Straw and earth were thrown into this rude vault to cover the dead.

Among the wounded who recovered were Isaac Laney, Nathan K. Knight, Mr. Yokum, two brothers by the name of Myers, Tarlton Lewis, Mr. Haun and several others, besides Miss Mary Stedwell, who was shot through the hand while fleeing with me, and who, fainting, fell over the log into which the mob shot upwards of twenty balls.

The crawling of my boys under the bellows in the blacksmith's shop where the tragedy occurred, is an incident familiar to all our people. Alma's hip was shot away while thus hiding. Sardius was discovered after the massacre by the monsters who came in to despoil the bodies. The eldest, Willard, was not discovered. In cold blood, one, Glaze, of Carroll county, presented a rifle near the head of Sardius and literally blew off the upper part of it, leaving the skull empty and dry while the brains and hair of the murdered boy were scattered around and on the walls.

At this one of the men, more merciful than the rest, observed:

"It was a d—d shame to kill those little boys."

"D—n the difference!" retorted the other; "nits make lice!"

My son who escaped, also says that the mobocrat William Mann took from my husband's feet, before he was dead, a pair of new boots. From his hiding place, the boy saw the ruffian drag his father across the shop in the act of pulling off his boot.

"Oh! you hurt me!" groaned my husband. But the murderer dragged him back again, pulling off the other boot; "and there," says the boy, "my father fell over dead."

Afterwards this William Mann showed the boots on his own feet, in Far West, saying: "Here is a pair of boots that I pulled off before the d—d Mormon was done kicking!"

The murderer Glaze also boasted over the country, as a heroic deed, the blowing off the head of my young son.

But to return to Alma, and how the Lord helped me to save his life.

I removed the wounded boy to a house, some distance off, the next day, and dressed his hip; the Lord directing me as before. I was reminded that in my husband's trunk there was a bottle of balsam. This I poured into the wound, greatly soothing Alma's pain.

"Alma, my child," I said, "you believe that the Lord made your hip?"

"Yes, mother."

"Well, the Lord can make something there in the place of your hip, don't you believe he can, Alma?"

"Do you think that the Lord can, mother?" inquired the child, in his simplicity.

"Yes, my son," I replied, "he has showed it all to me in a vision."

Then I laid him comfortably on his face, and said: "Now you lay like that, and don't move, and the Lord will make you another hip."

So Alma laid on his face for five weeks, until he was entirely recovered—a flexible gristle having grown in place of the missing joint and socket, which remains to this day a marvel to physicians.

On the day that he walked again I was out of the house fetching a bucket of water, when I heard screams from the children. Running back, in affright, I entered, and there was Alma on the floor, dancing around, and the children screaming in astonishment and joy.

It is now nearly forty years ago, but Alma has never been the least crippled during his life, and he has traveled quite a long period of the time as a missionary of the gospel and a living miracle of the power of God.

I cannot leave the tragic story without relating some incidents of those five weeks when I was a prisoner with my wounded boy in Missouri, near the scene of the massacre, unable to obey the order of extermination.

All the Mormons in the neighborhood had fled out of the State, excepting a few families of the bereaved women and children who had gathered at the house of Brother David Evans, two miles from the scene of the massacre. To this house Alma had been carried after that fatal night.

In our utter desolation, what could we women do but pray? Prayer was our only source of comfort; our Heavenly Father our only helper. None but he could save and deliver us.

One day a mobber came from the mill with the captain's fiat:

"The captain says if you women don't stop your d—d praying he will send down a posse and kill every d—d one of you!"

And he might as well have done it, as to stop us poor women praying in that hour of our great calamity.

Our prayers were hushed in terror. We dared not let our voices be heard in the house in supplication. I could pray in my bed or in silence, but I could not live thus long. This godless silence was more intolerable than had been that night of the massacre.

I could bear it no longer. I pined to hear once more my own voice in petition to my Heavenly Father.

I stole down into a corn-field, and crawled into a "stout of corn." It was as the temple of the Lord to me at that moment. I prayed aloud and most fervently.

When I emerged from the corn a voice spoke to me. It was a voice as plain as I ever heard one. It was no silent, strong impression of the spirit, but a *voice*, repeating a verse of the saint's hymn:

That soul who on Jesus hath leaned for repose,
I cannot, I will not desert to its foes;
That soul, though all hell should endeavor to shake,
I'll never, no never, no never forsake!

From that moment I had no more fear. I felt that nothing could hurt me. Soon after this the mob sent us word that unless we were all out of the State by a certain day we should be killed.

The day came, and at evening came fifty armed men to execute the sentence.

I met them at the door. They demanded of me why I was not gone? I bade them enter and see their own work. They crowded into my room and I showed them my wounded boy. They came, party after party, until all had seen my excuse. Then they quarreled among themselves and came near fighting.

At last they went away, all but two. These I thought were detailed to kill us. Then the two returned.

"Madam," said one, "have you any meat in the house?"

"No," was my reply.

"Could you dress a fat hog if one was laid at your door?"

"I think we could!" was my answer.

And then they went and caught a fat hog from a herd which had belonged to a now exiled brother, killed it and dragged it to my door, and departed.

These men, who had come to murder us, left on the threshold of our door a meat offering to atone for their repented intention.

Yet even when my son was well I could not leave the State, now accursed indeed to the saints.

The mob had taken my horses, as they had the drove of horses, and the beeves, and the hogs, and wagons, and the tents, of the murdered and exiled.

So I went down into Daviess county (ten miles) to Captain Comstock, and demanded of him my horses. There was one of them in his yard. He said I could have it if I paid five dollars for its keep. I told him I had no money.

I did not fear the captain of the mob, for I had the Lord's promise that nothing should hurt me. But his wife swore that the mobbers were fools for not killing the women and children as well as the men—declaring that we would "breed up a pack ten times worse than the first."

I left without the captain's permission to take my horse, or giving pay for its keep; but I went into his yard and took it, and returned to our refuge unmolested.

Learning that my other horse was at the mill, I next yoked up a pair of steers to a sled and went and demanded it also.

Comstock was there at the mill. He gave me the horse, and then asked if I had any flour.

"No; we have had none for weeks."

He then gave me about fifty pounds of flour and some beef, and filled a can with honey.

But the mill, and the slaughtered beeves which hung plentifully on its walls, and the stock of flour and honey, and abundant spoil besides, had all belonged to the murdered or exiled saints.

Yet was I thus providentially, by the very murderers and mobocrats themselves, helped out of the State of Missouri.

The Lord had kept his word. The soul who on Jesus had leaned for succor had not been forsaken even in this terrible hour of massacre, and in that infamous extermination of the Mormons from Missouri in the years 1838–39.

One incident more, as a fitting close.

Over that rude grave—that well—where the nineteen martyrs slept, where my murdered husband and boy were entombed, the mobbers of Missouri, with an exquisite fiendishness, which no savages could have conceived, had constructed a rude privy. This they constantly used, with a delight which demons might have envied, if demons are more wicked and horribly beastly than were they.

Thus ends my chapter of the Haun's Mill massacre, to rise in judgment against them! (As cited in Edward W. Tullidge, *The Women of Mormondom* [New York: Tullidge & Crandall, 1877], 121–32; spelling standardized).

Willard Gilbert Smith

(Years later, Willard described an experience he had as stake president in Morgan County, Utah, when two members of his stake were murdered while serving as missionaries in the Southern states. The murder of his father and brother at Haun's Mill helped him console the members of his stake.)

At 2 o'clock P.M. on Sunday, the people of Morgan County attended the solemn services held in the Stake meetinghouse in memory of the martyrs Gibbs and Berry. After singing and prayer, S. Francis read a full account of the killing of the martyrs by the brutal mob.

President W. G. Smith delivered a very impressive address and while expressing condolence for the bereaved said he thought no one could sympathize with the bereaved better than himself. The killing of these servants of God brought back to memory what he witnessed at the massacre of Haun's Mill when his father and brother were murdered and another of his brothers was seriously wounded. He was but a boy then, but he would never forget the horrid butchery. Himself and six more children were in a house at the time the mob commenced firing, and the bullets passed through the house in every direction. They all crept under a bed that was in the room and stayed there for a while. The thick casing of oak around the house, about two feet high, protected them from the shower of bullets fired upon them by the mob. As there was no let-up to the continuous firing they agreed to leave the house to find a place, if possible. On emerging from the house the mob occupied a semi-circle around them, but they passed out of the door, traversed the millrace on a plank to a house by the mill, where they found Brother (the reporter forgot the name) who had got into the cellar. He was shot through the body eight times.

"He begged me," the speaker continued, "to lift him out of the cellar. I did so, and notwithstanding the many times he had been shot, he lived some time after. From this house we made our way to a cornfield, dodging behind the shocks of corn, the mob firing on us little children as they had done during the whole of the time. The children who stayed behind in the blacksmith shop were killed. When the firing was all over, we found eighteen dead bodies, among them my father and brother. Our family was journeying to find a new home at the time. We had no means of getting coffins for the dead, and had to bury them all together in a dry well. Myself and Joseph Young dragged them to this improvised grave and put them in; but when we came to my brother, Joseph Young turned so sick at the sight that he said he could not help any longer, so I called my mother to help me carry my brother to the well. She did so, and helped me to bury the rest.

After we had covered them up, we made haste to leave, as the mob was still there, anxious to complete their bloody work by murdering the rest of us. We took along my wounded brother, and by my mother's wonderful faith, God raised up my brother and he is still alive.

With the Mormon Battalion I went to Mexico to defend my country, although its officers in the time of my greatest trouble afforded me no protection. After our discharge on the Pacific Coast, I went to Oregon, and while there at work with some companions, a man who appeared to be a tramp, dressed in a pair of overalls and shirt, stated that he had been traveling for years hoping to find some one to kill him, that he was one of the mob who murdered the Mormons and little children at the Haun's Mill massacre, that he had never known one minute's peace since, that his life was a burden to him, and he wanted some one to kill him. He asked if there were any Mormons there. Some one told him there was; that a young man was there who was present at the massacre, and who had a brother killed at the time under the bellows at the blacksmith's shop. The individual uttered a terrible groan, and said that he was the one who killed him. He was led into my presence, and as he approached me, he bared his breast and said, "Shoot me; kill me, that I may be at rest." I said, "No sir; I will do no such thing. If you were wicked enough to kill my little innocent brother and others without cause and are suffering the just penalty of such a horrid crime I would not stain my hands with your blood but leave you in the hands of a just God." He trembled from head to foot and went away. I have never heard of him since.

I have told you this much of my experience of the Haun's Mill massacre, but I can never tell you all of it. I feel now towards the murderers of Bros. Gibbs and Berry as I did towards the murderer of my brother.

Let God deal with them; I do not envy them their feelings. They will never more be happy on the earth. We leave these men in the hands of God. Amen ("Haun's Mill," *Journal History* [August 27, 1884]: 7; spelling standardized).

William Smith

William Smith
(Courtesy of the Church Archives, The Church of Jesus Christ of Latter-day Saints)

It was astonishing to think that the humane Governor [Lilburn W. Boggs of Missouri] would endanger the lives of his citizens by sending out only fifteen thousand men to exterminate a small handful of "Mormons," men, women, and children. While one division of the Governor's mob were on their way to Far West, under the command of one Comstock, they came across a company of the Saints who were encamped on Shoal Creek, on their way to Far West from Ohio, who were in a great measure ignorant of the extent of the difficulty and entirely innocent of any charge that could be preferred against them by the Missourians. Comstock, on learning that there was a company of Saints encamped on Shoal Creek, sent a committee of men to require them to give up all arms and ammunition that they might have with them, to which they replied, "We will, provided that we can be assured that the Missourians will not molest us;" stating at the same time, that peace was what they desired. An article of agreement was signed to that effect, in which the Missourians pledged their honor for the faithful fulfillment of the same. Articles of this nature have in all ages of the word been held sacred both by heathen and civilized nations; and [an] individual or a nation that was so base as to forfeit their oaths or solemn pledges was considered too base to deserve notice, but merited the vengeance of the gods. I would ask, how faithfully did Comstock and his men keep their vows, which they had so solemnly pledged themselves to do? On the day following, they showed themselves capable of perpetrating the most barbarous acts, as well as violating their solemn pledges; for while the Saints were engaged in solemn prayer to God, these lawless desperadoes came upon them with the fury of demons and commenced firing upon them while they were thus solemnly engaged. The Saints cried for quarters but in vain, they then endeavored to escape by flight, but were surrounded; the Missourians continued to shoot them. They would even place their guns to the heads of their victims, and thus barbarously take their lives. After the firing had partially subsided, one of Comstock's men found an old Revolutionary soldier by the name of McBride under the bank of the creek. On finding him he exclaimed, "You old grey headed Mormon, I will fix you." The old man got on his knees and begged for his life, but neither age, nor innocence could afford any protection; he was inhumanly butchered and thrown into the creek. During the slaughter a small boy endeavored to conceal himself in the blacksmith shop under a bellows, but one of the assassins, seeing him, was in the act of shooting him when one of the company cried out, "Do not shoot the boy." Another said "Shoot him, d—m him, he will make a big Mormon some day;" so he put the gun to the child's head, and blew out his brains. There were, in this slaughter, eighteen of the Saints killed and thirteen wounded out of a company of Saints who were on their way moving to Far West, who had never violated the laws of the State; a company who had never taken any part in the past difficulties; a company whom Gov. Boggs himself cannot (as base and unprincipled as he is) contend had violated even one clause of the law of the state, or had even acted in concert with their brethren when engaged in self-defense, butchered too, by his command, and their wagons plundered of their contents, and their dead bodies robbed of their coats, watches, money, hats, and boots (William Smith, "Infatuated & Deluded Sect," *Times & Seasons* [February 15, 1841]: 315–16; spelling, capitalization, and punctuation standardized).

John Hammer

In the fall of 1838 the mob threatened to burn this mill because it ground grain for the Mormons, and all the mills in that section of the country . . . refused to grind for them, hoping by so doing to starve the Mormons out. In consequence of these threats a few of the brethren assisted in guarding the mill. This duty they had performed for several days and nights. The mob kept repeating their threats of violence. Finally some of our leading men interviewed the mob leaders who agreed upon a certain day when they would send a committee to the mill to confer with our brethren and see if terms could be agreed upon whereby a compromise could be arranged. On the day thus fixed . . . a number of our brethren were at the mill hoping to have something of a reasonable talk, being of course anxious that peace and security might be restored. . . . No violence from the mob party on that day was anticipated, and the brethren stacked their arms. The mob committee, however, did not make their appearance: but as the day was drawing to a close a company of the mob, some two or three hundred strong, were seen partly sheltered from observation by the heavy timber near by. Our brethren immediately hoisted a white flag. When the mob saw the flag they knew they were discovered. They rode rapidly on, led by Boregard and Comstock, and on their arrival at the mill one of them—without saying a word to our men—gave orders for their men to fire, which order was obeyed. Their leader then said to the brethren: "All who desire to save their lives and make peace run into the blacksmith shop;" . . . which was immediately surrounded by the infuriated assailants who commenced firing between the logs, as there was no chinking between them. They also fired through a long opening made at one side of the shop by one of the logs having been sawed out to admit light . . . Several were killed in the shop, my father being one of the number, seven balls being shot into his body, breaking both thigh bones. Some of the brethren thus shot down were dragged out into the yard so that their murderers might have a better chance and more room to strip them of their clothing . . . My father had on a new pair of boots that fitted him tightly and in the efforts to get them off, he was dragged and pulled out of the shop and about the yard in a barbarous manner. In his mangled condition, this cruel treatment must have caused him the most excruciating pain.

The brethren, seeing that the mob party were so numerous and bloodthirsty, concluded that it was useless to make any defense. Their only safety was in every one making their escape the best way they could, which they did by fleeing into the woods and brush, or wherever they could secrete themselves. When the mob had murdered all they could find and robbed a number of their clothing, they retreated.

After darkness of night had come on, the brethren who were in hiding began to make search for those who had been killed and wounded. My father was found and carried into Haun's house, where he died about 12 o'clock that night. During that night they kept up the search as well as the darkness would permit, but were only able to find the wounded by their groans. All they were able in this manner to find were taken into Mr. Haun's house as soon as possible so as to be protected from being torn or mangled by the hogs with which the woods at that place were full. When daylight had fully come, the brethren who had been spared had to move with great caution, knowing that the mob were liable to fall upon them at any moment, for the purpose of finishing their bloody and damnable work.

Of course, there was no opportunity for affording the dead a decent and respectable burial. There was an old dry well near by . . . and the only burial clothes with which they could be clothed were just what this rapacious band of murderous vampires had left upon them. In this manner seventeen bodies of our brethren found there their place of rest, my father and my uncle York being among the number. At the time of this sad occurrence I was in the ninth year of my age.

I wish here to record a circumstance which occurred exactly at the time this bloody deed was being enacted. I stood in the yard with my mother, my aunt York, my cousin Isaiah York and some of the smaller children of our two families. Our anxiety, of course, was great as to the fate of the brethren at Haun's mill, knowing also that my father and uncle had gone there to aid in its protection and assist those of our friends who lived there. . . . Looking eagerly in the direction of the mill . . . a crimson colored vapor like a mist or thin cloud, ascended up from the precise place where we knew the mill to be located and was carried or streamed upward into the sky apparently as high as our sight could extend. This singular phenomenon—like a transparent pillar of blood—remained there for a long time—how long I am not now able correctly to state; but it was to be seen by us far into that fatal night. . . . At that hour we had not heard a word of what had taken place at the mill; but as quick as my mother and aunt saw this red, blood-like token, they commenced to wring their hands and moan, declaring they knew that their husbands had been murdered. Our uneasiness through that night was too great to be described, and when daylight came, my cousin rode to the mill in order to learn the facts in relation to what had taken place. On his arrival there, he learned concerning the massacre and brought us word back as soon as possible. The following morning my cousin and myself went to the mill and found that the dead had all been buried in the well. . . . We found the hat of my uncle York with a bullet hole made through it on the two sides at or near the place usually occupied by the band, showing that my uncle must have been shot through the head.

We, at this time, went into the blacksmith shop . . . the floor the earth constituted and in places where there were small hollows in the soil the blood stood in pools from two or three inches deep. A boy had tried to hide by creeping under the bellows, but was discovered by the ruffians and killed. . . . His brains dashed out, which were plain to be [seen] upon the logs at the time of my visit. . . .

The death of my father left our family in a very helpless and unprotected condition. It would have been an event sufficiently melancholy had he died of sickness, at home, where his family could have administered to his wants . . . But to be cut down in his prime, and torn thus suddenly and ruthlessly from wife and children so intensified the gloom which rested down upon our bereaved circle, that for a time it seemed that no ray of hope or joy would ever be able to penetrate our bosoms. And could we have been left, uninterrupted, to pass our season of grief—that would have been a boon which we had not the privilege to enjoy. Those prowling fiends who—like the demons of hell—murdered the innocent and robbed them of their raiment, were still lurking around watching for new victims. Especially all the male members of the neighborhood had to keep concealed. The moment the mob got sight of them they were shot at. The women were not quite so closely hunted and they, by being extremely cautious, managed to convey water and food to their husbands, sons and brothers. . . . Myself and cousin had to sleep in shocks of corn or in the brush for two or three weeks, not daring to enter the house. . . . The nights were cold and frosty, which added seriously to our affliction.

After about three weeks from the time of the massacre the mob sent our people word that we were all to leave that country inside of ten days or we would all be killed. They were doubtless stimulated to make this announcement because of the order of extermination which was issued by Governor Boggs. . . . It affected our family equally with other members of the church. The burden of all this preparation and removal, on our part, rested first upon my mother. A less healthy and resolute woman could not have had the courage and endurance to grapple successfully with the obstacles that lay in her path (in Lyman Littlefield, *Reminiscences of Latter-day Saints* [Logan, Utah: Utah Journal Co., 1888], 66–71; spelling standardized).

Margaret Foutz

We ran about three miles into the woods, and there huddled together, spreading what few blankets or shawls we chanced to have on the ground for the children; and here we remained until two o'clock the next morning (as cited in *The Women of Mormondom,* 171).

George Washington Gill Averett

Difficulty occurred betwixt the Saints and the mob in the neighborhood of Haun's Mill and the two parties met together and held a treaty of peace, and agreed to be at peace with each other and before the Saints who [were] assembled at the treaty of peace. The mobbers, contrary to their solemn agreement, returned and commenced some 200 . . . of them to fire on the unsuspecting Saints, men, women and children, massacring them in a most brutal manner so much so that my ability is inadequate to describe the extent of the same after satisfying their hellish desires by the shedding of blood. And some of them mangling the bodies of the slain after death; one man, by the name of McBride whose body was horribly mangled by being cut to pieces with a mowing scythe. It was also told that some of the mobbers fired at some of the women of that place, shutting them in their place after they had done all the meanness by killing all the men they could find alive. They murdered two small boys to satisfy their hellish disposition. All of this shouting happening at or near the Haun's Mill where there was a small . . . of houses and amongst the worst, one blacksmith's shop in which the most part, as I am informed of the murder, was committed and after the affair was all over 17 of the slain [were] buried in an old well near the shop by the few men that [were] left and the women of the place (George Washington Gill Averett, "Autobiography of George Washington Gill Averett," *Writings of Early Latter-day Saints and Their Contemporaries, a Database Collection,* comp. Milton V. Backman [Provo, Utah: BYU Religious Studies Center, 1996], 5).

The Siege of Far West
(October 30, 1838)

As word of the extermination order issued by Governor Boggs spread, Saints in Far West, Missouri, lay in wait for the mob they knew would inevitably come. Their fears were actualized in the early morning hours of October 30, 1838, when a mob attacked the settlement.

George Q. Cannon

At Far West, Missouri, on the 4th day of July, 1838, the liberty pole was struck by lightning and shattered into splinters. Joseph walked around the fragments saying:

"As that pole was splintered, so shall the nations of the earth be" (George Q. Cannon, *The Life of Joseph Smith, the Prophet* [Salt Lake City: Deseret Book Co., 1986], 529).

Emily Dow Partridge Young

On the fourth of July, 1838, the Saints assembled in Far West to celebrate the day, and I think the spot for the temple was that day dedicated. Our national flag, the stars and stripes, attached to the liberty-pole, floated gaily in the breeze. All were happy and joyful, as none but the Saints know how to be.

Shortly after the fourth a terrible storm arose; the thunder and lightning were terrific; the liberty was struck and shattered by a bolt, foreshadowing coming events, as the sequel proved.

Not long after this rumors came to Far West, from different settlements of the Saints, of threats, and depredations being committed by small parties of Missourians. There was trouble in Daviess County—a battle was fought on Crooked River, and Brother David Patten, one of the Twelve, and some others of the brethren were killed. Then came the news of the terrible massacre at Haun's Mill, and before we were hardly aware of it a large army of the mob were marching towards Far West, with an exterminating order from the Governor. The brethren hastily got together wagons, logs, boards and whatever they could find that would do, and threw up a breastwork to protect themselves, in a measure, from the bullets of the murderous mob. The mob halted when within about half a mile of Far West. A white flag was sent out by the mob, and were met by a party of our brethren, also carrying a white flag . . .

The days following another flag was sent by the mob, and some of our brethren met them and learned that they were commissioned by the chief executive, and were authorized to exterminate the Mormons en masse, and they had three thousand troops under command to carry these orders into effect. Col. Hinkle went out to meet the flag of truce, and secretly made arrangements to deliver up the leaders of the Church to be tried and punished; to have the property of the Saints delivered over to the mob to pay their expenses and all damages done them, and also arranged that the Saints should leave the state, and their arms be delivered up to the enemy.

In the evening of the same day the first step in this base treachery was taken. Hinkle represented to the Prophet, that the officers of the militia desired an interview with him, in the hope that a settlement might be brought about without carrying out the Governor's exterminating orders. . . .

Brother Joseph and others complied with the request, and were delivered into the hands of the mob as prisoners of war by the treacherous and cowardly George M. Hinkle. The brethren were put into a hollow square and strongly guarded. The mob . . . set up a most horrid, unearthly yell, and one might well imagine that it came from the throats of demons of the lower regions. It was a sound long to be remembered, and one that no person could desire to hear but once in their lives, especially under like circumstances.

On the morning of the 1st of November [1838], the bugle sounded for the brethren to assemble. Every man went well armed and was paraded and delivered over to the mob. The brethren were surrounded and required to surrender their arms and were guarded all day, while the soldiers went from house to house, plundering, pillaging, destroying, and driving, in some instances, women and children from their homes. Before the mob disbanded, after securing the arms of the brethren, they rode through the city, and passed so close to our house that we could hear their remarks (Emily Dow Partridge Young, "Autobiography," *Writings of Early Latter-day Saints,* 18).

Anson Call

(Anson reports what happened to the Saints in Adam-ondi-Ahman at the time of the siege of Far West.)

After supper we were all called together at general orders and received instructions from Lyman Wight and Reynolds Cahoon. They said that in consequence of the much fatigue the brethren had had we might all go to our lodgings with the exception of 25 men whom they had selected. They said they had been expecting an attack from the mob for the last three days and we must load our arms and lay them under our heads and not take off our clothes. If the bugle sounded we might consider that the mob was upon us and all hands were immediately to rally at that place. About one o'clock the next morning the bugle sounded; there was the running of horses, the hollering, "Turn out, turn out, the mob is upon us." The brethren immediately rallied. The women dressed themselves and children and prepared for the conflict. We immediately rushed, as we supposed, toward our enemies, but we found it to be a company of brethren from Far West. We then learned that Far West was surrendered and that the presidency was given up in the hands of the mob. We were informed that we would be called upon to surrender about 10 o'clock in the morning.

Presently Colonel Parks made his appearance with 500 armed men; forming a hollow square they ordered, "Within one hour every man is to be within the square with all his arms and ammunition." This, we learned, was the order of Brother Joseph. We accordingly obeyed the order. After our surrender General Parks left 200 men to guard us from those that he said would injure us, but those he left were the worst men in all the land. He gave us 10 days to leave the country. The General gave me a passport to Far West that we might travel and not be killed, to-wit: I permit Anson Call to remove to Far West and from thence out of the state. Signed General Parks.

While tarrying at Diahman two of the guard came to the tree top where I and my family were sitting, eating our dinner and asked me some questions. He said I was a damned liar and said he would shoot me. He cocked his gun and put it to his face. My family screamed, and he lowered his gun and rode off. The second night after the surrender the snow fell about six inches deep. I then started with my family to Far West. My children nearly froze to death. One of them froze his fingers so that he lost a part of his nails. His name was Maroni. After riding to

Far West the weather continued severely cold so that many of the mob were obliged to leave. They killed our cattle, stole our horses, burned our houses, constantly killing and abusing all that they met with; insulted our women and murdered some of our children.

We were not permitted to leave Far West only to get our firewood. We had not the privilege of hunting our cattle and horses, yet we were told that we had immediately to leave the state. We were deprived of holding meetings of any kind. Joseph Smith senior and Brigham Young were our principal counselors. We received two or three epistles from Joseph who was at that time in Liberty Jail, Clay County. Some few times in the course of the winter we slyly congregated ourselves in a schoolhouse about two miles from Far West to receive instructions from Joseph and others (Anson Call, *Autobiography and Sketch of the Life of Anson Call* [Provo, Utah: n.p., 1960], 9–10; spelling and capitalization standardized).

Heber C. Kimball

(The mobs took over Far West once the Church's leaders were arrested. Heber C. Kimball recounts the barbarity of the mobs.)

Judge Cameron drove in the hogs belonging to the brethren (many of which were identified), shot them down in the street, and without further bleeding, they were half dressed, cut up and distributed by Mr. McHenry to the poor, at the rate of four or five cents per pound, which, together with a few pieces of refuse calicoes at double and [triple] prices, soon consumed the appropriation (Heber C. Kimball, *Journal of Heber C. Kimball, an Elder of The Church of Jesus Christ of Latter-day Saints,* comp. R. B. Thompson [Salt Lake City: Juvenile Instructor Office, 1882], 65).

Hyrum Smith

(Recounting the barbarity of the mob at Far West.)

On the return of this messenger, we learned that several persons had been killed by some of the soldiers, who were under the command of General Lucas.

One Mr. Carey had his brains knocked out by the breach of a gun, and he lay bleeding several hours, but his family were not permitted to approach him, nor any one else allowed to administer relief to him whilst he lay upon the ground in the agonies of death. Mr. Carey had just arrived in the country, from the state of Ohio, only a few hours previous to the arrival of the army. He had a family consisting of a wife and several small children. He was buried by Lucius N. Scovil, who is now [1843] the senior warden of the Nauvoo [Masonic] Legion.

Another man, of the name of John Tanner, was knocked on the head at the same time, and his skull laid bare to the width of a man's hand, and he lay, to all appearances, in the agonies of death for several hours; but by the permission of General Doniphan, his friends brought him out of the camp, and with good nursing he slowly recovered, and is now living.

There was another man, whose name is Powell, who was beaten on the head with the breech of a gun until his skull was fractured. He is now alive, and resides in this [Hancock] county, but has lost the use of his senses. Several persons of his family were also left for dead, but have since recovered (Lucy Mack Smith, *The Revised and Enhanced History of Joseph Smith by His Mother*, ed. Scot Facer Proctor and Maurine Jensen Proctor [Salt Lake City: Bookcraft, 1996], 379).

The Arrest of Joseph and Hyrum
(October 31, 1838)

The repercussions of the Extermination Order were widespread, reaching from the massacre of Haun's Mill to the siege of Far West. In the midst of all the turmoil, Joseph and Hyrum Smith were arrested at Far West and sent to Independence, then to Richmond Jail, and finally to Liberty Jail. Several other men were arrested with Joseph and Hyrum. Some of these managed to escape, some stayed in Richmond, and others (Lyman Wight, Caleb Baldwin, Alexander McRae, and Sidney Rigdon) were taken with Joseph and Hyrum to Liberty Jail.

Mary Fielding Smith

Mary Fielding Smith
(Courtesy of the Church Archives, The Church of Jesus Christ of Latter-day Saints)

My husband was taken from me by an armed force, at a time when I needed, in a particular manner, the kindest care and attention of such a friend, instead of which, the care of a large family was suddenly and unexpectedly left upon myself, and, in a few days after, my dear little Joseph F. was added to the number. Shortly after his birth I took a severe cold, which brought on chills and fever: this, together with the anxiety of mind I had to endure, threatened to bring me to the gates of death. I was at least four months entirely unable to take any care either of myself or child; but the Lord was merciful in so ordering things that my dear sister could be with me all the time. Her child was five months old when mine was born; so she had strength given her to nurse them both (Mary Fielding Smith, "To the Editor of the Star," *Millennial Star* [June 1840]: 40).

Lyman Wight

(Wight related the following heartrending account of what took place when Joseph and Hyrum Smith were taken prisoner in Far West.)

About the hour the prisoners were to have been shot on the public square in Far West, they were exhibited in a wagon in the town, all of them having families there, but myself; and it would have broken the heart of any person possessing an ordinary share of humanity, to have seen the separation. The aged father and mother of Joseph Smith were not permitted to see his face, but to reach their hands through the curtains of the wagon, and thus take leave of him. When passing his own house, he was taken out of the wagon and permitted to go into the house, but not without a strong guard, and not permitted to speak with his family but in the presence of his guard and his eldest son, Joseph, about six or eight years old, hanging to the tail of his coat, crying father, is the mob going to kill you? The guard said to him, "you damned little brat, go back, you will see your father no more" (Lyman Wight, "Trial of Joseph Smith," *Times and Seasons* [July 1, 1843]: 4:268).

Parley P. Pratt

The haughty general [Lucas] rode up, and without speaking to us, instantly ordered his guard to surround us. They did so very abruptly, and we were marched into camp surrounded by thousands of savage looking beings, many of whom were dressed and painted like Indian warriors. These all set up a constant yell, like so many bloodhounds let loose upon their prey, as if they had achieved one of the most miraculous victories that ever graced the annals of the world (Parley P. Pratt, *Autobiography of Parley P. Pratt, revised and enhanced,* ed. Scot Facer Proctor and Maurine Jensen Proctor [Salt Lake City: Deseret Book, 2000], 159–60).

George Q. Cannon

The next morning was the Sabbath; and the people along the road came out in their best attire to view the "Mormon" Prophet, for the news had preceded his advent, and the whole country was aroused. While they were yet in camp on that morning a number of ladies and gentlemen visited them; and one woman inquired of the guards, "Which of the captives is the Lord worshiped by the Mormons?"

The mobocrat pointed to Joseph with a significant smile and said, "That is he." After gazing upon the Prophet for a moment, the lady candidly asked whether he professed to be the Lord and Savior Jesus Christ. Joseph answered:

"I am only a man, a humble minister of salvation sent by the Redeemer to preach His gospel."

Astounded at this reply, so different from what she had been led to expect, the lady pressed question after question upon the Prophet. As he responded, many listeners gathered around, including a company of the wondering soldiers; and there on that Sabbath morning, with hundreds of spectators and his captors for a congregation, the Prophet preached as impressive a discourse as ever before in his life. He set forth the doctrines of faith in Jesus Christ, repentance, baptism for the remission of sin, with a promise of the gift of the Holy Ghost—as recorded in the Acts of the Apostles. . . .

His listeners were filled with strange emotions; this man spoke as no other had ever talked in their hearing. The woman who had first asked to see the Prophet was wrought upon by a spirit of conviction. When Joseph finished his remarks, she arose and praised God in solemn tones, and she went away praying that the Lord would protect and deliver His servants (George Q. Cannon, *Life of Joseph Smith the Prophet* [Salt Lake City: Deseret Book, 1986], 282–83; punctuation standardized).

Joseph Fielding Smith

"[On] November 1, 1838, Hyrum Smith and Amasa Lyman were brought as prisoners into the camp. The prisoners were placed under a strong guard . . .

"On the night of November 1, 1838, a court martial was held."

The prisoners were held that night in General Doniphan's camp. General Doniphan had been a friend to the Saints in the past and remained on that night. Many of the militia officers at the hearing in camp thought the prisoners should be killed the next morning. General Lucas issued the following order to General Doniphan:

"Brigadier—General Doniphan—Sir: You will take Joseph Smith and the other prisoners into the public square of Far West, and shoot them at 9 o'clock tomorrow morning."

General Doniphan returned the following reply to his superior:

"It is cold-blooded murder. I will not obey your order. My brigade shall march for Liberty tomorrow morning, at 8 o'clock; and if you execute these men, I will hold you responsible before an earthly tribunal, so help me God!" (Joseph Fielding Smith, *Church History and Modern Revelation,* 4 vols. [Salt Lake City: The Church of Jesus Christ of Latter-day Saints, 1946–49], 3:165–67).

Joseph Smith Jr.

(Recalling the separation from his family.)

We were delivered up as prisoners of war and taken into their camp . . . The next day they held a court-martial upon us and sentenced me with the rest of the prisoners to be shot which sentence was to be carried into effect on Friday morning in the public square . . . The militia then went and selected to my house and drove my family out of doors under sanction of General Clark and carried away all my property . . . We were led into the public square and after considerable entreaty we were permitted to see our family's being attended with a strong guard. I found my family in tears . . . they clung to my garments with weeping. Requesting to have an proper interview with my wife and [children] in an adjoining room, but was refused. When taking my departure from my family it was almost too painful for me. My child[ren] clung to me and were thrust away at the point of the swords of the soldiery [punctuation added] (Clark V. Johnson, *Mormon Redress Petitions: Documents of the 1833–1838 Missouri Conflict* [Provo, Utah: BYU Religious Studies Center, 1992], 349; capitalization standardized).

Parley P. Pratt

On the night of the betrayal of Joseph and his friends, Elder Brigham Young and Heber C. Kimball ordered a strong barricade built between the defenders of Far West and the enemy. The barricade was completed that night, and artillery and ammunition were gathered. Women helped in preparing to defend the city by pouring lead into bullet molds. At the break of day Mormon defenders with rifles in hand stood behind the barricade, ready to fire upon the enemy in the event of an attack. To the beat of drums the army of General Lucas marched within rifle shot of the defenders and halted. An orderly presented the defenders a dispatch from Lucas ordering surrender. Without the defenders' knowledge, Colonel Hinkle had previously made a treaty of surrender with General Lucas. The Mormons were marched to the public square where about 600 guns, besides swords and pistols, were delivered up to the enemy, among whom were some of the apostates. . . .

William E. McLellin, once an apostle, now an apostate, was among a mob which entered a number of homes, driving out wives and children, in order to steal whatever valuables could be found. From the Prophet's home he stole a roll of linen cloth, a number of valuable books, buttons, a horse and gig, and other items (as cited in Ivan Barrett, *Joseph Smith and the Restoration* [Provo, Utah: Brigham Young University Press, 1967], 413–14).

October 31, 1838.—In the afternoon we were informed that the Governor had ordered this force against us, with orders to exterminate or drive every "*Mormon*" from the State. As soon as these facts were ascertained we determined not to resist anything in the shape of authority, however abused. We had now nothing to do but to submit to be massacred, driven, robbed or plundered, at the option of our persecutors.

Colonel George M. Hinkle, who was at that time the highest officer of the militia assembled for the defense of Far West, waited on Messrs. J. Smith, S. Rigdon, Hyrum Smith, L. Wight, George Robinson and myself, with a request from General Lucas that we would repair to his camp, with the assurance that as soon as peaceable arrangements could be entered into we should be released. We had no confidence in the word of a murderer and robber, but there was no alternative but to put ourselves into the hands of such monsters, or to have the city attacked, and men, women and children massacred. We, therefore, commended ourselves to the Lord, and voluntarily surrendered as sheep into the hands of wolves. As we approached the camp of the enemy General Lucas rode out to meet us with a guard of several hundred men.

The haughty general rode up, and, without speaking to us, instantly ordered his guard to surround us. They did so very abruptly, and we were marched into camp surrounded by thousands of savage looking beings, many of whom were dressed and painted like Indian warriors. These all set up a constant yell, like so many bloodhounds let loose upon their prey, as if they had achieved one of the most miraculous victories that ever graced the annals of the world. If the vision of the infernal regions could suddenly open to the mind, with thousands of malicious fiends, all clamoring, exulting, deriding, blaspheming, mocking, railing, raging and foaming like a troubled sea, then could some idea be formed of the hell which we had entered.

In camp we were placed under a strong guard, and were without shelter during the night, lying on the ground in the open air, in the midst of a great rain. The guards during the whole night kept up a constant tirade of mockery, and the most obscene blackguardism and abuse. They blasphemed God; mocked Jesus Christ; swore the most dreadful oaths; taunted brother Joseph and others; demanded miracles; wanted signs, such as: "Come, Mr. Smith, show us an angel." "Give us one of your revelations." "Show us a miracle." "Come, there is one of your brethren here in camp whom we took prisoner yesterday in his own house, and knocked his brains out with his own rifle, which we found hanging over his fireplace; he lays speechless and dying; speak the word and heal him, and then we will all believe." "Or, if you are Apostles or men of God, deliver yourselves, and then we will be Mormons." Next would be a volley of oaths and blasphemies; then a tumultuous tirade of lewd boastings of having defiled virgins and wives by force, etc., much of which I dare not write; and, indeed, language would fail me to attempt more than a faint description. Thus passed this dreadful night, and before morning several other captives were added to our number, among whom was brother Amasa Lyman.

We were informed that the general officers held a secret council during most of the night, which was dignified by the name of court martial; in which, without a hearing, or, without even being brought before it, we were all sentenced to be shot. The day and hour was also appointed for the execution of this sentence, viz: next morning at 8 o'clock, in the public square at Far West. Of this we were informed by Brigadier-General Doniphan, who was one of the council, but who was so violently opposed to this cool blooded murder that he assured the council that he would revolt and withdraw his whole brigade, and march them back to Clay County as soon as it was light, if they persisted in so dreadful an undertaking. Said he, "It is cold blooded murder, and I wash my hands of it." His firm remonstrance, and that of a few others, so alarmed the haughty murderer and his accomplices that they dare not put the decree in execution.

Thus, through a merciful providence of God our lives were spared through that dreadful night. It was the common talk, and even the boast in the camp, that individuals lay here and there unburied, where they had shot them down for sport. The females they had ravished; the plunder they had taken; the houses they had burned; the horses they had stolen; the fields of grain they had laid waste, were common topics; and were dwelt on for mere amusement, or, as if these deeds were a step-stone to office; and it is a fact that such deeds were so considered.

No pen need undertake to describe our feelings during that terrible night, while there confined—not knowing the fate of our wives and children, or of our fellow Saints, and seeing no way for our lives to be saved except by the miraculous power of God. But, notwithstanding all earthly hopes were gone, still we felt a calmness indescribable. A secret whispering to our inmost soul seemed to say: "Peace, my sons, be of good cheer, your work is not yet done; therefore I will restrain your enemies, that they shall not have power to take your lives" (*Autobiography of Parley P. Pratt, revised and enhanced,* 234–36).

Hyrum Smith

Hyrum Smith
(Courtesy of the Church Archives, The Church of Jesus Christ of Latter-day Saints)

The next day, the soldiers were permitted to patrol the streets, to abuse and insult the people at their leisure, and enter into houses and pillage them, and ravish the women, taking away every gun and every other kind of arms or military implements. About twelve o'clock on that day, Colonel Hinkle came to my house with an armed force, opened the door and called me out of doors and delivered me up as a prisoner unto that force. They surrounded me and commanded me to march into the camp. I told them that I could not go; my family was sick, and I was sick myself, and could not leave home. They said they did not care for that—I must go and should go. I asked when they would permit me to return. They made me no answer, but forced me along with the point of the bayonet into the camp, and put me under the same guard as my brother Joseph; and within about half an hour . . . Amasa Lyman was also brought and placed under the same guard. There we were compelled to stay all that night and lie on the ground. But some time in the same night, Colonel Hinkle came to me and told me that he had been pleading my case before the court-martial, but he was afraid he would not succeed.

He said there was a court-martial then in session, consisting of thirteen or fourteen officers; Circuit Judge Austin A. King, and Mr. Birch, district attorney; also Sashiel Woods, Presbyterian priest, and about twenty other priests of the different religious denominations in that country. He said they were determined to shoot us . . . the next morning in the public square in Far West. I made him no reply. . . .

After our arrival in Independence, we were driven all through the town for inspection, and then we were ordered into an old log house and there kept under guard as usual until supper, which was served up to us as we sat upon the floor or on billets of wood, and we were compelled to stay in that house all that night and the next day.

They continued to exhibit us to the public by letting the people come in and examine us, and then go away and give place for others alternately, all that day and the next night. But on the morning of the following day, we were all permitted to go to the tavern to eat and sleep; but afterward they made us pay our own expenses for board, lodging, and attendance, and . . . made a most exorbitant charge. . . .

We arrived there [Richmond] on Friday evening, the ninth day of November, and were thrust into an old log house with a strong guard placed over us.

After we had been there for the space of half an hour, there came in a man who was said to have some notoriety in the penitentiary, bringing in his hands a quantity of chains and padlocks. He said he was commanded by General Clark to put us in chains.

Immediately the soldiers rose up, and pointing their guns at us, placed their thumb on the cock, and their finger on the trigger, and the state's prison keeper went to work putting a chain around the leg of each man and fastening it on with a padlock, until we were all chained together, seven of us.

In a few moments General Clark came in. We requested to know . . . the cause of all this harsh and cruel treatment. He refused to give us any information at that time, but said he would in a few days; so we were compelled to continue in that situation—camping on the floor, all chained together, without any change or means to be made comfortable, having to eat our victuals as they were served up to us, using our fingers and teeth instead of knives and forks.

Whilst we were in this situation, a young man of the name of Jedediah M. Grant, brother-in-law to my brother, William Smith, came to see us and put up at the tavern where General Clark made his quarters. He happened to come in time to see General Clark make choice of his men to shoot us on Monday morning, the twelfth day of November. He saw them make choice of their rifles and load them with two balls in each; and after they had prepared their guns, General Clark saluted them by saying, *"Gentlemen, you shall have the honor of shooting the "Mormon" leaders on Monday morning at eight o'clock!"*

But in consequence of the influence of our friend, the inhuman general was intimidated so that he durst not carry his murderous designs into execution, and sent a messenger immediately to Fort Leavenworth to obtain the military code of laws. . . .

The judge made out a subpoena and inserted the names of those men and caused it to be placed in the hands of Bogart, the notorious Methodist minister; and he took fifty armed soldiers and started for

Far West. I saw the subpoenas given to him and his company, when they started.

In the course of a few days, they returned with most of all those forty men, whose names were inserted in the subpoena, and thrust them into jail, and we were not permitted to bring one of them before the court; but the judge turned upon us, with an air of indignation, and said, "Gentlemen, you must get your witnesses, or you shall be committed to jail immediately, for we are not going to hold the court open, on expense, much longer for you, anyhow."

We felt very much distressed and oppressed at that time. Colonel Wight said, "What shall we do? Our witnesses are all thrust into prison, and probably will be, and we have no power to do anything; of course we must submit to this tyranny and oppression; we cannot help ourselves."

Several others made similar expressions, in the agony of their souls, but my brother Joseph did not say anything, he being sick at that time with the toothache, and pain in his face, in consequence of a severe cold brought on by being exposed to the severity of the weather. However, it was considered best by General Doniphan and Lawyer Rees that we should try to get some witnesses, before the pretended court.

Accordingly, I myself gave the names of about twenty other persons; the judge inserted them in a subpoena, and caused it to be placed in the hands of Bogart, the Methodist priest, and he again started off with his fifty soldiers, to take those men prisoner, as he had done to the forty others.

The judge sat and laughed at the good opportunity of getting the names, that they might the more easily capture them, and so bring them down to be thrust into prison in order to prevent us from getting the truth before the pretended court, of which himself was the chief inquisitor or conspirator. Bogart returned from his second expedition, with one witness only, whom he also thrust into prison.

The people at Far West had learned the intrigue and had left the state, having been made acquainted with the treatment of the former witnesses. But we, on learning that we could not obtain witnesses, whilst privately consulting with each other what we should do, discovered a Mr. Allen, standing by the window on the outside of the house. We beckoned to him as though we would have him come in. He immediately came in.

At that time Judge King retorted upon us again, saying, "Gentlemen, are you not going to introduce some witnesses?"—also saying it was the last day he should hold the testimony open for us, and if we did not rebut the testimony that had been given against us, he should have to commit us to jail.

I had then got Mr. Allen into the house, and before the court (so called) I told the judge we had one witness, if he would be so good as to put him under oath. He seemed unwilling to do so, but after a few moments' consultation, the state's attorney arose and said, he should object to that witness being sworn, and that he should object to that witness giving his evidence at all, stating that this was not a court to try the case, but only a court of investigation on the part of the state.

Upon this, General Doniphan arose, and said he would be G—d d—d, if the witness should not be sworn, and that it was a d—d shame, that these defendants should be treated in this manner, that they could not be permitted to get one witness before the court, whilst all their witnesses, even forty at a time, had been taken by force of arms and thrust into the "bull pen," in order to prevent them from giving their testimony.

After Doniphan sat down, the judge permitted the witness to be sworn and enter upon his testimony. But as soon as he began to speak, a man by the name of Cook, who was a brother-in-law to priest Bogart, the Methodist, and who was a lieutenant, [in the state militia], and whose place at that time was to superintend the guard, stepped in before the pretended court, and took him by the nape of his neck and jammed his head down under the pole or log of wood that was placed up around the place where the inquisition was sitting, to keep the bystanders from intruding upon the majesty of the inquisitors, and jammed him along to the door, and kicked him out of doors. He instantly turned to some soldiers, who were standing by him, and said to them, "Go and shoot him, d—n him; shoot him, d—n him."

The soldiers ran after the man to shoot him. He fled for his life, and with great difficulty made his escape. The pretended court immediately arose, and we were ordered to be carried to Liberty, Clay County, and there to be thrust into jail. We endeavored to find out for what cause, but, all that we could learn was, [that it was] because we were "Mormons." . . .

As we journeyed along on the road, we were exhibited to the inhabitants, and this course was adopted all the way, thus making a public exhibition of us until we arrived at Liberty, Clay County.

There we were thrust into prison again and locked up and were held there in close confinement for the space of six months, and our place of lodging [bed] was the square side of a hewed white oak log, and our food was anything but good and decent. Poison was administered to us three or four times. The effect it had upon our system was that it vomited us almost to death, and then we would lay some two or three days in a torpid, stupid state, not even caring or wishing for life—the poison being administered in too large doses, or it would inevitably have proved fatal, had not the power of Jehovah interposed on our behalf to save us from their wicked purpose. . . .

I do know that the "Mormon" people, en masse, were driven out of that state after being robbed of all they had, and they barely escaped with their lives, as well as my brother Joseph, who barely escaped with his life. His family also was robbed of all they had, and barely escaped with the skin of their teeth, and all this in consequence of the exterminating order of Governor Boggs, the same being confirmed by the legislature of that state.

And I do know, so does this court, and every rational man who is acquainted with the circumstances, and every man who shall hereafter become acquainted with the particulars thereof will know, that Governor Boggs, and Generals Clark, Lucas, Wilson, and Gillium, also Austin A. King, have committed treason upon the citizens of Missouri and did violate the Constitution of the United States and also the constitution and laws of the state of Missouri and did exile and expel, at the point of bayonet, some twelve or fourteen thousand inhabitants from the state and did murder some three or four hundred . . . men, women and children in cold blood, and in the most horrid and cruel manner possible; and the whole of it was caused by religious bigotry and persecution, because the "Mormons" dared to worship Almighty God according to the dictates of their own consciences, and agreeable to his divine will, as revealed in the scriptures of eternal truth, and had turned away from following the vain traditions of their fathers and would not worship according to the dogmas and commandments of those men who preach for hire and divine for money and teach for doctrine the precepts of men, [the Saints] expecting that the Constitution of the United States would have protected them therein.

But notwithstanding the "Mormon" people had purchased *upwards of two hundred thousand dollars' worth of land,* most of which was entered and paid for at the land office of the United States in the state of Missouri; and although the President of the United States has been made acquainted with these facts and the particulars of our persecutions and oppressions by petition to him and to Congress, yet they have not even attempted to restore the "Mormons" to their rights, or given any assurance that we may hereafter expect redress from them. And I do also know most positively and assuredly, that my brother Joseph Smith, has not been in the state of Missouri since the spring of the year 1839. And further this deponent saith not.

[Signed] HYRUM SMITH (*History of Joseph Smith by His Mother,* 383–96; italics added; grammar standardized).

Lyman Wight

Rumors were immediately sent to the Governor, with the news that the Mormons were killing and burning every thing before them, and that great fears were entertained that they would reach Jefferson city before the runners could bring the news. This was not known by the Church of Latter-day Saints, until 2200 of the militia had arrived within half a mile of Far West, and they then supposed the militia to be a mob. I was sent for from Ondiahman to Far West—reached there the sun about one hour high in the morning of the 29th of October, 1838, called upon Joseph Smith, enquired the cause of the great uproar, he declared he did not know, but feared the mob had increased their numbers, and was endeavoring to destroy us—I enquired of him if he had had any conversation with any one concerning the matter—he said he had not, as he was only a private citizen of the county—that he did not interfere with any such matters. I think that he told me there had been an order from General Acheson or Doniphan, one to the Sheriff to call out the militia in order to quell the riots, and to go to him he could give me any information on this subject, on enquiring for him I found him not. That between 3 and 4 o'clock, P. M., George M. Hinkle Colonel of the militia in that place called on me in company with Joseph Smith, and . . . Hinkle said he had been in the camp in order to learn the intention of the same, he said they greatly desired to see Joseph Smith, Lyman Wight, Sidney Rigdon, P. P. Pratt, and George W. Robinson; Joseph Smith first enquired why they should desire to see him as he held no office either civil or military. I next enquired why it was they should desire to see a man out of his own county. Colonel Hinkle here observed there is no time for controversy, if you are not into the camp immediately they are determined to come upon Far West before the setting of the sun, and said they did not consider us as military bodies, but religious bodies. He said that if the aforesaid persons went into the camp they would be liberated that night or very early next morning, that there should be no harm done.—We consulted together and agreed to go down—on going about half the distance from the camp, I observed it would be well for Generals Lucas, Doniphan, and others, to meet us and not have us go in so large a crowd of soldiers—accordingly the Generals moved onwards, followed by 50 Artillery men with a four-pounder. The whole 2200 moved in steady pace on the right and left keeping about even with the former.—General Lucas approached the aforesaid designated persons with a vile, base, and treacherous look in his countenance—I shook hands with him and saluted him thus: "we understand General you wish to confer with us a few moments, will not tomorrow morning do as well." At this moment George M. Hinkle spake and said, here General are the prisoners I agreed to deliver to you. General Lucas then brandished his sword with a most hideous look, and said you are my prisoners, and there is no time for talking at the present, you will march into the camp. At this moment I believe that there was 500 guns cocked and not less than 20 caps burst, and more hideous yells were never heard, even if the description of the yells of the damned in hell is true as given by the modern sects of the day. The aforesaid designated persons were there introduced into the midst of 2200 mob militia. They then called out a guard of 90 men, placing 30 around the prisoners who were on duty 2 hours and 4 off—prisoners were placed on the ground with nothing to cover but the heavens, and they were overshadowed by clouds that moistened them before morning.—Sidney Rigdon was of a delicate constitution, received a slight shock of Apoplectic fits which excited great laughter and much ridicule in the guard and mob militia. Thus the prisoners spent a doleful night in the midst of a prejudiced and diabolical community. Next day Hyrum Smith and Amasa Lyman were dragged from their families and brought prisoners into the camp—they alleging no other reason for taking Hyrum Smith than that he was brother to Joe Smith the Prophet, and one of his counselors as President of the Church. The prisoners spent this day as comfortably as could be expected under the existing circumstances. Night came on and under the dark shadows of the night, General Wilson, subaltern of General Lucas, took me one side, and said we do not wish to hurt you nor kill you, neither shall you be, by G— d— but we have one thing against you, and that is you are too friendly to Joe Smith, and we believe him to be a G—d d—d rascal! and Wight you know all about his character—I said, I do sir—will you swear all you know concerning him said Wilson—I will sir, was the answer I gave—give us the outlines said Wilson—I then told said Wilson I believed said Joseph Smith to be the most philanthropic man he ever saw and possessed of the most pure and republican principles, a friend to mankind, a maker of peace, and sir, had it not been that I had given heed to his counsel I would have given you hell before this time with all your mob forces, he then observed: Wight, I fear your life is in danger for there is no end to the prejudice against Joe Smith—kill and be d—d sir, was my answer. He answered and said there is to be a court martial held this night, and will you attend sir? I will not, unless compelled by force, was my reply. He returned about 11 o'clock that night and took me aside, and said I regret to tell you your die is cast, your doom is fixed, you are sentenced to be shot to-morrow morning on the public square, in Far West, at 8 o'clock. I answered, shoot, and be d—d.

We were in hopes said he, you would come out against Joe Smith, but as you have not, you will have to share the same fate with him. I answered, you may thank Joe Smith that you are not in hell this night; for had it not been for him, I would have put you there. Somewhere about this time General Doniphan came up and said to me; Colonel, the decision is a damned hard one, and I have washed my hands against such cool and deliberate murder. He further told me, that General Graham and several others, (names not recollected,) were with him in the decision, and opposed it with all their power; that he should move his soldiers away by day light, in the morning; that they should not witness such a heartless murder, Colonel, I wish you well. I then returned to my fellow prisoners, to spend another night on the cold damp earth, and the canopy of heaven to cover us. The night again proved a damp one. At the removal of General Doniphan's part of the army, the camp was thrown into the utmost confusion and consternation. General Lucas, fearing the consequence of such hasty and inconsiderate measures, revoked the decree of shooting the prisoners, and determined to take them to Jackson county. Consequently, he delivered the prisoners over to General Wilson, ordering him to see them safe to Independence, Jackson county. About the hour the prisoners were to have been shot on the public square in Far West, they were exhibited in a wagon in the town . . . The prisoners then set out for Jackson county, accompanied by Generals Lucas and Wilson, and about three hundred troops for a guard. We remained in Jackson county two or three days and nights, during most of which time, the prisoners were treated in a gentlemanly manner, and boarded at a hotel, for which they had afterwards, when confined in Liberty jail, to pay the most extravagant price, or have their property, if any they had, attached for the same.—At this time General Clark had arrived at Richmond, and by orders from the governor, took on himself the command of the whole of the militia, notwithstanding General Atchison's commission was the oldest, but he was supposed to be too friendly to the Mormons: and therefore dismounted, and General Clark sanctioned the measures of General Lucas, however cruel they might have been; and said, he should have done the same had he been there himself. Accordingly he remanded the prisoners from Jackson county, and they were taken and escorted by a strong guard to Richmond; threatened several times on the way with violence and death. They were met five miles before they reached Richmond, by about one hundred armed men, and when they arrived in town they were thrust into an old cabin under a strong guard. I was informed by one of the guards, that two nights previous to their arrival, General Clark had a court-martial, and the prisoners were again sentenced to be shot; but he being made a little doubtful of his authority, sent immediately to Fort Leavenworth for the military law, and a decision from the United State's officers, where he was duly informed, that any such proceeding would be a cool blooded and heartless murder. On the arrival of the prisoners at Richmond, Joseph Smith and myself sent for General Clark; to be informed by him what crimes were alleged against us. He came in and said he would see us again in a few minutes; shortly he returned and said he would inform us of the crimes alleged against us by the state of Missouri.

"Gentlemen, you are charged with treason, murder, arson, burglary, larceny, theft, and stealing, and various other charges too tedious to mention, at this time;" and he left the room. In about twenty minutes, there came in a strong guard, together with the keeper of the penitentiary of the state, who brought with him two common trace chains, noozed together by putting the small end through the ring; and commenced chaining us up one by one, and fastening with padlocks, about two feet apart. In this unhallowed situation, the prisoners remained fifteen days, and in this situation, General Clark delivered us to the professed civil authorities of the state, without any legal process being served on us at all, during the whole time we were kept in chains, with nothing but exparte evidence, and that either by the vilest apostates, or by the mob who had committed murder in the state of Missouri. Notwithstanding all of this exparte evidence, Judge King did inform our lawyer, ten days previous to the termination of the trial, who he should commit and who he should not; and I heard Judge King say on his bench, in the presence of hundreds of witnesses, that there was no law for Mormons, and they need not expect any. Said he, if the governor's exterminating order had been directed to me, I would have seen it fulfilled to the very letter ere this time.

After a tedious trial of fifteen days, with no other witnesses but exparte ones, the witnesses, for prisoners were either kicked out of doors or put on trial for themselves. The prisoners were now committed to Liberty jail, under the care and direction of Samuel Tillery, jailor.—Here we were received with a shout of indignation and scorn, by the prejudiced populace. Prisoners were here thrust into jail without a regular mittimus; the jailor having to send for one some days after. . . . In this situation we were kept until about the month of April, when we were remanded to Davies county for trial before the grand jury.—We were kept under the most loathsome and despotic guards they could produce in that county of lawless mobs. After six or eight days the grand jury, (most of whom by the by, were so drunk that they had to be carried out and into their rooms as though they were lifeless,) formed a fictitious indictment, which was sanctioned by Judge Birch, who was the State's Attorney under Judge King at our exparte trial, and who at that time stated that the Mormons ought to be hung without judge or jury, he the said judge, made out a mittimus without day or date, ordering the sheriff to take us to Columbia. The sheriff selected four men to guard five of us. We then took a circuitous route, crossing prairies sixteen miles without houses, and after traveling three days the sheriff and I were together, by ourselves five miles from any of the rest of the company, for sixteen miles at a stretch. The sheriff here observed to me, that he wished to God he was at home, and your friends and you also. The sheriff then showed me the mittimus, and he found it had neither day or date to it; and said the inhabitants of Davies county would be surprised that the prisoners had not left them sooner; and said he, by God, I shall not go much further. We were then near Yellow creek, and there were no houses nearer one way than sixteen miles and eleven another way; except right on the creek. Here a part of the guard took a spree while the balance helped us to mount our horses, which we purchased of them and for which they were paid. Here we took a change of venue and went to Quincy without difficulty, where we found our families who had been driven out of the state under the exterminating order of Governor Boggs. I never knew of Joseph Smith's holding any office, civil or military, or using any undue influence in religious matters during the whole routine of which I have been speaking (Lyman Wight, "Trial of Joseph Smith," *Times and Seasons* [July 15, 1843]: 266–69; spelling standardized).

Brigham Young

(Describing the vindictiveness of Judge Austin A. King.)

Joseph Smith was arraigned before Judge Austin A. King, on a charge of treason. The Judge inquired of Mr. Smith, "Do you believe and teach the doctrine that in the course of time the Saints will possess the earth?" Joseph replied that he did. "Do you believe that the Lord will raise up a kingdom that will fill the whole earth and rule over all other kingdoms, as the Prophet Daniel has said?" "Yes sir, I believe that Jesus Christ will reign king of nations as he does king of Saints." "Write that down, clerk; we want to fasten upon him the charge of treason, for if he believes this, he must believe that the State of Missouri will crumble and fall to rise no more." Lawyer Doniphan said to the Judge, " . . . Judge, you had better make the Bible treason and have done with it" (in *Journal of Discourses,* 26 vols. [London: Latter-day Saints' Book Depot, 1854–86], 9:331; spelling standardized).

Parley P. Pratt

In order to show some pretense of respect for some of the forms of law, Judge Austin A. King now entered our prison and took our testimony, preparatory to a change of venue. I shall never forget this interview. There stood our Judge, face to face with those who, by his cruelty and injustice, had lived a cold half year in a dungeon. He refused to look us in the eye; hung his head and looked like a culprit before his betters about to receive his doom. The looks of guilt and misery portrayed in his countenance during that brief interview bespoke more of misery than we had suffered during our confinement. I actually pitied him in my heart. With an extraordinary effort and a voice scarcely audible, he administered the oaths and withdrew (*Autobiography of Parley P. Pratt*, 297).

The Saints Are Driven from the State of Missouri

While Joseph and others were imprisoned in Liberty Jail, the Saints were forced to flee the state of Missouri, during the cold, late months of 1838.

Hyrum Smith

The "Mormon" people throughout the country were in a great state of alarm, and also in great distress. They saw themselves completely surrounded with armed forces on the north, and on the northwest, and on the south. Bogart, who was a Methodist preacher and who was then a captain over a militia company of fifty soldiers, but who had added to his number out of the surrounding counties about a hundred more, which made his force about one hundred and fifty strong, was stationed at Crooked Creek, sending out his scouting parties, taking men, women, and children prisoners, driving off cattle, hogs, and horses, entering into every house on Log and Long Creeks, rifling their houses of their most precious articles, such as money, bedding, and clothing, taking all their old muskets and their rifles or military implements, threatening the people with instant death if they did not deliver up all their precious things and enter into a covenant to leave the state or go into the city of

Far West by the next morning, sating that they "calculated to drive the people into Far West, and then drive them to hell." Gillium also was doing the same on the northwest side of Far West; and Sashiel Woods, a Presbyterian minister, was the leader of the mob in Daviess County; and a very noted man of the same society was the leader of the mob in Carroll County. And they were also sending out their scouting parties, robbing and pillaging houses, driving away hogs, horses, and cattle, taking men, women and children, and carrying them off, threatening their lives, and subjecting them to all manner of abuses that they could invent or think of.

Under this state of alarm, excitement and distress, the messengers returned from the governor, and from the other authorities, bringing the fatal news that the "Mormons" could have no assistance. They stated that the governor said that the "Mormons" had got into a difficulty with the citizens, and they might fight it out for all what he cared. He could not render them any assistance.

The people of DeWitt were obliged to leave their homes and go into Far West; but did not do so until after many of them had starved to death for want of proper sustenance, and several died on the road there and were buried by the wayside without a coffin or a funeral ceremony. The distress, sufferings, and privations of the people cannot be expressed.

All the scattered families of the "Mormon" people, in all the counties except Daviess were driven into Far West, with but few exceptions. This only increased their distress, for many thousands who were driven there had no habitations or houses to shelter them and were huddled together, some in tents and others under blankets, while others had no shelter from the inclemency of the weather. Nearly two months the people had been in this awful state of consternation, many of them had been killed, whilst others had been whipped until they had to swathe up their bowels to prevent them from falling out (*History of Joseph Smith by His Mother*, 373–75).

Lucy Mack Smith

The first day we arrived at a place called Tinney's Grove, where we lodged in an old log house, spending a rather uncomfortable time. The day after, I traveled on foot half the day, and at night came to the house of one Mr. Thomas, who was then a member of the Church. My husband was very much out of health, as he had not recovered from the shock occasioned by the capture of Hyrum and Joseph, and he suffered much with a severe cough.

The third day in the afternoon, it commenced raining. When night arrived, we stopped at a house and asked permission to stay over. The man of the house showed us a miserable outhouse, filthy enough to sicken the stomach, even to look at, and told us if we would clean this place out and haul our own wood, we might lodge there. We cleaned out the place so as to be able to lay our beds down, and here we spent the night without a fire. The next morning the landlord charged us seventy-five cents for the use of this shed, and we went on in the pouring rain. We asked for shelter at many places but were refused admittance until near night. We traveled through the rain and mud without finding anyone who was willing to take us in. At last we came to one other place very much like where we had spent the night before. Here we stayed all night, again without a fire.

The day after, which was the fifth from the time we started, just before we got to Palmyra, Missouri, Don Carlos called to us and said, "Father, this exposure is too bad and I will not bear it any longer. And the first place I come to that looks comfortable, I shall drive up to the house and go in, and do follow me."

We soon came to a handsome, neat-looking farmhouse which was surrounded with every appearance of comfort. The house stood a short distance from the road, but there was a large gate which opened into the field in front of it. Don Carlos opened the gate, drove into the field, and then, after he had assisted us through, he started to see the landlord, who met him before he came to the house. "Landlord," said Don Carlos, "I do not know but that I am trespassing, but I have with me an aged father, who is sick, besides my mother and a number of women with small children. We have now traveled two days and a half in the rain, and we shall die if we are compelled to go much further. If you will allow us to stay with you overnight, we will pay you any price for our accommodations."

"Why, what do you mean, sir?" said the gentleman. "Do you not consider us human beings? Do you think that we would turn anything that was flesh and blood away from our doors in such a time as this? Where are your parents? Drive your wagons to the door and help your wife and children out. I will attend to the others." He then assisted Mr. Smith and myself into the room where his lady was sitting, but as she was not well and he was afraid the dampness of the room might cause her to take cold, he ordered a . . . servant to make her a fire in another room. He then helped each one of the family into the house and hung their cloaks and shawls up to dry, saying he never in his life saw a family so uncomfortable from the effects of rainy weather.

At this house we had everything that could conduce to our comfort as this gentleman, whose name was Esquire Mann, did all that he could do to assist us. He brought us milk for our children, hauled us water to wash with, furnished good beds to sleep in, and more. In short, he left nothing undone. . . .

After spending the night here with this good man, we set out again the next morning, although it continued raining, for we were obliged to travel in order to avoid being detained by high water. We went on through mud and rain until we arrived within six miles of the Mississippi River. Here the ground was low and swampy, so much so that a person on foot would sink in above his ankles at every step. The weather grew colder and it began snowing and hailing, but still we were compelled to go on foot as the horses were not able to draw us. As we were crossing this place, Lucy lost her shoes several times, and her father had to thrust his cane into the mud to ascertain where they were, because they were so completely covered with mud and water.

When we came to the Mississippi River, we could not cross nor yet find a place of shelter, for there were many Saints there waiting to go over into Quincy. The snow was now six inches deep and still falling, but we were very tired, and we made up our beds on the snow and went to rest with what comfort we might under such circumstances. The next morning, our beds were covered with snow, but we rose and after considerable pains succeeded in folding up our frozen bedding. We tried to light a fire, but finding it impossible, we resigned ourselves to our situation and waited patiently for some opportunity to cross the river.

Soon after, Samuel came over from Quincy, and he, with Seymour Brunson's assistance, obtained permission of the ferryman to have us cross that day. About sunset we landed in Quincy, where Samuel had hired a house into which we moved. Our household included five other families, namely, Mr. Smith and myself with our daughter, Henry and Hyrum Hoit, also the families of Samuel Smith, Jenkins Salisbury, William McLeary, and Brother Graves (*History of Joseph Smith by His Mother*, 411–14).

Petitions to the Government for Redress

During the 1838–39 persecutions in Missouri, the Prophet Joseph instructed the Saints to do as the Lord had commanded: "to take statements and affidavits" of the abuses and losses they had suffered (D&C 123:1–4). In response, the Saints wrote almost 1,000 affidavits between 1839 and 1845, with the intent of submitting them to government officials. In 1839–40, Joseph Smith presented these claims to the United States Congress. Of the almost 1,000 claims submitted, 773 are currently known. They paint a graphic picture of the unjust devestation that wrecked the lives of the Saints in Missouri.

Clark V. Johnson

In his 1843 affidavit, Caleb Baldwin reported that because of the abuses that he and his family had suffered, he sought and obtained an interview, in November 1838, with Judge Austin A. King, at Richmond, Missouri, prior to the court of inquiry presided over by Judge King himself. Baldwin petitioned Judge King for a "fair trial," whereupon the judge, Baldwin testified, replied that "there was no law for the Mormons" and that "they must be exterminated." Baldwin explained to Judge King "that his family composed of helpless females had been plundered and driven out into the prairie and asked Judge King what he should do." Judge King answered that "if he [Baldwin] would renounce his religion and forsake [Joseph] Smith he would be released and protected." Baldwin further wrote that "the same offer was made to the other prisoners all of whom however [also] refused to do so and were in reply told that they would be put to death." Alanson Ripley, who was with Baldwin and Joseph Smith during the interview, also said that "the same offer was made to him [Ripley] by Mr. Birch the prosecuting attorney, that if he would forsake the mormons he should be released and Restored to his home and suffer to remain [in Missouri]; to which he returned." Joseph Smith recorded that "he and Mr. Baldwin were chained together at the time of the conversation ... recited by Mr. Baldwin, which conversation he heard and which is correctly stated." Joseph also testified "that no such offer was made to him it being understood as certain that he was to be shot." These two men who chose to continue their belief in the teachings of Joseph Smith, as exemplified in the Book of Mormon, were confined in Liberty Jail, Liberty, Missouri, from December 1838 through April 1839 by Judge King's court of inquiry, to await trial (*Mormon Redress Petitions*, 685–86).

Petition to the Missouri Legislature

We, the undersigned petitioners and inhabitants of Caldwell county, Missouri, in consequence of the late calamity that has come upon us taken in connection with former afflictions, feel it a duty we owe to ourselves and our country to lay our case before your honorable body for consideration. It is a well known fact, that a society of our people commenced settling in Jackson county, Missouri, in the summer of 1831, where they, according to their ability, purchased lands, and settled upon them, with the intention and expectation of becoming permanent citizens in common with others.

Soon after the settlement began, persecution commenced; and as the society increased, persecution also increased, until the society at last was compelled to leave the county; and although an account of these persecutions has been published to the world, yet we feel that it will not be improper to notice a few of the most prominent items in this memorial.

On the 20th of July, 1833, a mob convened at Independence—a committee of which called upon a few of the men of our Church there, and stated to them that the store, printing office, and indeed all other mechanic shops must be closed forthwith, and the society leave the county immediately.

These propositions were so unexpected, that a certain time was asked for to consider on the subject, before an answer should be returned, which was refused, and our men being individually interrogated, each one answered that he could not consent to comply with their propositions. One of the mob replied that he was sorry, for the work of destruction would commence immediately.

In a short time the printing-office, which was a two story brick building, was assailed by the mob and soon thrown down, and with it much valuable property destroyed. Next they went to the store for the same purpose; but Mr. Gilbert, one of the owners, agreeing to close it, they abandoned their design. Their next move was the dragging of Bishop Partridge from his house and family to the public square, where, surrounded by hundreds, they partially stripped him of his clothes, and tarred and feathered him from head to foot. A man by the name of Allen was also tarred at the same time. This was Saturday, and the mob agreed to meet the following Tuesday, to accomplish their purpose of driving or massacring the society.

Tuesday came, and the mob came also, bearing with them a red flag in token of blood. Some two or three of the principal men of the society offered their lives, if that would appease the wrath of the mob, so that the rest of the society might dwell in peace upon their lands. The answer was, that unless the society would leave *en masse*, every man should die for himself. Being in a defenseless situation, to save a general massacre, it was agreed that one half of the society should leave the county by the first of the next January, and the remainder by the first of the following April. A treaty was entered into and ratified, and all things went on smoothly for awhile. But sometime in October, the wrath of the mob began again to be kindled, insomuch that they shot at some of our people, whipped others, and threw down their houses, and committed many other depredations; indeed the society of Saints were harassed for some time both day and night; their houses were brick-batted and broken open and women and children insulted. The store-house of A. S. Gilbert and Company was broken open, ransacked, and some of the goods strewed in the streets.

These abuses, with many others of a very aggravated nature, so stirred up the indignant feelings of our people, that when a party of them, say about thirty, met a company of the mob of about double their number, a skirmish took place, in which some two or three of the mob, and one of our people, were killed. This raised, as it were, the whole county in arms, and nothing would satisfy the mob but an immediate surrender of the arms of our people, who forthwith were to leave the county. Fifty-one guns were given up, which have never been returned, or paid for, to this day. The next day, parties of the mob, from fifty to seventy, headed by priests, went from house to house, threatening women and children with death if they were not gone before they returned. This so alarmed our people that they fled in different directions; some took shelter in the woods, while others wandered in the prairies till their feet bled; and the weather being very cold, their sufferings in other respects were great.

The society made their escape to Clay county as fast as they possibly could, where the people received them kindly, and administered to their wants. After the society had left Jackson county, their buildings, amounting to about two hundred, were either burned or otherwise destroyed, and much of their crops, as well as furniture and stock; which if properly estimated would make a large sum, for the loss of which they have not as yet received any remuneration.

The society remained in Clay county nearly three years; when, at the suggestion of the people there, they removed to that section of the state known as Caldwell county. Here the people bought out most of the former inhabitants, and also entered much of the wild land. Many soon owned a number of eighties [an eighty acre] while there was scarcely a man who did not secure to himself at least a forty [a forty acre]. Here we were permitted to enjoy peace for a season; but as our society increased in numbers, and settlements were made in Daviess and Carroll counties, the mob spirit spread itself again. For months previous to our giving up our arms to General Lucas' army, we heard little else than rumors of mobs collecting in different places and threatening our people. It is well known that the people of our Church, who had located themselves at De Witt, had to give up to a mob, and leave the place, notwithstanding the militia were called out for their protection.

From De Witt the mob went towards Daviess county, and while on their way there took they two of our men prisoners, and made them ride upon the cannon, and told them that they would drive the "Mormons" from Daviess to Caldwell, and from Caldwell to hell; and that they would give them no quarter, only at the cannon's mouth. The threats of the mob induced some of our people to go to Daviess to help to protect their brethren who had settled at Adam-ondi-Ahman, on Grand river. The mob soon fled from Daviess county; and after they were dispersed and the cannon taken, during which time no blood was shed, the people of Caldwell returned to their homes, in hopes of enjoying peace and quiet; but in this they were disappointed; for a large mob was soon found to be collecting on the Grindstone fork of Grand river from ten to fifteen miles off, under the command of Cornelius Gillium, a scouting party of which came within four miles of Far West, in open daylight, and drove off stock belonging to our people.

About this time, word came to Far West that a party of the mob had come into Caldwell county to the south of Far West; that they were taking horses and cattle, burning houses and ordering the inhabitants to leave their homes immediately; and that they had then actually in their possession three men prisoners. This report reached Far West in the evening, and was confirmed about midnight. A company of about sixty men went forth under the command of David W. Patten to disperse the mob, as they supposed. A battle was the result, in which Captain Patten and three of his men were killed, and others wounded. Bogart, it appears, had but one killed and others wounded. Notwithstanding the unlawful acts committed by Captain Bogart's men previous to the battle, it is now asserted and claimed that he was regularly ordered out as a militia captain, to preserve the peace along the line of Ray and Caldwell counties. That battle was fought four or five days previous to the arrival of General Lucas and his army. About the time of the battle with Captain Bogart, a number of our people who were living near Haun's mill, on Shoal creek, about twenty miles below Far West, together with a number of emigrants who had been stopped there in consequence of the excitement, made an agreement with the mob in that vicinity that neither party should molest the other, but dwell in peace. Shortly after this agreement was made a mob party of from two to three hundred, many of whom are supposed to be from Chariton county, some from Daviess, and also those who had agreed to dwell in peace, came upon our people there, whose number in men was about forty, at a time they little expected any such thing, and without any ceremony, notwithstanding they begged for quarter, shot them down as they would tigers or panthers. Some few made their escape by fleeing. Eighteen were killed and a number more were severely wounded.

This tragedy was conducted in the most brutal and savage manner. An old man [Father Thomas McBride] after the massacre was partially over, threw himself into their hands and begged for quarter, when he was instantly shot down; that not killing him, they took an old corn cutter and literally mangled him to pieces. A lad of ten years of age, after being shot down, also begged to be spared, when one of the mob placed the muzzle of his gun to the boy's head and blew out his brains. The slaughter of these not satisfying the mob, they then proceeded to rob and plunder. The scene that presented itself after the massacre, to the widows and orphans of the killed, is beyond description. It was truly a time of weeping, mourning and lamentation.

As yet we have not heard of any one being arrested for these murders, notwithstanding there are men boasting about the county that they did kill on that occasion more than one "Mormon;" whereas all our people who were in the battle with Captain Patten against Bogart, that can be found, have been arrested, and are now confined in jail to await their trial for murder.

When General Lucas arrived near Far West, and presented the Governor's order, we were greatly surprised; yet we felt willing to submit to the authorities of the state. We gave up our arms without reluctance. We were then made prisoners, and confined to the limits of the town for about a week, during which time the men from the country were not permitted to go to their families, many of whom were in a suffering condition for want of food and firewood, the weather being very cold and stormy.

Much property was destroyed by the troops in town during their stay there, such as burning house logs, rails, corn-cribs, boards; the using of corn and hay, the plundering of houses, the killing of cattle, sheep and hogs, and also the taking of horses not their own; and all this without regard to owners, or asking leave of any one. In the meantime men were abused, women insulted and abused by the troops; and all this while we were kept prisoners.

Whilst the town was guarded, we were called together by the order of General Lucas, and a guard placed close around us, and in that situation we were compelled to sign a deed of trust for the purpose of making our individual property, all holden, as they said, to pay all the debts of every individual belonging to the Church, and also to pay for all damages the old inhabitants of Daviess may have sustained in consequence of the late difficulties in that country.

General Clark now arrived, and the first important move made by him was the collecting of our men together on the square and selecting about fifty of them, whom he immediately marched into a house, and placed in close confinement. This was done without the aid of the sheriff, or any legal process. The next day forty-six of those taken, were driven off to Richmond, like a parcel of menial slaves, not knowing why they were taken, or what they were taken for. After being confined in Richmond more than two weeks, about one half were liberated; the rest, after another week's confinement, were required to appear at court, and have since been let to bail. Since General Clark withdrew his troops from Far West, parties of armed men have gone through the country, driving off horses, sheep and cattle, and also plundering houses;

the barbarity of General Lucas' troops ought not to be passed over in silence. They shot our cattle and hogs merely for the sake of destroying them, leaving them for the ravens to eat. They took prisoner an aged man by the name of John Tanner, and without any reason for it, he was struck over the head with a gun, which laid his skull bare. Another man by the name of Carey was also taken prisoner by them, and without any provocation had his brains dashed out by a gun. He was laid in a wagon and there permitted to remain for the space of twenty-four hours; during which time no one was permitted to administer to him comfort or consolation; and after he was removed from that situation, he lived but a few hours.

The destruction of property at and about Far West is very great. Many are stripped bare, as it were, and others partially so; indeed take us as a body at this time, we are a poor and afflicted people; and if we are compelled to leave the state in the Spring, many, yes a large portion of our society, will have to be removed at the expense of the state; as those who might have helped them are now debarred that privilege in consequence of the deed of trust we were compelled to sign; which deed so operated upon our real estate, that it will sell for but little or nothing at this time.

We have now made a brief statement of some of the most prominent features of the troubles that have befallen our people since our first settlement in the state; and we believe that these persecutions have come in consequence of our religious faith, and not for any immorality on our part. That instances have been, of late, where individuals have trespassed upon the rights of others, and thereby broken the laws of the land, we will not pretend to deny; but yet we do believe that no crime can be substantiated against any of the people who have a standing in our Church of an earlier date than the difficulties in Daviess county. And when it is considered that the rights of this people have been trampled upon from time to time with impunity, and abuses almost innumerable heaped upon them it ought in some degree to palliate for any infraction of the law which may have been made on the part of our people.

The late order of Governor Boggs to drive us from the state, or exterminate us, is a thing so novel, unlawful, tyrannical, and oppressive, that we have been induced to draw up this memorial, and present this statement of our case to your honorable body, praying that a law may be passed, rescinding the order of the governor to drive us from the state, and also giving us the sanction of the legislature to possess our lands in peace. We ask an expression of the legislature, disapproving the conduct of those who compelled us to sign a deed of trust, and also disapproving of any man or set of men taking our property in consequence of that deed of trust, and appropriating it to the payment of debts not contracted by us or for the payment of damages sustained in consequence of trespasses committed by others.

We have no common stock; our property is individual property, and we feel willing to pay our debts as other individuals do; but we are not willing to be bound for other people's debts. The arms which were taken from us here, which we understand to be about six hundred and thirty, besides swords and pistols, we care not so much about, as we do the pay for them; only we are bound to do military duty, which we are willing to do, and which we think was sufficiently manifested by the raising of a volunteer company last fall at Far West when called upon by General Parks to raise troops for the frontier.

The arms given up by us, we consider were worth between twelve and fifteen thousand dollars; but we understand they have been greatly damaged since taken, and at this time probably would not bring near their former value. And as they were, both here and in Jackson county, taken by the militia, and consequently by the authority of the state, we therefore ask your honorable body to cause an appropriation to be made by law, whereby we may be paid for them, or otherwise have them returned to us, and the damages made good.

The losses sustained by our people in leaving Jackson county are such that it is impossible to obtain any compensation for them by law, because those who have sustained them are unable to prove those trespasses upon individuals. That the facts do exist that the buildings, crops, stock, furniture, rails, timber, etc., of the society have been destroyed in Jackson county, is not doubted by those who are acquainted in this upper country [the part of the state north of the Missouri river was so called]; and since these trespasses cannot be proven upon individuals, we ask your honorable body to consider this case; and if in your liberality and wisdom you can conceive it to be proper to make an appropriation by law to these sufferers, many of whom are still pressed down with poverty in consequence of their losses, they would be able to pay their debts, and also in some degree be relieved from poverty and woe; whilst the widow's heart would be made to rejoice, and the orphan's tears measurably dried up, and the prayers of a grateful people ascend on high, with thanksgiving and praise to the Author of our existence for such [a] beneficent act.

In laying our case before your honorable body, we say that we are willing, and ever have been, to conform to the Constitution and laws of the United States, and of this state. We ask, in common with others, the protection of the laws. We ask for the privilege guaranteed to all free citizens of the United States, and of this state, to be extended to us that we may be permitted to settle and live where we please, and worship God according to the dictates of our conscience without molestation. And while we ask for ourselves this privilege, we are willing all others should enjoy the same.

We now lay our case at the feet of your legislatures, and ask your honorable body to consider it, and do for us, after mature deliberation, that which your wisdom, patriotism and philanthropy may dictate. And we, as in duty bound, will ever pray.

EDWARD PARTRIDGE,
HEBER C. KIMBALL,
JOHN TAYLOR,
THEODORE TURLEY,
BRIGHAM YOUNG,
ISAAC MORLEY,
GEORGE W. HARRIS,
JOHN MURDOCK,
JOHN M. BURK.

A committee appointed by the citizens of Caldwell county, to draft the memorial and sign it in their behalf.

Far West, Caldwell county, Missouri, December 10, 1838 (*History of the Church*, 3:217–24).

Orson F. Whitney

The only recognition given by the Legislature to this pathetic appeal, this soul-harrowing recital of "bitter, burning wrongs," enough to melt a heart of stone . . . was the appropriation of the paltry sum of two thousand dollars, to be distributed among the people of Daviess and Caldwell Counties, *"the Mormons not excepted."*

Oh lavish generosity! Two thousand dollars for a city sacked and pillaged, fields and farms laid waste, and homes given to the flames; not to mention murders, rapes, expulsions and other outrages nameless for their enormity, committed upon a helpless people by a ruthless mob in the sovereign name of the state of Missouri!

"THE MORMONS NOT EXCEPTED!"

Oh world-wide philanthropy! Magnanimity unparalleled! As though the Mormons had not been the main, and well-nigh only sufferers from this horrible and hellish invasion. Indeed, the only other losses sustained—barring those inflicted by the oppressed people in sheer self-defense—were from depredations by the mobocrats themselves upon their own sympathizers, committed in such a way as to seem the work of Mormons, who were falsely accused of the devilish deeds and the public mind thus inflamed against them. . . .

And thus did the great state of Missouri redress the wrongs of ten thousand innocent people, robbed and trampled on without provocation by its mob militia, led on and fired to their deeds of blood and plunder by political demagogues and hireling priests of Christendom. And this in the broad daylight of the nineteenth century, in a land of religious liberty, on soil consecrated by the blood of patriots—ancestors of the people thus trampled on and despoiled—and in the presence of American judges, magistrates and priests, affecting the calling, but disgracing the name, of Christian! (Orson F. Whitney, *Life of Heber C. Kimball* [Salt Lake City: Deseret Book, 2001], 234–36).

Eliza R. Snow

What aileth thee, O Missouri! that thy face should gather blackness? and why are thy features so terribly distorted?

Rottenness has seized upon thy vitals, corruption is preying upon thy inward parts, and the breath of thy lips is full of destructive contagion.

Eliza R. Snow
(Courtesy of the Church Archives, The Church of Jesus Christ of Latter-day Saints)

Thou has violated the laws of our sacred constitution; thou hast unsheathed the sword against thy dearest national rights, by rising up against thine own citizens, and moistening thy soil with the blood of those that legally inherited it.

When thou hadst torn from helpless innocence its rightful protectors thou didst pollute the holy sanctuary of female virtue, and barbarously trampled upon the most scared gems of domestic felicity.

Though thou shouldst be severed from the body of the Union, like a mortified member—though the lion from the thicket should devour thee, thy doings will be perpetuated; mention will be made of them by the generations to come.

Thou art already associated with Herod, Nero, and the bloody Inquisition; thy name has become synonymous with oppression, cruelty, treachery, and murder.

Thou wilt rank high with the haters of righteousness and the shedders of innocent blood: the hosts of tyrants are waiting beneath to meet thee at thy coming.

For the cries of the widow and fatherless, the groans of the oppressed and the prayers of the suffering exile have come up before the God of hosts (As cited in Ted Gibbons, *The Road to Carthage: Conspiracy and Betrayal* [Provo, Utah: Maasai, Inc., 2001], 10–11).

9

Richmond and Liberty Jails

From November 1838 to April 6, 1839, Joseph and Hyrum Smith, Sidney Rigdon, Caleb Baldwin, Lyman Wight, and Alexander McRae awaited trial, first in the Richmond Jail and then in Liberty Jail. Joseph was not killed during his arrest and imprisonment, but for several weeks he and his associates were abused and insulted, forced to march to Independence and then to Richmond, and finally placed in Liberty Jail on November 30, 1838. These men had not been convicted of any crime, but they were held in Liberty Jail for over five months, under terrible and inhuman conditions. During this time, the Prophet communicated with Church members by way of letters, and he received many disturbing and harrowing accounts of the treatment of the Saints. Unable to help his people, the Prophet Joseph Smith lamented the suffering of the Saints of God. During a period of deep reflection and grief, Joseph Smith received divine inspiration and instruction from his Heavenly Father.

Richmond Jail

Parley P. Pratt

(Richmond, November 30, 1838)

In one of those tedious nights we had lain as if in sleep till the hour of midnight had passed, and our ears and hearts had been pained, while we had listened for hours to the obscene jests, the horrid oaths, the dreadful blasphemies and filthy language of our guards, Colonel Price at their head, as they recounted to each other their deeds of rapine, murder, robbery, etc., which they had committed among the "*Mormons*" while at Far West and vicinity. They even boasted of defiling by force wives, daughters and virgins, and of shooting or dashing out the brains of men, women, and children.

I had listened till I became so disgusted, shocked, horrified, and so filled with the spirit of indignant justice that I could scarcely refrain from rising upon my feet and rebuking the guards; but had said nothing to Joseph, or any one else, although I lay next to him and knew he was awake. On a sudden he arose to his feet, and spoke in a voice of thunder, or as the roaring lion, uttering, as near as I can recollect, the following words:

"SILENCE, ye fiends of the infernal pit. In the name of Jesus Christ I rebuke you, and command you to be still; I will not live another minute and bear such language. Cease such talk, or you or I die THIS INSTANT!"

He ceased to speak. He stood erect in terrible majesty. Chained, and without a weapon; calm, unruffled and dignified as an angel, he looked upon the quailing guards, whose weapons were lowered or dropped to the ground; whose knees smote together, and who, shrinking into a corner, or crouching at his feet, begged his pardon, and remained quiet till a change of guards.

I have seen ministers of justice, clothed in magisterial robes, and criminals arraigned before them, while life was suspended on a breath, in the Courts of England; I have witnessed a Congress in solemn session to give laws to nations; I have tried to conceive of kings, of royal courts, of thrones and crowns; and of emperors assembled to decide the fate of kingdoms; but dignity and majesty have I seen but *once*, as it stood in chains, at midnight, in a dungeon in an obscure village of Missouri (Parley P. Pratt, *Autobiography of Parley P. Pratt, revised and enhanced*, ed. Scot Facer Proctor and Maurine Jensen Proctor [Salt Lake City: Deseret Book, 2000], 262–63).

Parley P. Pratt

(Joseph Smith, Parley P. Pratt, and other Church leaders sought to negotiate with the Missouri militia in an attempt to peaceably end the persecution the Saints faced in Missouri. Upon meeting with them, however, they were immediately seized and later incarcerated at Independence and Ray Counties, where they were falsely accused of murder, treason, arson, larceny, burglary, and robbery. After the November 28 inquiry, Joseph

was sent to Liberty Jail, while Parley was taken to Richmond Jail. He was later transferred to a jail in Columbia, Missouri, where on July 4, he finally escaped to Illinois, after being imprisoned for more than eight months.)

We had prevailed on the keeper [of the prison] to furnish us with a long pole, on which to suspend a flag, and also some red stripes of cloth. We then tore a shirt in pieces, and took the body of it for the ground work of a flag, forming with the red stripes of cloth an eagle and the word "*Liberty*," in large letters. This rude flag of red and white was suspended on the pole from the prison window, directly in front of the public square and court house, and composed one of the greatest attractions of the day. Hundreds of the people from the country, as well as villagers who were there at the celebration, would come up and stare at the flag, and reading the motto, would go swearing or laughing away, exclaiming, "Liberty! Liberty! What have the Mormons to do with celebrating *liberty* in a damned old prison?" . . .

The [prison's] large, heavy door had always to be opened when food, drink, or other articles were handed in; and while open, the inner door served as a temporary guard to prevent prisoners from escaping, and was not always opened on such occasions, the food being handed through the hole in the top of the door, while the door itself remained locked. However, as a fortunate circumstance for us, the coffee pot when filled would not easily slip through the hole in the door, and, rather than spill the coffee and burn his fingers, the keeper would sometimes unlock and open the inner door, in order to set in this huge and obstinate pot; and once in, the door would immediately close, and the key be turned, while the outer door would perhaps stand open till the supper was finished, and the dishes handed out.

Now, our whole chance of escape depended on the question, whether the inner door would be opened that evening, or the coffee pot squeezed in at the hole in the top. . . .

As the sun began to decline behind the long range of forest which bounded the western horizon, and the lengthened shadows of the tall trees were thrown over our prison, we called upon the Lord to prosper us and open our way, and then sang aloud . . . but the doctrine of spiritualizing had become so prevalent that neither this, nor the flag of liberty, nor any other Scripture seemed to them to have any literal meaning, till they found too late the true interpretation by the fulfillment.

The sun was now setting, and the footsteps of the old keeper were heard on the stairs—the key turned, the outer door grated on its huge hinges, while at the same moment we sprang upon our feet, hats and coats on . . . and stood by the door to act the part of waiters in receiving the dishes and food for supper, and placing them on the table. Dish after dish was handed in through the small aperture in the door, and duly received and placed upon the table by us, with as much grace and as calm countenances as if we thought of nothing else but our suppers. And I will now venture to say that famishing men never watched the movements of a coffee pot with more anxiety than we did on this occasion. At length the other dishes all being handed in, the huge pot made its appearance in the hole in the top of the door, but one of us cried out to the keeper—"Colonel, you will only spill the coffee by attempting to put it through, besides, it burns our fingers; it will be more convenient to unlock and hand it in at the door." With this it was lowered again, and the key turned on the inner door.

In this, as in most other fields of battle, where liberty and life depend on the issue, every one understood the part assigned to him and exactly filled it. . . .

No sooner was the key turned than the door was seized by Mr. Follett with both hands; and with his foot placed against the wall, he soon opened a passage, which was in the same instant filled by Mr. Phelps, and followed by myself and Mr. Follett. The old jailer strode across the way, and stretched out his arms like Bunyan's Apollion, or like the giant Despair in Doubting Castle, but all to no purpose. One or two leaps brought us to the bottom of the stairs, carrying the old gentleman with us headlong, helter skelter. . . . We found ourselves in the open air, in front of the prison and in full view of the citizens, who had already commenced to rally, while Mr. Phelps and the jailer still clinched fast hold of each other like two mastiffs. However, in another instant he cleared himself, and we were all three scampering off through the fields towards the thicket. . . .

As soon as the prisoners drew near, they were hailed by their friends, and conducted to the horses. They were breathless and nearly ready to faint . . . In another instant we were all separated from each other, and each one was making the best shift he could for his own individual safety (Parley P. Pratt, *Autobiography of Parley P. Pratt,* ed. Parley P. Pratt Jr. [Salt Lake City: Deseret Book, 1985], 210–17).

Parley P. Pratt

(The experience in Richmond was not the only time Parley P. Pratt had to use ingenious means to escape unfair imprisonment and unjust persecution. The following is a well-loved story of an earlier escape by Parley while he was serving a mission in 1830 about fifty miles from Kirtland, Ohio.)

We had stopped for the night at the house of Simeon Carter . . . and were in the act of reading to him and explaining the Book of Mormon, when there came a knock at the door, and an officer entered with a warrant from a magistrate by the name of Byington, to arrest me on a very frivolous charge. . . . We arrived at the place of trial late in the evening; found false witnesses in attendance, and a Judge who boasted of his intention to thrust us into prison, for the purpose of testing the powers of our apostleship, as he called it . . . The Judge boasting thus, and the witnesses being entirely false in their testimony, I concluded to make no defense, but to treat the whole matter with contempt.

I was soon ordered to prison, or to pay a sum of money which I had not in the world. It was now a late hour, and I was still retained in court, tantalized, abused and urged to settle the matter, to all of which I made no reply for some time. This greatly exhausted their patience. . . .

The court adjourned, and I was conducted to a public house over the way, and locked in till morning; the prison being some miles distant.

In the morning the officer appeared and took me to breakfast; this over, we sat waiting in the inn for all things to be ready to conduct me to prison. . . .

After sitting awhile by the fire in charge of the officer, I requested to step out. I walked out into the public square accompanied by him. Said I, "Mr. Peabody, are you good at a race?" "No," said he, "but my big bull dog is, and he has been trained to assist me in my office these several years; he will take any man down at my bidding." "Well, Mr. Peabody, you compelled me to go a mile, I have gone with you two miles. You have given me an opportunity to preach, sing, and have also entertained me with lodging and breakfast. I must now go on my journey; if you are good at a race you can accompany me. I thank you for all your kindness—good day, sir."

I then started on my journey, while he stood amazed and not able to step one foot before the other. Seeing this, I halted, turned to him and again invited him to a race. He still stood amazed. I then renewed my exertions, and soon increased my speed to something like that of a deer. He did not awake from his astonishment sufficiently to start in pursuit till I had gained, perhaps, two hundred yards . . . He now came hallooing after me, and shouting to his dog to seize me. The dog, being one of the largest I ever saw, came close on my footsteps with all his fury; the officer behind still in pursuit, clapping his hands and hallooing, "stu-boy, stu-boy—take him—watch—lay hold of him, I say—down with him," and pointing his finger in the direction I was running. The dog was fast overtaking me, and in the act of leaping upon me, when, quick as lightning, the thought struck me, to assist the officer, in sending the dog with all fury to the forest a little distance before me. I pointed my finger in that direction, clapped my hands, and shouted in imitation of the officer. The dog hastened past me with redoubled speed towards the forest; being urged by the officer and myself, and both of us running in the same direction (Parley P. Pratt, *Autobiography of Parley P. Pratt, revised and enhanced*, ed. Scot Facer Proctor and Maurine Jensen Proctor [Salt Lake City: Deseret Book, 2000], 52–55).

TRANSFER TO LIBERTY JAIL

On November 30, 1838, Joseph Smith and five other prisoners entered Liberty Jail, twenty-five miles to the west of Richmond, in Clay County. These men were charged with "overt acts of treason" (as cited in *Personal Writings of Joseph Smith*, ed. Dean C. Jessee [Salt Lake City: Deseret Book, 2002], 410).

Liberty Jail was a small, two-story building, consisting of twenty-two square feet. This jail was like a dungeon with dirt floors and heavy stone walls that were timbered inside with logs, the low ceiling resting on these thick stone walls. The interior was divided into two rooms, consisting of an upper and lower level. The lighting was very dim, due to the fact that it was lighted only by two small windows in the upper room. The temperature inside was as cold as it was outside, and when the prisoners built a fire the smoke choked them, because there was no chimney. The prison food was described as "so filthy that we could not eat it until we were driven to it by hunger" (Joseph Smith, *History of The Church of Jesus Christ of Latter-day Saints*, 7 vols., ed. B. H. Roberts [Salt Lake City: Deseret Book, 1980], 3:257). For four winter months, the Prophet and his companions suffered from cold, filthy conditions, smoke inhalation, loneliness, bad treatment, and filthy food (James B. Allen and Glen M. Leonard, *The Story of the Latter-day Saints* [Salt Lake City: Deseret Book, 1992], 141–42).

The Prophet and the other men were occasionally allowed visitors, and the experience there was highlighted only by sporadic visits from relatives and friends. Immediately after receiving the first letter written by Joseph in the jail, Emma took young Joseph and Sidney Rigdon's wife to the prison to visit. Rough guards allowed the three visitors inside, and the hinges creaked as the heavy door swung shut behind them. They spent the night with the prisoners in the damp half-lit cellar but had to leave the following day. Emma returned soon after and spent two days confined with Joseph.

In an effort to end their imprisonment, or at least hasten their trial, the prisoners petitioned the Missouri legislature, the Supreme Court of the state, and the Clay County Court—all to no avail. Finally, in desperation, they made two attempts at escape, both ending in failure. In April the remaining prisoners were ordered to Daviess County for trial. A grand jury brought in a bill against them for "murder, treason, burglary, arson, larceny, theft, and stealing" (*History of the Church,* 3:315). The accused were unable to obtain a change of venue for trial on these charges, but as they were being taken to Boone County, the prisoners were allowed to escape to Illinois to rejoin their families—a guard even assisting them in saddling their horses.

As bad as this experience was, Liberty Jail will always be known as a temple-prison, because of the revelations received there. The Prophet had time to pray and meditate about the Church and its meaning, time to formulate new ideas and put them into writing. Some of his most profound revelations and writings come from this jail, such as the long letter he wrote to the Church, parts of which now appear as sections 121, 122, and 123 of the Doctrine and Covenants. Liberty Jail has now become a sacred place, in which revelations were received for the comfort and instruction of the prisoners, other Saints, and generations to come.

George Q. Cannon

Joseph and his companions were carried to Liberty, Clay County, in irons. As they entered the town considerable excitement prevailed among people desirous to view them. Arrived at the jail, they descended from the vehicle and walked up the steps to a landing or platform in front of the entrance of the prison building. Joseph wore a suit of black and had a cloak of dark-colored material hanging on his arm. Hyrum followed him and the others stood close around. The gaze of the spectators was concentrated upon Joseph, and his majestic air made a deep impression upon them. One lady in the crowd cried: "Their Prophet looks like a gentleman!" Another looking at the group expressed the opinion: "Well, they are fine looking men if they are Mormons."

It was on the 30th day of November, 1838, that they were incarcerated in Liberty Jail; and at once an order was made to cut off all communication between them and their friends, while every effort was put forth to drive away or frighten any witnesses whose testimony might be desirable for the defendants. And at the same time the threat went out through all that region that if judges or juries or courts of any kind should clear the prisoners, they would be slaughtered (George Q. Cannon, *Life of Joseph Smith the Prophet* [Salt Lake City: Deseret Book, 1986], 290–91).

Conditions in Liberty Jail

Joseph Fielding Smith

After the mock trial in Richmond, Joseph Smith and his five companions were imprisoned in Liberty, Clay County, for a period of six months. Here they suffered, during that time, many untold hardships. Much of the time they were bound in chains. Their food was often not fit to eat, and never wholesome or prepared with the thought of proper nourishment. Several times poison was administered to them in their food, which made them sick nigh unto death, and only the promised blessings of the Lord

Joseph Fielding Smith

(Courtesy of the Church Archives, The Church of Jesus Christ of Latter-day Saints)

saved them. Their bed was on the floor, or on the flat side of a hewn white oak log, and in this manner they were forced to suffer (Joseph Fielding Smith, *Essentials in Church History* [Salt Lake City: Deseret Book, 1979], 210).

Hyrum Smith

We are often inspected by fools who act as though we were elephants or dromedarys or sea hogs or some monstrous whale or sea serpents. We have never had our teeth examined like an old horse, but expect [to] every day when . . . a new swarm come that have never seen us (as cited in Neal A. Maxwell, *But for a Small Moment* [Salt Lake City: Bookcraft, 1986], 109).

Hyrum Smith

I traversed my prison house for hours, thinking of their [former friends and mobocrats] cruelty to my family, and the afflictions they brought upon the saints (Hyrum Smith, "Communications to the Saints scattered abroad," *Times and Seasons* [December 1839]: 23).

Hyrum Smith

I . . . endured almost everything but death, from the nauseous cell, and the wretched food we were obliged to eat (*History of the Church*, 3:374).

Lyman Wight

The mercies of the jailor were intolerable, feeding us with a scanty allowance, on the dregs of coffee and tea, from his own table, and fetching the provisions in a basket, on which the chickens had roosted the night before, without being cleaned; five days he fed the prisoners on human flesh, and from extreme hunger I was compelled to eat it (Lyman Wight, "Trial of Joseph Smith," *Times and Seasons* [July 1, 1843]: 269).

Mercy Fielding Thompson

Mercy Fielding Thompson
(Courtesy of the Church Archives, The Church of Jesus Christ of Latter-day Saints)

In February 1839, while Joseph and Hyrum Smith, with four other brethren were incarcerated in Liberty Jail, I accompanied my sister Mary from Far West, to visit them. It would be beyond my power to describe my feelings when we were admitted into the jail by the keeper and the door was locked behind us. We could not help feeling a sense of horror on realizing that we were locked up in that dark and dismal den, fit only for criminals of the deepest dye; but there we beheld Joseph, the Prophet, the man chosen of God, in the dispensation of the fullness of time to hold the keys of His kingdom on the earth, with power to bind and to loose as God should direct, confined in a loathsome prison for no other cause or reason than that he claimed to be inspired of God to establish His church among men. There also we found his noble brother, Hyrum, who, I believe was not charged with any other crime than that of being a friend to his brother Joseph. There also were four other brethren whose offenses were similar to that of Hyrum's. The night was spent in fearful forebodings, owing to a false rumor having gone out that the prisoners contemplated making an attempt to escape, which greatly enraged the jailor and the guards (Mercy Fielding Thompson, "Recollections of the Prophet Joseph Smith," *Writings of Early Latter-day Saints and Their Contemporaries, a Database Collection*, comp. Milton V. Backman [Provo, Utah: BYU Religious Studies Center, 1996], 398).

Orson F. Whitney
(Courtesy of the Church Archives, The Church of Jesus Christ of Latter-day Saints)

Orson F. Whitney

I bear in mind another incident in his history, when he and some of his brethren were lying in a dungeon, Liberty jail, Missouri, during the winter of 1838–9, after the Saints, fifteen thousand men, women and children, had been driven from the state of Missouri. These brethren were treated with great cruelty in prison. It is said that the depravity of their jailers descended so low that they even cooked human flesh, taken from the body of a negro who had been killed, and offered it to these prisoners to eat; and the Prophet, warned by the Lord, told his brethren not to partake of it. It was in the midst of these circumstances that one of the brethren was asked to pray; and he prayed that God would damn the men who were treating them thus cruelly. When he got through, the others were laughing at him. He asked, "What is the matter?" They said, "We are laughing at your prayer." "Well," he replied, "if you want any better praying than that, you can do it yourselves." The Prophet then told him, "You yourself will yet see the day when you will pity these very men who are inflicting these injuries upon you. God has shown to me in vision the sufferings of the ungodly, and I had to pray to Him to close the vision when I saw the terrible judgments that would come upon the wicked." The Prophet taught the principle of patient submission to wrong. And it is this that lifts men up above other men. When men injure us they put themselves in our debt, and that debt remains until we cancel it by an act of retaliation (*Collected Discourses*, 5 vols., ed. Brian H. Stuy [Burbank, California: B. H. S. Publishing, 1992], 5:429).

Alexander McRae

(Alexander, a fellow prisoner, related the following.)

Orin P. Rockwell brought us refreshments many times; and Jane Bleven and her daughter brought cakes, pies, etc., and handed them in at the window. These things helped us much, as our food was very coarse, and so filthy that we could not eat it until we were driven to it by hunger (*History of the Church*, 3:257).

Joseph Smith Jr.

Be of good cheer, . . . the word of the Lord came to me last night that, whatever we may suffer during this captivity, not one of our lives should be taken (as cited in Susan Evans McCloud, *Joseph Smith, A Photobiography* [Salt Lake City: Aspen Books, 1992], 91).

Letters to and from Joseph Smith While Incarcerated in Liberty Jail

Joseph Smith Jr.

(Writing to his wife, Emma.)

With emotions known only to God, do I write this letter. The contemplations of the mind under these circumstances defies the pen, or tongue, or angels to describe, or paint to the human being who never experience[d] what we experience (Joseph Smith Jr., *Letter to Emma Smith, April 4, 1839* [Beinecke Rare Book and Manuscript Library, Yale University, New Haven, Connecticut]; as cited in *Personal Writings of Joseph Smith*, 463; spelling, capitalization, and punctuation standardized).

Joseph Smith Jr.

(Writing to the Saints.)

[We are] surrounded with a strong guard, who continually watch day and night as indefatigable as the devil does in tempting and laying snares for the people of God (*History of the Church*, 3:290).

Joseph Smith Jr.

(Writing to his wife, Emma)

Liberty Jail,
Clay County, Missouri
March 21, 1839
Affectionate Wife,

I have sent an epistle to the Church directed to you because I wanted you to have the first reading of it, and then I want Father and Mother to have a copy of it. Keep the original yourself, as I dictated the matter myself and shall send another as soon as possible. I want to be with you very much but the powers of mobocracy [are] too many for me at present. I would ask if Judge Cleaveland will be kind enough to let you and the children tarry there until [I] can learn something further concerning my fate. I will reward him well if he will, and see that you do not suffer for anything. I shall have a little money left when I come, my dear Emma. I very well know your toils and sympathize with you. If God will spare my life once more to have the privilege of taking care of you, I will ease your care and endeavor to comfort your heart. I want you to take the best care of the family you can, which I believe you will do all you can. I was sorry to learn that Frederick was sick but I trust he is well again, and that you are all well. I want you to try to gain time and write to me a long letter, and tell me all you can, and even if Old Major is alive yet, and what those little prattlers say that cling around your neck. Do you tell them I am in prison that their lives might be saved? I want all the church to make out a bill of damages and apply to the United States Court as soon as possible. However, they will find out what can be done themselves. You expressed my feelings concerning the order and I believe that there is a way to get redress for such things, but God ruleth all things after the council of his own will. My trust is in him. The salvation of my soul is of the most importance to me, for as much as I know for a certainty of eternal things, if the heavens linger, it is nothing to me. I must steer my bark safe, which I intend to do. I want you to do the same. . . .

I want you to have the epistle copied immediately and let it go to the brethren, first into the hands of Father, for I want the production for my record. If you lack for money or for bread, do let me know it as soon as possible. My nerve trembles from long confinement, but if you feel as I do, you don't care for the imperfections of my writings. For my part, a word of consolation from any source is cordially received by me. I feel like Joseph in Egypt. Doth my friends yet live? If they live, do they remember me? Have they regard for me? If so, let me know it in time of trouble. My dear Emma, do you think that my being cast into prison by the mob renders me less worthy of your friendship? No, I do not think so. But when I was in prison and ye visited me, inasmuch as you have done it to the least of these you have done it to me. These shall enter into life eternal. But no more.

Your Husband,

J Smith Jr. (as cited in *Messages of the First Presidency,* 6 vols., ed. James R. Clark [Salt Lake City: Bookcraft, 1965], 1:87; spelling, punctuation, and capitalization standardized).

Emma Smith

(Writing to her husband, Joseph.)

Emma Smith
(Public Domain, Courtesy of BYU Online Collections)

I shall not attempt to write my feelings altogether, for the situation in which you are, the walls, bars, and bolts, rolling rivers, running streams, rising hills, sinking valleys and spreading prairies that separate us, and the cruel injustice that first cast you into prison and still holds you there, with many other considerations, places my feelings far beyond description. Was it not for conscious innocence, and the direct interposition of divine mercy, I am very sure I never should have been able to have endured the scenes of suffering that I have passed through, since what is called the Militia, came into Far West, under the ever to be remembered Governor's notable order. . . . We are all well at present, except Frederick, who is quite sick. Little Alexander who is now in my arms is one of the finest little fellows, you ever saw in your life, he is so strong that with the assistance of a chair he will run all round the room. . . . No one but God, knows the reflections of my mind and the feelings of my heart when I left our house and home, and almost all of every thing that we possessed excepting our little children, and took my journey out of the State of Missouri, leaving you shut up in that lonesome prison. But the recollection is more than human nature ought to bear. . . . The daily sufferings of our brethren in traveling and camping out nights, and those on the other side of the river would beggar the most lively description. The people in this state are very kind indeed, they are doing much more than we ever anticipated they would; I have many more things I could like to write but have not time and you may be astonished at my bad writing and incoherent manner, but you will pardon all when you reflect how hard it would be for you to write, when your hands were stiffened with hard work, and your heart convulsed with intense anxiety. But I hope there is better days to come to us yet (Emma Smith, "Emma Smith to Joseph Smith, 7 March 1839," *Joseph Smith Letterbook* [LDS Church Archives, The Church of Jesus Christ of Latter-day Saints, Salt Lake City, Utah], 2; as cited in *Personal Writings of Joseph Smith,* 429).

Joseph Smith Jr.

(Excerpts from this lengthy letter were later canonized as D&C 121, 122, and 123. The entire letter has been reproduced below. Those portions of the letter that are now part of D&C 121–23 are italicized. The headings were later added by Elder Joseph Fielding Smith.)

The Prophet's Epistle to the Church, Written in Liberty Prison.

Liberty Jail, Clay County, Missouri,

March 25, 1839

To the Church of Latter-day Saints at Quincy, Illinois, and Scattered Abroad, and to Bishop Partridge in Particular:

Your humble servant, Joseph Smith, Jun., prisoner for the Lord Jesus Christ's sake, and for the Saints, taken and held by the power of mobocracy, under the exterminating reign of his excellency, the governor, Lilburn W. Boggs, in company with his fellow prisoners and beloved brethren, Caleb Baldwin, Lyman Wight, Hyrum Smith, and Alexander McRae, send unto you all greeting. May the grace of God the Father, and of our Lord and Savior Jesus Christ, rest upon you all, and abide with you forever. May knowledge be multiplied unto you by the mercy of God. And may faith and virtue, and knowledge and temperance, and patience and godliness, and brotherly kindness and charity be in you and abound, that you may not be barren in anything, nor unfruitful.

Joseph Smith Jr.
(Courtesy of the Church Archives, The Church of Jesus Christ of Latter-day Saints)

The Sustaining Love of God

For inasmuch as we know that the most of you are well acquainted with the wrongs and the high-handed injustice and cruelty that are practiced upon us; whereas we have been taken prisoners charged falsely with every kind of evil, and thrown into prison, enclosed with strong walls, surrounded with a strong guard, who continually watch day and night as indefatigable as the devil does in tempting and laying snares for the people of God.

Therefore, dearly beloved brethren, we are the more ready and willing to lay claim to your fellowship and love. For our circumstances are calculated to awaken our spirits to a sacred remembrance of everything, and we think that yours are also, and that nothing therefore can separate us from the love of God and fellowship one with another; and that every species of wickedness and cruelty practiced upon us will only tend to bind our hearts together and seal them together in love. We have no need to say to you that we are held in bonds without cause, neither is it needful that you say unto us, We are driven from our homes and smitten without cause. We mutually understand that if the inhabitants of the state of Missouri had let the Saints alone, and had been as desirable of peace as they were, there would have been nothing but peace and quietude in the state unto this day; we should not have been in this hell, surrounded with demons (if not those who are damned, they are those who shall be damned) and where we are compelled to hear nothing but blasphemous oaths, and witness a scene of blasphemy, and drunkenness and hypocrisy, and debaucheries of every description.

The Persecution of the Saints

And again, the cries of orphans and widows would not have ascended up to God against them. Nor would innocent blood have stained the soil of Missouri. But oh! the unrelenting hand! The inhumanity and murderous disposition of this people! It shocks all nature; it beggars and defies all description; it is a tale of woe; a lamentable tale; yea a sorrowful tale; too much to tell; too much for contemplation; too much for human beings; it cannot be found among the heathens; it cannot be found among the nations where kings and tyrants are enthroned; it cannot be found among the savages of the wilderness; yea, and I think it cannot be found among the wild and ferocious beasts of the forest—that a man should be mangled for sport! women be robbed of all that they have—their last morsel for subsistence, and then be violated to gratify the hellish desires of the mob, and finally left to perish with their helpless offspring clinging around their necks.

But this is not all. After a man is dead, he must be dug up from his grave and mangled to pieces, for no other purpose than to gratify their spleen against the religion of God.

They practice these things upon the Saints, who have done them no wrong, who are innocent and virtuous; who loved the Lord their God, and were willing to forsake all things for Christ's sake. These things are awful to relate, but they are verily true. It must needs be that offenses come, but woe unto them by whom they come.

A Righteous Appeal to Heaven

Oh God! where art Thou? And where is the pavilion that covereth Thy hiding place? How long shall Thy hand be stayed, and Thine eye, yea Thy pure eye, behold from the eternal heavens, the wrongs of Thy people, and of Thy servants, and Thy ear be penetrated with their cries? Yea, O Lord, how long shall they suffer these wrongs and unlawful oppressions, before Thine heart shall be softened towards them, and Thy bowels be moved with compassion towards them?

O Lord God Almighty, Maker of Heaven, Earth and Seas, and of all things that in them are, and who controllest and subjectest the devil, and the dark and benighted dominion of Sheol! Stretch forth Thy hand, let Thine eye pierce; let Thy pavilion be taken up; let Thy hiding place no longer be covered; let Thine ear be inclined; let Thine heart be softened, and Thy bowels moved with compassion towards us, let Thine anger be kindled against our enemies; and in the fury of Thine heart, with Thy sword avenge us of our wrongs; remember Thy suffering Saints, O our God! and Thy servants will rejoice in Thy name forever.

Perilous Times

Dearly and beloved brethren, we see that perilous times have come, as was testified of. We may look, then, with most perfect assurance, for the fulfillment of all those things that have been written, and with more confidence than ever before, lift up our eyes to the luminary of day, and say in our hearts, Soon thou wilt veil thy blushing face. He that said "Let there be light," and there was light, hath spoken this word. And again, Thou moon, thou dimmer light, thou luminary of night, shalt turn to blood.

We see that everything is being fulfilled; and that the time shall soon come when the Son of Man shall descend in the clouds of heaven. Our hearts do not shrink, neither are our spirits altogether broken by the grievous yoke which is put upon us. We know that God will have our oppressors in derision; that He will laugh at their calamity, and mock when their fear cometh.

O that we could be with you, brethren, and unbosom our feelings to you! We would tell, that we should have been liberated at the time Elder Rigdon was, on the writ of habeas corpus, had not our own lawyers interpreted the law, contrary to what it reads, against us; which prevented us from introducing our evidence before the mock court.

They have done us much harm from the beginning. They have of late acknowledged that the law was misconstrued, and tantalized our feelings with it, and have entirely forsaken us, and have forfeited their oaths and their bonds; and we have a come-back on them, for they are co-workers with the mob.

Change of Public Opinion

As nigh as we can learn, the public mind has been for a long time turning in our favor, and the majority in now friendly; and the lawyers can no longer browbeat us by saying that this or that is a matter of public opinion, for public opinion is not willing to brook it; for it is beginning to look with feelings of indignation against our oppressors, and to say that the "Mormons" were not in the fault in the least. We think that truth, honor, virtue and innocence will eventually come out triumphant. We should have taken a habeas corpus before the high judge and escaped the mob in a summary way; but unfortunately for us, the timber of the wall being very hard, our auger handles gave out, and hindered us longer than we expected; we applied to a friend, and a very slight incautious act gave rise to some suspicions, and before we could fully succeed, our plan was discovered; we had everything in readiness, but the last stone, and we could have made our escape in one minute, and should have succeeded admirably, had it not been for a little imprudence or over-anxiety on the part of our friend.

The sheriff and jailer did not blame us for our attempt; it was a fine breach, and cost the county a round sum; but public opinion says that we ought to have been permitted to have made our escape; that then the disgrace would have been on us, but now it must come on the state; that there cannot be any charge sustained against us; and that the conduct of the mob, the murders committed at Haun's Mills, and the exterminating order of the governor, and the one-sided, rascally proceedings of the legislature, have damned the state of Missouri to all eternity. I would just name also that General Atchison has proved himself as contemptible as any of them.

We have tried for a long time to get our lawyers to draw us some petitions to the supreme judges of this state, but they utterly refused. We have examined the law, and drawn the petitions ourselves, and have obtained abundance of proof to counteract all the testimony that was against us, so that if the supreme judge does not grant us our liberty, he has to act without cause, contrary to honor, evidence, law or justice, sheerly to please the devil, but we hope better things and trust before many days God will so order our case, that we shall be set at liberty and take up our habitation with the Saints.

The Sympathy of Friends

We received some letters last evening—one from Emma, one from Don C. Smith, and one from Bishop Partridge—all breathing a kind and consoling spirit. We were much gratified with their contents. We had been a long time without information; and when we read those letters they were to our souls as the gentle air is refreshing, but our joy was mingled with grief, because of the sufferings of the poor and much injured Saints. And we need not say to you that the floodgates of our hearts were lifted and our eyes were a fountain of tears, but those who have not been enclosed in the walls of prison without cause or provocation, can have but little idea how sweet the voice of a friend is; one token of friendship from any source whatever awakens and calls into action every sympathetic feeling; it brings up in an instant everything that is passed; it seizes the present with the avidity of lightning; it grasps after the future with the fierceness of a tiger; it moves the mind backward and forward, from on thing to another, until finally all enmity, malice and hatred, and past differences, misunderstandings and mismanagements are slain victorious at the feet of hope; and when the heart is sufficiently contrite, then the voice of inspiration steals along and whispers,

The Value of Tribulation

My son, peace be unto thy soul; thine adversity and thine afflictions shall be but a small moment; and then if thou endure it well, God shall exalt thee on high; thou shalt triumph over all thy foes; thy friends do stand by thee, and they shall hail thee again, with warm hearts and friendly hands; thou art not yet as Job; thy friends do not contend against thee, neither charge thee with transgression, as they did Job; and they who do charge thee with transgression, their hope shall be blasted and their prospects shall melt away as the hoar frost melteth before the burning rays of the rising sun; and also that God hath set His hand and seal to change the times and seasons, and to blind their minds, that they may not understand His marvelous workings, that He may prove them also and take them in their own craftiness; also because their hearts are corrupted, and the things which they are willing to bring upon others, and love to have others suffer, may come upon themselves to the very uttermost; that they may be disappointed also, and their hopes may be cut off; and not many years hence, that they and their posterity shall be swept from under heaven, saith God, that not one of them is left to stand by the wall. Cursed are all those that shall lift up the heel against mine anointed, saith the Lord, and cry they have sinned when they have not sinned before me, saith the Lord, but have done that which was meet in mine eyes, and which I commanded them; but those who cry transgression do it because they are the servants of sin and are the children of disobedience themselves; and those who swear falsely against my servants, that they might bring them into bondage and death; wo unto them; because they have offended my little ones; they shall be severed from the ordinances of mine house; their basket shall not be full, and their houses and their barns shall perish, and they themselves shall be despised by those that flattered them; they shall not have right to the Priesthood, nor their posterity after them, from generation to generation; it had been better for them that a millstone had been hanged about their necks, and they drowned in the depth of the sea.

Wo unto all those that discomfort my people, and drive and murder, and testify against them, saith the Lord of Hosts; a generation of vipers shall not escape the damnation of hell. Behold mine eyes see and know all their works, and I have in reserve a swift judgment in the season thereof, for them all; for there is a time appointed for every man according as his work shall be.

A Tried People

And now, beloved brethren, we say unto you, that inasmuch as God hath said that He would have a tried people, that He would purge them as gold, now we think that this time He has chosen His own crucible, wherein we have been tried; and we think if we get through with any degree of safety, and shall have kept the faith, that it will be a sign to this generation, altogether sufficient to leave them without excuse; and we think also, it will be a trial of our faith equal to that of Abraham, and that the ancients will not have whereof to boast over us in the day of judgment, as being called to pass through heavier afflictions; that we may hold an even weight in the balance with them; but now, after having suffered so great sacrifice and having passed through so great a season of sorrow, we trust that a ram may be caught in the thicket speedily, to relieve the sons and daughters of Abraham from their great anxiety, and to light up the lamp of salvation upon their countenances, that they may hold on now, after having gone so far unto everlasting life.

A Location for the Saints

Now, brethren, concerning the places for the location of the Saints, we cannot counsel you as we could if we were present with you; and as to the things that were written heretofore, we did not consider them anything very binding, therefore we now say once for all, that we think it most proper that the general affairs of the Church, which are necessary to be considered, while your humble servant remains in bondage, should be transacted by a general conference of the most faithful and the most respectable of the authorities of the Church, and a minute of those transactions may be kept, and forwarded from time to time, to your humble servant; and if there should be any corrections by the word of the Lord, they shall be freely transmitted, and your humble servant will approve all things whatsoever is acceptable unto God. If anything should have been suggested by us, or any names mentioned, except by commandment, or thus saith the Lord, we do not consider it binding; therefore our hearts shall not be grieved if different arrangements should be entered into. Nevertheless we would suggest the propriety of being aware of an aspiring spirit, which spirit has oftentimes urged men forward to make foul speeches, and influence the Church to reject milder counsels, and has eventually been the means of bringing much death and sorrow upon the Church.

Beware of Pride

We would say, beware of pride also; for well and truly hath the wise man said, that pride goeth before destruction, and a haughty spirit before a fall. And again, outward appearance is not always a criterion by which to judge our fellow man; but the lips betray the haughty and overbearing imaginations of the heart; by his words and his deeds let him be judged. Flattery also is a deadly poison. A frank and open rebuke provoketh a good man to emulation; and in the hour of trouble he will be your best friend; but on the other hand, it will draw out all the corruptions of corrupt hearts, and lying and the poison of asps is under their tongues; and they do cause the pure in heart to be cast into prison, because they want them out of their way.

A fanciful and flowery and heated imagination beware of; because the things of God are of deep import; and time, and experience, and careful and ponderous and solemn thoughts can only find them out. Thy mind, O man! if thou wilt lead a soul unto salvation, must stretch as high as the utmost heavens, and search into and contemplate the darkest abyss, and the broad expanse of eternity—thou must commune with God. How much more dignified and noble are the thoughts of God, than the vain imaginations of the human heart! None but fools will trifle with the souls of men.

How vain and trifling have been our spirits, our conferences, our councils, our meetings, our private as well as public conversations—too low, too mean, too vulgar, too condescending for the dignified characters of the called and chosen of God, according to the purposes of His will, from before the foundation of the world! We are called to hold the keys of the mysteries of those things that have been kept hid from the foundation of the world until now. Some have tasted a little of these things, many of which are to be poured down from heaven upon the heads of babes; yea, upon the weak, obscure and despised ones of the earth. Therefore we beseech of you, brethren, that you bear with those who do not feel themselves more worthy than yourselves, while we exhort one another to a reformation with one and all, both old and young, teachers and taught, both high and low, rich and poor, bond and free, male and female; let honesty, and sobriety, and candor, and solemnity, and virtue, and pureness, and meekness, and simplicity crown our heads in every place; and in fine, become as little children, without malice, guile or hypocrisy.

Revelation of Eternal Truth

And now, brethren, after your tribulations, if you do these things, and exercise fervent prayer and faith in the sight of God always, *He shall give unto you knowledge by His Holy Spirit, yea by the unspeakable gift of the Holy Ghost, that has not been revealed since the world was until now; which our forefathers have waited with anxious expectation to be revealed in the last times, which their minds were pointed to by the angels, as held in reserve for the fullness of their glory; a time to come in the which nothing shall be withheld, whether there be one God or many Gods, they shall be manifest; all thrones and dominions, principalities and powers, shall be revealed and set forth upon all who have endured valiantly for the Gospel of Jesus Christ; and also if there be bounds set to the heavens, or to the seas; or to the dry land, or to the sun, moon or stars; all the times of their revolutions; all the appointed days, months and years, and all the days of their days, months and years, and all their glories, laws, and set times, shall be revealed, in the days of the dispensation of the fullness of times, according to that which was ordained in the midst of the Council of the Eternal God of all other Gods, before this world was, that should be reserved unto the finishing and the end thereof, when every man shall enter into His eternal presence, and into His immortal rest.*

Ignorance Retards the Church

But I beg leave to say unto you, brethren, that ignorance, superstition and bigotry placing itself where it ought not, is oftentimes in the way of the prosperity of this Church; like the torrent of rain from the mountains, that floods the most pure and crystal stream with mire, and dirt, and filthiness, and obscures everything that was clear before, and all rushes along in one general deluge; but time weathers tide; and notwithstanding we are rolled in the mire of the flood for the time being, the next surge peradventure, as time rolls on, may bring to us the fountain as clear as crystal, and as pure as snow; while the filthiness, flood-wood and rubbish is left and purged out by the way.

The Hand of the Lord Cannot Be Stayed

How long can rolling water remain impure? What power shall stay the heavens? As well might man stretch forth his puny arm to stop the Missouri river in its decreed course, or to turn it up stream, as to hinder the Almighty from pouring down knowledge from heaven, upon the heads of the Latter-day Saints.

What is Boggs or his murderous party, but wimbling willows upon the shore to catch the flood-wood? As well might we argue that water is not water, because the mountain torrents send down mire and roil the crystal stream, although afterwards render it more pure than before;

or that fire is not fire, because it is of a quenchable nature, by pouring on the flood; as to say that our cause is down because renegades, liars, priests, thieves and murderers, who are all alike tenacious of their crafts and creeds, have poured down, from their spiritual wickedness in high places, and from their strongholds of the devil, a flood of dirt and mire and filthiness and vomit upon our heads.

No! God forbid. Hell may pour forth its rage like the burning lava of mount Vesuvius, or of Etna, or of the most terrible of the burning mountains; and yet shall "Mormonism" stand. Water, fire, truth and God are all realities. Truth is "Mormonism." God is the author of it. He is our shield. It is by Him we received our birth. It was by His voice that we were called to a dispensation of His Gospel in the beginning of the fullness of times. It was by Him we received the Book of Mormon; and it is by Him that we remain unto this day; and by Him we shall remain, if it shall be for our glory; and in His Almighty name we are determined to endure tribulation as good soldiers unto the end.

But, brethren, we shall continue to offer further reflections in our next epistle. You will learn by the time you have read this, and if you do not learn it, you may learn it, that walls and irons, doors and creaking hinges, and half-scared-to-death guards and jailers, grinning like some damned spirits, lest an innocent man should make his escape to bring to light the damnable deeds of a murderous mob, are calculated in their very nature to make the soul of an honest man feel stronger than the powers of hell.

But we must bring our epistle to a close. We send our respects to fathers, mothers, wives and children, brothers and sisters; we hold them in the most sacred remembrance.

We feel to inquire after Elder Rigdon; if he has not forgotten us, it has not been signified to us by his writing. Brother George W. Robinson also; and Elder Cahoon, we remember him, but would like to jog his memory a little on the fable of the bear and the two friends who mutually agreed to stand by each other. And perhaps it would not be amiss to mention uncle John [Smith], and various others. A word of consolation and a blessing would not come amiss from anybody, while we are being so closely whispered by the bear. But we feel to excuse everybody and everything, yea the more readily when we contemplate that we are in the hands of persons worse than a bear, for the bear would not prey upon a dead carcass.

Our respects and love and fellowship to all the virtuous Saints. We are your brethren and fellow-sufferers, and prisoners of Jesus Christ for the Gospel's sake, and for the hope of glory which is in us. Amen.

Continued Reflections

We continue to offer further reflections to Bishop Partridge, and to The Church of Jesus Christ of Latter-day Saints, whom we love with a fervent love, and do always bear them in mind in all our prayers to the throne of God.

It still seems to bear heavily on our minds that the Church would do well to secure to themselves the contract of the land which is proposed to them by Mr. Isaac Galland, and to cultivate the friendly feelings of that gentleman, inasmuch as he shall prove himself to be a man of honor and a friend to humanity; also Isaac Van Allen, Esq., the attorney-general of Iowa Territory, and Governor Lucas, that peradventure such men may be wrought upon by the providence of God, to do good unto His people. We really think that Mr. Galland's letter breathes that kind of a spirit, if we may judge correctly. Governor Lucas also. We suggest the idea of praying fervently for all men who manifest any degree of sympathy for the suffering children of God.

We think that the United States Surveyor of the Iowa Territory may be of great benefit to the Church, if it be the will of God to this end; and righteousness should be manifested as the girdle of our loins.

Preparation against the Wrath of God

It seems to be deeply impressed upon our minds that the Saints ought to lay hold of every door that shall seem to be opened unto them, to obtain foothold on the earth, and be making all the preparation that is within their power for the terrible storms that are now gathering in the heavens, "a day of clouds, with darkness and gloominess, and of thick darkness," as spoken of by the Prophets, which cannot be now of a long time lingering, for there seems to be a whispering that the angels of heaven who have been entrusted with the counsel of these matters for the last days, have taken counsel together; and among the rest of the general affairs that have to be transacted in their honorable council, they have taken cognizance of the testimony of those who were murdered at Haun's Mills, and also those who were martyred with David W. Patten, and elsewhere, and have passed some decisions peradventure in favor of the Saints, and those who were called to suffer without cause.

These decisions will be made known in their time; and the council will take into consideration all those things that offend.

We have a fervent desire that in your general conferences everything should be discussed with a great deal of care and propriety, lest you grieve the Holy Spirit, which shall be poured out at all times upon your heads, when you are exercised with those principles of righteousness that are agreeable to the mind of God, and are properly affected one toward another, and are careful by all means to remember, those who are in bondage, and in heaviness, and in deep affliction for your sakes. And if there are any among you who aspire after their own aggrandizement, and seek their own opulence, while their brethren are groaning in poverty, and are under sore trials and temptations, they cannot be benefited by the intercession of the Holy Spirit, which maketh intercession for us day and night with groanings that cannot be uttered.

We ought at all times to be very careful that such high-mindedness shall never have place in our hearts; but condescend to men of low estate, and with all long-suffering bear the infirmities of the weak.

Many Called but Few Chosen

Behold, there are many called, but few are chosen. And why are they not chosen? Because their hearts are set so much upon the things of this world, and aspire to the honors of men, that they do not learn this one lesson—that the rights of the Priesthood are inseparably connected with the powers of heaven, and that the powers of heaven cannot be controlled nor handled only upon the principles of righteousness. That they may be conferred upon us, it is true; but when we undertake to cover our sins, or to gratify our pride, our vain ambition, or to exercise control, or dominion, or compulsion, upon the souls of the children of men, in any degree of unrighteousness, behold, the heavens withdraw themselves; the Spirit of the Lord is grieved; and when it is withdrawn, Amen to the Priesthood, or the authority of that man. Behold! ere he is aware, he is left unto himself, to kick against the pricks; to persecute the Saints, and to fight against God.

We have learned by sad experience that it is the nature and disposition of almost all men, as soon as they get a little authority, as they suppose, they will immediately begin to exercise unrighteous dominion. Hence many are called, but few are chosen.

The Priesthood Gentle and Long-suffering

No power or influence can or ought to be maintained by virtue of the Priesthood, only by persuasion, by long-suffering, by gentleness, and meekness, and by love unfeigned; by kindness, and pure knowledge, which shall greatly enlarge the soul without hypocrisy, and without guile, reproving betimes with sharpness, when moved upon by the Holy Ghost, and then showing forth afterwards an increase of love toward him whom thou hast reproved, lest he esteem thee to be his enemy; that he may know that thy faithfulness is stronger than the cords of death; let thy bowels also be full of charity towards all men, and to the household of faith, and [let] virtue garnish thy thoughts unceasingly, then shall thy confidence wax strong in the presence of God, and the doctrine of the Priesthood shall distil upon thy soul as the dews from heaven. The Holy Ghost shall be thy constant companion, and thy sceptre an unchanging sceptre of righteousness and truth, and thy dominion shall be an everlasting dominion, and without compulsory means it shall flow unto thee forever and ever.

The ends of the earth shall inquire after thy name, and fools shall have thee in derision, and hell shall rage against thee, while the pure in heart, and the wise, and the noble, and the virtuous, shall seek counsel, and authority and blessings constantly from under thy hand, and thy people shall never be turned against thee by the testimony of traitors; and although their influence shall cast thee into trouble, and into bars and walls, thou shalt be had in honor, and but for a small moment and thy voice shall be more terrible in the midst of thine enemies, than the fierce lion, because of thy righteousness; and thy God shall stand by thee forever and ever.

Experience through Suffering

If thou art called to pass through tribulations; if thou art in perils among false brethren; if thou art in perils among robbers; if thou art in perils by land or by sea; if thou art accused with all manner of false accusations; if thine enemies fall upon thee; if they tear thee from the society of thy father and mother and brethren and sisters; and if with a drawn sword thine enemies tear thee from the bosom of thy wife, and of thine offspring, and thine elder son, although but six years of age, shall cling to thy garments, and shall say, My father, my father, why can't you stay with us? O, my father, what are the men going to do with you? and if then he shall be thrust from thee by the sword, and thou be dragged to prison, and thine enemies prowl around thee like wolves for the blood of the lamb; and if thou shouldst be cast into the pit, or into the hands of murderers, and the sentence of death passed upon thee; if thou be cast into the deep; if the billowing surge conspire against thee; if fierce winds become thine enemy; if the heavens gather blackness, and all the elements combine to hedge up the way; and above all, if the very jaws of hell shall gape open the mouth wide after thee, know thou, my son, that all these things shall give thee experience, and shall be for thy good. The Son of Man hath descended below them all; art thou greater than he?

Gathering of the Saints

Therefore, hold on thy way, and the Priesthood shall remain with thee, for their bounds are set, they cannot pass. Thy days are known, and thy years shall not be numbered less; therefore, fear not what man can do, for God shall be with you forever and ever.

Now, brethren, I would suggest for the consideration of the conference, its being carefully and wisely understood by the council or conferences that our brethren scattered abroad, who understood the spirit of the gathering, that they fall into the places and refuge of safety that God shall open unto them, between Kirtland and Far West. Those from the east and from the west, and from far countries, let them fall in somewhere between those two boundaries, in the most safe and quiet places they can find; and let this be the present understanding, until God shall open a more effectual door for us for further considerations.

And again, we further suggest for the considerations of the Council, that there be no organization of large bodies upon common stock principles, in property, or of large companies of firms, until the Lord shall signify it in a proper manner, as it opens such a dreadful field for the avaricious, the indolent, and the corrupt hearted to prey upon the innocent and virtuous, and honest.

We have reason to believe that many things were introduced among the Saints before God had signified the times; and notwithstanding the principles and plans may have been good, yet aspiring men, or in other words, men who had not the substance of godliness about them, perhaps undertook to handle edged tools. Children, you know, are fond of tools, while they are not yet able to use them.

Time and experience, however, are the only safe remedies against such evils. There are many teachers, but, perhaps, not many fathers. There are times coming when God will signify many things which are expedient for the well-being of the Saints; but the times have not yet come, but will come, as fast as there can be found place and reception for them.

The Gathering of False Reports

And again, we would suggest for your consideration the propriety of all the Saints gathering up a knowledge of all the facts and sufferings and abuses put upon them by the people of this state; and also of all the property and amount of damages which they have sustained, both of character and personal injuries, as well as real property; and also the names of all persons that have had a hand in their oppressions, as far as they can get hold of them and find them out; and perhaps a committee can be appointed to find out these things, and to take statements, and affidavits, and also to gather up the libelous publications that are afloat, and all that are in the magazines, and in the encyclopedias, and all the libelous histories that are published, and are writing, and by whom, and present the whole concatenation of diabolical rascality, and nefarious and murderous impositions that have been practiced upon this people, that we may not only publish to all the world, but present them to the heads of government in all their dark and hellish hue, as the last effort which is enjoined on us by our Heavenly Father, before we can fully and completely claim that promise which shall call Him forth from His hiding place, and also that the whole nation may be left without excuse before He can send forth the power of His mighty arm.

A Duty to Wives and Children

It is an imperative duty that we owe to God, to angels, with whom we shall be brought to stand, and also to ourselves, to our wives and children, who have been made to bow down with grief, sorrow, and care, under the most damning hand of murder, tyranny, and oppressions, supported and urged on and upheld by the influence of that spirit which has so strongly riveted the creeds of the fathers, who have inherited lies, upon the hearts of the children, and filled the world with confusion, and has been growing stronger and stronger, and is now the very main-spring of all corruption, and the whole earth groans under the weight of its iniquity.

It is an iron yoke, it is a strong band; they are the very hand-cuffs, and chains, and shackles, and fetters of hell.

Therefore it is an imperative duty that we owe, not only to our own wives and children, but to the widows and fatherless, whose husbands and fathers have been murdered under its iron hand; which dark and blackening deeds are enough to make hell itself shudder, and to stand aghast and pale, and the hands of the very devil to tremble and palsy. And also it is an imperative duty that we owe to all the rising generation, and to all the pure in heart, (for there are many yet on the earth among all sects, parties, [and] denominations, who are blinded by the subtle craftiness of men, whereby they lie in wait to deceive, and who are only kept from the truth because they know not where to find it); therefore, that we should waste and wear out our lives in bringing to light all the hidden things of darkness, wherein we know them; and they are truly manifest from heaven.

These should then be attended to with great earnestness. Let no man count them as small things; for there is much which lieth in futurity, pertaining to the Saints, which depends upon these things. You know, brethren, that a very large ship is benefited very much by a very small helm in the time of a storm, by being kept workways with the wind and the waves.

Therefore, dearly beloved brethren, let us cheerfully do all things that lie in our power, and then may we stand still with the utmost assurance, to see the salvation of God, and for His arm to be revealed.

Counsel against Secrecies

And again, I would further suggest the impropriety of the organization of bands or companies, by covenant or oaths, by penalties or secrecies; but let the time past of our experience and sufferings by the wickedness of Doctor Avard suffice and let our covenant be that of the Everlasting Covenant, as is contained in the Holy Writ and the things that God hath revealed unto us. Pure friendship always becomes weakened the very moment you undertake to make it stronger by penal oaths and secrecy.

Your humble servant or servants, intend from henceforth to disapprobate everything that is not in accordance with the fullness of the Gospel of Jesus Christ, and is not of a bold, and frank, and upright nature. They will not hold their peace—as in times past when they see iniquity beginning to rear its head—for fear of traitors, or the consequences that shall follow by reproving those who creep in unawares, that they may get something with which to destroy the flock. We believe that the experience of the Saints in times past has been sufficient, that they will from henceforth be always ready to obey the truth without having men's persons in admiration because of advantage. It is expedient that we should be aware of such things; and we ought always to be aware of those prejudices which sometimes so strangely present themselves, and are so congenial to human nature, against our friends, neighbors, and brethren of the world, who choose to differ from us in opinion and in matters of faith. Our religion is between us and our God. Their religion is between them and their God.

There is a love from God that should be exercised toward those of our faith, who walk uprightly, which is peculiar to itself, but it is without prejudice; it also gives scope to the mind, which enables us to conduct ourselves with greater liberality towards all that are not of our faith, than what they exercise towards one another. These principles approximate nearer to the mind of God, because it is like God, or Godlike.

The Principle of Religious Freedom

Here is a principle also, which we are bound to be exercised with, that is, in common with all men, such as governments, and laws, and regulations in the civil concerns of life. This principle guarantees to all parties, sects, and denominations, and classes of religion, equal, coherent, and indefeasible rights; they are things that pertain to this life; therefore all are alike interested; they make our responsibilities one towards another in matters of corruptible things, while the former principles do not destroy the latter, but bind us stronger, and make our responsibilities not only one to another, but unto God also. Hence we say, that the Constitution of the United States is a glorious standard . . .

We, brethren, are deprived of the protection of its glorious principles, by the cruelty of the cruel, by those who only look for the time being, for pasturage like the beasts of the field, only to fill themselves; and forget that the "Mormons," as well as the Presbyterians, and those of every other class and description, have equal rights to partake of the fruits of the great tree of our national liberty. But notwithstanding we see what we see, and feel what we feel, and know what we know, yet that fruit is no less precious and delicious to our taste; we cannot be weaned from the milk, neither can we be driven from the breast; neither will we deny our religion because of the hand of oppression; but we will hold on until death.

We say that God is true; that the Constitution of the United States is true; that the Bible is true; that the Book of Mormon is true; that the Book of Covenants is true; that Christ is true; that the ministering angels sent forth from God are true, and that we know that we have an house not made with hands eternal in the heavens, whose builder and maker is God; a consolation which our oppressors cannot feel, when fortune, or fate, shall lay its iron hand on them as it has on us.

Now, we ask, what is man? Remember, brethren, that time and chance happen to all men.

We shall continue our reflections in our next.

We subscribe ourselves, your sincere friends and brethren in the bonds of the everlasting Gospel, prisoners of Jesus Christ, for the sake of the Gospel and the Saints.

We pronounce the blessings of heaven upon the heads of the Saints who seek to serve God with undivided hearts, in the name of Jesus Christ. Amen.

JOSEPH SMITH, JUN.,
HYRUM SMITH,
LYMAN WIGHT,
CALEB BALDWIN,
ALEXANDER McRAE (*History of the Church*, 3:289–305; spelling standardized).

B. H. Roberts

The succession of these unpleasantries was occasionally broken by the coming of a friend or a group of them to express their sympathy for the prisoners, and their confidence in the Prophet. All the prisoners, and especially the latter, appreciated these visits. "I was in prison and ye visited me," had a real meaning in his experience. "Those who have not been enclosed in the walls of a prison," he writes, "can have but little idea how sweet the voice of a friend is. One token of friendship from any source whatever awakens and calls into action every sympathetic feeling; it brings up in an instant everything that is passed; it seizes the present with the avidity of lightning; it grasps after the future with the fierceness of a tiger; it moves the mind backward and forward, from one thing to another, until finally all enmity, malice and hatred, and past differences, misunderstanding and mismanagement are slain victorious at the feet of hope."

These visiting friends also brought information concerning the progress of the church in leaving the state, which enabled the Prophet to give the saints counsel from time to time. Also he communicated with them by letter several times, and in these communications he loosened the flood tide of his over-wrought emotions, and in them the greatness of his soul is often revealed (B. H. Roberts, *A Comprehensive History of The Church of Jesus Christ of Latter-day Saints,* 6 vols. [Salt Lake City: Deseret Book, 1930], 1:523).

Brigham Young

(While Joseph Smith was in Liberty Jail, Brigham Young received revelation that the Saints who were driven from Missouri were to travel east rather than west, which led the Saints to the place they would later call Nauvoo. Below is Brigham Young's description of this revelation.)

The revelations which I receive are all upon natural principles. I will give you one revelation which I had in Far West, and it was upon the same principle that it would be for me to have a revelation now, while I am talking to you. It was in the spring of 1838, before there was any disturbance in Far West, or in Davis County.

This people, thought I, are obnoxious to these Missourians, our religion they hate, our Prophet they despise and would like to kill him; they are ignorant of the things of God; they have received the precepts of men and drank deep into them, and are so interwoven with their feelings that the true religion of heaven cannot abide in their minds. Therefore I saw, upon natural principles, that we would be driven from there, but when, I did not know; but still it was plain to me that we would have to leave the State, and that when we did leave it we would not go south, north or west, but east, back to the other States. That I saw upon natural principles, and I knew what those people were afraid of. I then saw that we would go north, as a Church and people, and then to the west, and that when they went to Jackson County, they would go from the west to the east. Mark my words, write them down, this people, as a Church and kingdom, will go from the west to the east. I can tell you more concerning what I saw upon natural principles; I saw that this people would have to gain a foothold, a strength, power, influence, and ability to walk by themselves and to take care of themselves, and power to contend with their enemies and overcome them, upon the same principle that the whites did when they first came to America and overcame the Indians (in *Journal of Discourses,* 26 vols. [London: Latter-day Saints' Book Depot, 1854–86], 3:209).

10

Missions to England

"At a time when the Church experienced great persecutions in Missouri and a widespread apostasy in Kirtland, the Lord inspired the Prophet Joseph Smith to call two apostles and five others to serve missions in England. During their remarkable eight-month mission more than two thousand people were baptized. This was a great blessing during a difficult period in the Church" (Thomas R. Valletta, *Church History for Latter-day Saint Families* [Salt Lake City: Deseret Book, 2004], 262).

The first mission to England in this dispensation began with a commandment from the Lord for the Twelve to meet at Far West to dedicate the cornerstones for the temple, before embarking on their journeys. This was particularly difficult because the Saints had earlier been driven out of Missouri with threats that they would be killed if they dared to return.

Importance of the Missions to Great Britain

These two apostolic missions to Great Britain had an incredible success rate and continued to flourish, even after the missionaries returned to the United States. Nearly one thousand British Saints immigrated to America in 1841, and within the next decade over ten thousand more arrived as the Church in England remained prosperous. Although the people were often receptive to the gospel message, many times the missionaries were forced to endure many hardships.

Charles A. Callis

(Regarding the first apostolic mission to Great Britain.)

In the days of Kirtland, in the darkest hour of the history of the Church, the very midnight of its history, when the powers of evil were attempting to destroy the Church, the word of the Lord came to the Prophet Joseph: "Something new must be done for the salvation of my Church." And then Joseph, always imbued with the spirit of sacrifice, sowed corns of wheat in the ground, so to speak. He took his choice servant, Heber C. Kimball, and he called upon Willard Richards, two stalwart defenders of the prophet and of the gospel; and these men with others, he sent to England to preach the gospel, because it was the will of the Lord that they should go. Oh, what a splendid spectacle—the prophet, surrounded by traitors, some, alas, in the Church, surrounded by enemies, voluntarily depriving himself of the support of these two pillars of the Church, whom he sent to Great Britain to open up the gospel door to the inhabitants of that great land. And when they arrived in Preston, behold, their eyes met this inscription written upon a banner: "Truth will prevail." It did prevail. It shall ever prevail, because this work is the truth of God, and truth is imperishable; it is of God, and like God, it is eternal and shall live forever (Charles A. Callis, in Conference Report, October 1918, 35).

Joseph Smith Jr.

(Regarding the second apostolic mission to Great Britain.)

The mission of the Twelve to England marks an epoch in the missionary experience of the Church. They undertook this mission in fulfillment of a commandment received of the Lord on the 8th of July, 1838, at Far West, Missouri, which revelation was given in answer to the question of the Prophet: "Show us thy will, O Lord, concerning the Twelve." In answer to that question the Lord directed that the several vacancies then existing in the quorum should be filled by the appointment of John Taylor, John E. Page, Wilford Woodruff, and Willard Richards. "And next spring," said the revelation, "let them [the Twelve] depart to go over the great waters and there promulgate my gospel, the fullness thereof, and bear record of my name. Let them take leave of my Saints in the City Far West on the 26th day of April next, on the building spot of my house saith the Lord."

Notwithstanding the fact that the Church had been expelled from the state of Missouri before the 26th day of April, 1839, a number of the Twelve accompanied by several of those who had been appointed to fill vacancies in the quorum, returned to Far West, held a meeting on the site of the Lord's house in the public square of that place, on the date appointed, sung some hymns, ordained those present who had been appointed to fill vacancies in the quorum, laid a corner stone of the Lord's house, took leave of a few of the brethren who were there, and thence started for foreign lands, stopping for a time en route at Nauvoo. Late in the summer of 1839 the Twelve began their departure, usually in pairs, for foreign lands. The work had already been introduced into England by the labors of Elder Heber C. Kimball and associates, Elder Orson Hyde of the quorum of the Twelve; also Elders Willard Richards, Isaac Russell, John Goodson, John Snyder; and Joseph Fielding, a priest. The mission of the Twelve to England as a quorum, however, established the work in the British Isles on a broader and more permanent basis, and thence forward the body religious was strengthened from this mission; and as much from the character as from the numbers of the British Saints (Joseph Smith, *History of The Church of Jesus Christ of Latter-day Saints*, 7 vols., ed. B. H. Roberts [Salt Lake City: Deseret Book, 1980], 4:30–31).

Heber C. Kimball's Call to England *(June 1837)*

Heber C. Kimball

A short time previous to starting, I was laid prostrate on my bed with a stitch in my back, which [had] suddenly seized me while chopping and drawing wood for my family. I could not stir a limb without crying out from the severeness of the pain. Joseph, hearing of it, came to see me, bringing Oliver Cowdery and Bishop Partridge with him; they prayed for and blessed me, Joseph being mouth, beseeching God to raise me up; he then took me by the right hand and said, "Brother Heber, I take you by your right hand in the name of Jesus Christ of Nazareth, and by virtue of the Holy Priesthood vested in me I command you in the name of Jesus Christ to arise, and be thou made whole." I arose from my bed, put on my clothes, and started with them and went up to the temple, and felt no more of the pain afterwards (Orson F. Whitney, *The Life of Heber C. Kimball* [Salt Lake City: Deseret Book, 2001], 106).

Joseph Smith Jr.

Brother Heber, the Spirit of the Lord has whispered to me: "Let my servant Heber go to England and proclaim my Gospel, and open the door of salvation to that nation" (*The Life of Heber C. Kimball*, 104).

Heber C. Kimball

The idea of being appointed to such an important mission was almost more than I could bear up under. I felt my weakness and was nearly ready to sink under it, but the moment I understood the will of my heavenly Father, I felt a determination to go at all hazards, believing that he would support me by his almighty power, and although my family were dear to me, and I should have to leave them almost destitute, I felt that the cause of truth, the gospel of Christ, outweighed every other consideration (as cited in Edward W. Tullidge, *The Women of Mormondom* [New York: Tullidge & Crandall, 1877], 112).

Robert B. Thompson

(Commenting on seeing Heber C. Kimball embark on his mission to England.)

The door [of the Kimball home] being partly open I entered and felt struck with the sight which presented itself to my view. I would have retired, thinking I was intruding, but I felt riveted to the spot. The father [Heber C. Kimball] was pouring out his soul to [God] . . . that he would grant unto him a prosperous voyage across the mighty ocean, and make him useful wherever his lot should be cast, and that he who careth for the sparrows, and feedeth the young ravens when they cry, would supply the wants of his wife and little ones in his absence. He then, like the patriarchs, and by virtue of his office, laid his hands upon their heads individually, leaving a father's blessing upon them, and commending them to the care and protection of God, while he should be engaged preaching the gospel in foreign lands. . . . His emotions were great, and he was obliged to stop at intervals, while the big tears rolled down his cheeks, an index to the feelings which reigned in his bosom. My heart was not stout enough to refrain; in spite of myself I wept and mingled my tears with theirs at the same time. I felt thankful that I had the privilege of contemplating such a scene. I realized that nothing could induce that man to tear himself from so affectionate a family group—from his partner and children who were so dear to him—but a sense of duty and love to God and attachment to his cause (*The Women of Mormondom,* 114–15).

Heber C. Kimball

[I felt] as though my very inmost parts would melt within me at leaving my family in such a condition, as it were almost in the arms of death. I felt as though I could not endure it. I asked the teamster to stop, and said to Brother Brigham, "This is pretty tough, isn't it; let's rise up and give them a cheer." We arose, and swinging our hats three times over our heads, shouted: "Hurrah, hurrah for Israel." Vilate, hearing the noise, arose from her bed and came to the door. She had a smile on her face. Vilate and Mary Anne Young cried out to us: "Goodbye, God bless you" (*The Life of Heber C. Kimball,* 265–66).

Heber C. Kimball

I felt that the cause of truth, the Gospel of Christ, outweighed every other consideration (*The Life of Heber C. Kimball,* 104).

Vilate Kimball

(Courtesy of the Church Archives, The Church of Jesus Christ of Latter-day Saints)

Vilate Kimball

At nine o'clock in the morning of this never-to-be-forgotten-day . . . Heber bade adieu to his brethren and friends and started without purse or scrip to preach the gospel in a foreign land. He was accompanied by myself and children, and some of the brethren and sisters, to Fairport. Sister Mary Fielding, who became afterwards the wife of Hyrum Smith, gave him five dollars, with which Heber paid the passage of himself and Brother Hyde to Buffalo. They were also accompanied by her and Brother Thompson and his wife (Mary Fielding's sister), who were going on a mission to Canada (*The Women of Mormondom*, 115).

Opposition from the Adversary

Heber C. Kimball

(On the morning of July 30, 1837, the day the first baptisms in England were to be performed, the missionaries were attacked by Satan and his hosts. Elder Isaac Russell came to Elder Heber C. Kimball, seeking relief from the torment of evil spirits. As Elders Orson Hyde and Heber C. Kimball laid their hands on him to bless him, Elder Kimball was knocked senseless to the floor by an invisible power. As he regained consciousness, he saw his brethren praying for him, and soon after, a vision was opened before them.)

I then arose and sat up on the bed, when a vision was opened to our minds, and we could distinctly see the evil spirits, who foamed and gnashed their teeth at us. We gazed upon them about an hour and a half (by Willard's watch). We were not looking towards the window, but towards the wall. Space appeared before us, and we saw the devils coming in legions, with their leaders, who came within a few feet of us. They came towards us like armies rushing to battle. They appeared to be men of full stature, possessing every form and feature of men in the flesh, who were angry and desperate; and I shall never forget the vindictive malignity depicted on their countenances as they looked me in the eye; and any attempt to paint the scene which then presented itself, or portray their malice and enmity, would be vain. I perspired exceedingly, my clothes becoming as wet as if I had been taken out of the river. I felt excessive pain, and was in the greatest distress for some time. I cannot even look back on the scene without feelings of horror; yet by it I learned the power of the adversary, his enmity against the servants of God, and got some understanding of the invisible world. We distinctly heard those spirits talk and express their wrath and hellish designs against us. However, the Lord delivered us from them, and blessed us exceedingly that day. . . .

Years later, narrating the experience of that awful morning to the Prophet Joseph, Heber asked him . . . whether there was anything wrong with him that he should have such a manifestation.

"No, Brother Heber," he replied, "at that time you were nigh unto the Lord; there was only a veil between you and Him, but you could not see Him. When I heard of it, it gave me great joy, for I then knew that the work of God had taken root in that land. It was this that caused the devil to make a struggle to kill you. . . . The nearer a person approaches the Lord, a greater power will be manifested by the adversary to prevent the accomplishment of His purposes" (*The Life of Heber C. Kimball*, 130–32).

Myrtle Hyde

Orson's vision unveiled, and he saw the throng of awful attackers. They rushed at him with knives, threats, imprecations, and hellish grins, Orson's astonishment [was] extreme at the sinister appearance. These full-statured, bizarrely-clothed devils, men and women, possessed every form and feature of mortals, but some had hideous distortions in face and body. They seemed infuriated, their words and actions expressing confusion and misery. The sight sickened Orson, but he stood between Heber and their venomous host. Summoning spiritual power, he eventually forced these fiends of hell to begin to retreat from the area of the room. As the last savage imp departed, he turned around and said, as if to appease Elder Hyde's strenuous opposition to them, "I never said anything against you!"

Orson replied, "It matters not to me whether you have or have not; you are a liar from the beginning! In the name of Jesus Christ, depart!"

Orson, Willard [Richards], and Isaac [Russell] turned their concerned attention to Heber, stretched out on the bed. They laid their hands on his head and, with priesthood authority, in the name of Jesus Christ, rebuked the influence of the evil spirits. Immediately Heber roused. Looking around, he began to get up.

In agonizing pain, drained of strength, Heber's body refused to stand, so he knelt, and he prayed. His energy beginning to return, he arose and sat on the bed with his companions, facing the room and fireplace. Before any significant discussion endued, the veil withdrew from the eyes of all four missionaries, apparently that they would *all* know with surety the reality of the occupants of the realms of darkness.

The space before them seemed to open up, and they watched the demoniac host advance toward them in legions, behind leaders, like armies surging to battle, the repulsive belligerents foaming and gnashing their teeth at the mortals. The evil horde pressed close—virulent and desperate, looks of vindictive malignity on their faces—within a few feet of the missionaries, making eye contact. In addition to human forms in this repulsive spectacle, Orson and the others saw snakes in both corners of the old fireplace, hissing, writhing, and crawling over each other, producing soul-racking effects on the observers (as cited in Roy B. Huff, "Orson Hyde: A Life of Lessons Learned," *The Religious Educator* [2002]: 172–73).

Heber C. Kimball

It is written, "resist the devil and he will flee from you." Some people do not believe that there are any devils. There are thousands of evil spirits that are just as ugly as evil can make them. The wicked die, and their spirits remain not far from where their tabernacles are. When I was in England . . . I saw more devils than there are persons here to-day; they came upon me with an intention to destroy me; they are the spirits of wicked men who, while in the flesh, were opposed to God and his purposes. I saw them with what we call the spiritual eyes, but what is in reality the natural eye. The atmosphere of many parts of these mountains is doubtless the abode of the spirits of Gadianton robbers, whose spirits are as wicked as hell, and who would kill Jesus Christ and every Apostle and righteous person that ever lived if they had the power. It is by the influence of such wicked spirits that men and women are all the time tempted to tell little lies, to steal a little, to take advantage of their neighbor a little, and they tell us there is no harm in it. It is by the influence and power of evil spirits that the minds of men are prejudiced against each other, until they are led to do each other an injury, and sometimes to kill each other (in *Journal of Discourses,* 26 vols. [London: Latter-day Saints' Book Depot, 1854–86], 11:84–85).

Heber C. Kimball

Where will those go to that reject this Gospel? Why, in reality they will not go anywhere. . . . They will remain where they are, in hell, where my spirit was for a short time, when I was in England. Where was my body during that brief period? It was in Preston, on the corner of Wilford-street, but my spirit could see and observe those evil spirits as plainly as it ever will after I die. Legions of disembodied evil spirits came against me, organized in companies that they might have more power, but they had not power over me to any great extent, because of the power that was in and sustaining me. I had the Priesthood, and the power of it was upon me. I saw the invisible world of the condemned spirits, those who were opposed to me and to this work, and to the lifting up of the standard of Christ in that country. Did I at the same time see or have a vision of the angels of God—of His legions? No, I did not; though they were there and stood in defense of me and my brethren, and I knew it. And all this not that there was any very great virtue in me, but there was virtue in the Priesthood and Apostleship which I held, and God would and did defend; and the evil spirits were dispersed by the power of God (in *Journal of Discourses*, 4:2).

Return to Far West, Missouri

Many faithful members of the Church were tested and tried in the fires of adversity and proved they would do anything to fulfill the commandments of the Lord—not excepting laying down their lives if necessary. In April 1838, the Lord revealed that Far West was a "holy and consecrated land" and commanded that a temple be built "for the gathering together of my Saints, that they may worship me." The Lord had commanded the Twelve Apostles to lay the cornerstone of the Far West Temple on a specific day—April 26, 1839—and then leave from there to serve a mission in Great Britain. But the Saints were driven from Missouri in the fall of 1838. The brethren were therefore faced with the decision of whether or not to return to Missouri, knowing that their very lives would be in danger if they did. Their enemies knew of the specified date and vowed to prevent the Saints from accomplishing what they had been commanded to do. The willingness of the Twelve to keep the commandment of the Lord is indicative of their courage and faith.

Doctrine and Covenants 115:7–10

(The commandment to return to Far West was given April 26, 1838.)

Let the city, Far West, be a holy and consecrated land unto me; and it shall be called most holy, for the ground upon which thou standest is holy.

Therefore, I command you to build a house unto me, for the gathering together of my saints, that they may worship me.

And let there be a beginning of this work, and a foundation, and a preparatory work, this following summer;

And let the beginning be made on the fourth day of July next [1839]; and from that time forth let my people labor diligently to build a house unto my name;

Captain Samuel Bogart

(Captain Bogart, one of the mobocrats of Missouri, challenged the revelation that instructed the Twelve to return to Missouri. He threatened Theodore Turley, saying the following.)

The Twelve are now scattered all over creation; let them come here if they dare; if they do, they will be murdered (*History of the Church*, 3:307).

Brigham Young

Many of the Authorities considered, in our present persecuted and scattered condition, the Lord would not require the Twelve to fulfill his words to the letter, and, under our present circumstances, he would take the will for the deed; but I felt differently and so did those of the Quorum who were with me. I asked them, individually, what their feelings were upon the subject. They all expressed their desired to fulfill the revelation. I told them the Lord God had spoken, and it was our duty to obey and leave the event in his hands and he would protect us (Elden Jay Watson, *Manuscript History of Brigham Young, 1801–1844* [Salt Lake City: Smith Secretarial Service, 1968], 35).

History of the Church

Shortly after midnight on April 26, five apostles and twenty Saints gathered on the spot in Far West designated for the Lord's House. The five apostles ordained Wilford Woodruff and George A. Smith as apostles to fill vacancies left by apostasy. Thirty-one apostates were excommunicated. The Saints sang the hymn "Adam-ondi-Ahman." Finally, the cornerstones for the Far West Temple were dedicated. Having kept the commandment and fulfilled the revelation, the Twelve took their leave of the Saints and started back to Illinois, en route to England. (*History of the Church*, 3:336–39).

Brigham Young

Thus was this revelation fulfilled, concerning which our enemies said, if all other revelations of Joseph Smith were fulfilled that one should not, as it had day and date to it (*Manuscript History of Brigham Young*, 39).

Joseph Smith Jr.

(Describing what happened immediately following the meeting in Far West.)

As the Saints were passing away from the meeting, Brother Turley said to Elders Page and Woodruff, "Stop a bit, while I bid Isaac Russell good bye;" and knocking at the door, called Brother Russell. His wife answered, "Come in, it is Brother Turley." Russell replied, "It is not; he left here two weeks ago;" and appeared quite alarmed; but on finding it was Brother Turley, asked him to sit down; but the latter replied, "I cannot, I shall lose my company." "Who is your company?" enquired Russell. "The Twelve." "*The Twelve!*" "Yes, don't you know that this is the twenty-sixth, and the day the Twelve were to take leave of their friends on the foundation of the Lord's House, to go to the islands of the sea? The revelation is now fulfilled, and I am going with them." Russell was speechless, and Turley bid him farewell (*History of the Church*, 3:339–40; spelling standardized).

DEPARTURE OF OTHERS TO ENGLAND *(1839)*

Wilford Woodruff

Early upon the morning of the 8th of August, I arose from my bed of sickness, laid my hands upon the head of my sick wife, Phoebe, and blessed her. I then departed from the embrace of my companion, and left her almost without food or the necessaries of life. She suffered my departure with the fortitude that becomes a saint, realizing the responsibilities of her companion. . . .

Although feeble, I walked to the banks of the Mississippi River. There President Young took me in a canoe . . . and paddled me across the river. When we landed, I lay down on a side of sole leather, by the post office, to rest. Brother Joseph, the Prophet of God, came along and looked at me. "Well, Brother Woodruff," said he, "you have started upon your mission." "Yes," said I, "but I feel and look more like a subject for the dissecting room than a missionary." Joseph replied: "What did you say that for? Get up, and go along; all will be right with you" (*Wilford Woodruff: History of His Life and Labors as Recorded in His Daily Journals*, ed. Matthias F. Cowley [Salt Lake City: Bookcraft, 1965], 109).

Parley P. Pratt

During the few days that we were together in New York we held many precious meetings in which the Saints were filled with joy, and the people more and more convinced of the truth of our message. Near forty persons were baptized and added to the Church in that city during the few days of our brethren's stay there (Parley P. Pratt, *Autobiography of Parley P. Pratt*, ed. Parley P. Pratt Jr. [Salt Lake City: Deseret Book, 1985], 261).

Joseph Smith Jr.

Perhaps no men ever undertook such an important mission under such peculiarly distressing and unpropitious circumstances. . . . However, notwithstanding their afflictions and trials, the Lord always interposed in their behalf, and did not suffer them to sink in the arms of death. Some way or other was made for their escape—friends rose up when they most needed them, and relieved their necessities; and thus they were enabled to pursue their journey and rejoice in the Holy One of Israel. They, truly, "went forth weeping, bearing precious seed," but have "returned with rejoicing, bearing their sheaves with them" (*History of the Church*, 4:390–91).

Orson Hyde

To travel two thousand miles on foot, teaching from house to house, and from city to city, without purse or scrip, often sleeping in school houses after preaching—in barns, in sheds, by the way side, under trees, &c., was something of a task. When one would be teaching in private families, the other would frequently be nodding in his chair, weary with toil, fatigue and want of sleep. We were often rejected in the after part of the day, compelling us to travel in the evening, and sometimes till people were gone to bed, leaving us to lodge where we could. We would sometimes travel until midnight or until nearly daylight before we could find a barn or shed in which we dare to lie down; must be away before discovered least suspicion rest upon us. Would often lie down under trees and sleep in day time to make up loss (Orson Hyde, "History of Orson Hyde," *Millennial Star* [November 19, 1864]: 776).

Joseph Smith Jr.

(Describing a vision given to the Prophet Joseph Smith regarding the Twelve in England.)

I saw the twelve, apostles of the Lamb, who are now up on the earth who hold the keys of this last ministry, in foreign lands, standing together in a circle much fatigued, with their clothes tattered and feet swollen, with their eyes cast downward, and Jesus standing in their midst, and they did not behold him, the Savior looked upon them and wept (*Personal Writings of Joseph Smith*, ed. Dean C. Jessee [Salt Lake City: Deseret Book, 2002], 176; spelling standardized).

Conversion Stories and Missionary Experiences in England

Descendent of George D. Watt

(Despite the terrors presented by Satan and his host, the first baptisms in England, held in the River Ribble, went on as scheduled. George D. Watt won a foot race to the river, which earned him the honor of being the first to be baptized in England. These baptisms began a flood of English converts. Years later, George D. Watt compiled the Journal of Discourses.)

Few of us recall the details of July 30th of 1837 at the River Ribble, but I know well the details because my ancestor was George Watt. At 9 o'clock on Sunday morning near the River, two of the nine baptismal candidates lined up for a foot race to the water's edge. It may have been a 24 mile marathon to their destination, but no less than a 6K. When the starter gun signaled the beginning of the race, the well-laid out track which charted the runners' destination, was surrounded by a cheering crowd of 9,000 breathlessly awaiting the victor. Speculation and even wagers were being called from the crowd as everyone hoped his favorite would win. George Watt was the younger man and more sure of foot. He easily out ran the other and won first place. As the cheering of the crowd ceased, they reverently watched as the first man in Britain was baptized (Susan Easton Black, "A Profile of a British Saint 1837–1848," Regional Studies in Latter-day Saint Church History, British Isles, ed. Donald Q. Cannon [Provo, Utah: Department of Church History and Doctrine, Brigham Young University, 1990], 104).

Heber C. Kimball

(In Chatburn, Heber baptized twenty-five people the first night he preached there. During the next five days, with the assistance of his companion, Joseph Fielding, Heber baptized about 110 people and organized branches in Downham, Chatburn, Waddington, and Clithero.)

I cannot refrain from relating an occurrence which took place while Brother Fielding and myself were passing through the village of Chatburn on our way to Downham. Having been observed approaching the village, the news ran from house to house, and immediately the noise of their looms was hushed, and the people flocked to their doors to welcome us and see us pass. More than forty young people of the place ran to meet us; some took hold of our mantles and then of each others' hands; several having hold of hands went before us singing the songs of Zion, while their parents gazed upon the scene with delight, and poured their blessings upon our heads, and praised the God of heaven for sending us to unfold the principles of truth and the plan of salvation to them. The children continued with us to Downham, a mile distant. Such a scene, and such gratitude, I never witnessed before. "Surely," my heart exclaimed, "out of the mouths of babes and sucklings thou hast perfected praise." What could have been more pleasing and delightful than such a manifestation of gratitude to Almighty God; and from those whose hearts were deemed too hard to be penetrated by the Gospel, and who had been considered the most wicked and hardened people in that region of country (*The Life of Heber C. Kimball*, 171–72).

Heber C. Kimball

I went through the streets of that town [Chatburn] feeling as I never before felt in my life. My hair would rise on my head as I walked through the streets, and I did not then know what was the matter with me. I pulled off my hat, and felt that I wanted to pull off my shoes, and I did not know what to think of it.

When I returned, I mentioned the circumstance to brother Joseph, who said, "Did you not understand it? That is a place where some of the old Prophets traveled and dedicated that land, and their blessing fell upon you" (in *Journal of Discourses*, 5:22).

Wilford Woodruff

The whole history of this Herefordshire mission shows the importance of listening to the still small voice of the Spirit of God and the revelations of the Holy Ghost. The Lord had a people there prepared for the gospel. They were praying for light and truth, and the Lord sent me to them, and I declared the gospel of life and salvation unto them, and some eight hundred souls received it, and many of them have been gathered to Zion in these mountains (Wilford Woodruff, *Leaves from My Journal* [Salt Lake City: Juvenile Instructor Office, 1881], 98–99).

Joseph Fielding Smith

Elder Wilford Woodruff and Elder Theodore Turley had a wonderful experience. Elder Woodruff had been laboring in Burslem, Hanley, Stoke and the Potteries from the time he arrived in England to the second of March, and many were baptized. While preaching on the Sabbath day, March 1, 1840, the anniversary of his birth, it was made known to him by the spirit that he was to move to the south. Acting on this impression, he journeyed to the farm communities of Herefordshire and stopped at the home of Mr. John Benbow at Castle Frome, Ledbury. Mr. Benbow was a prosperous farmer, cultivating some three hundred acres of land. Brother Woodruff introduced himself as a missionary from America representing The Church of Jesus Christ of Latter-day Saints, and said that he had been sent to preach the Gospel to Mr. Benbow in his household. Mr. Benbow was impressed by Elder Woodruff's story and said that there were in that place six hundred persons and more, who had broken off from the Methodists and had taken the name of "United Brethren." They had forty-five preachers and a number of meeting houses, duly licensed. These people were dissatisfied with the teachings of the churches and were looking for light and truth. On the morning of the 5th, at the request of Mr. Benbow, the people were invited to come to a large hall in the mansion of Mr. Benbow, to hear Elder Woodruff preach. The people flocked to the hall to hear the American stranger speak. Meetings continued to be held, and in a short time Elder Woodruff had baptized over six hundred persons, mostly from these dissenters from the Methodist church. On the 8th at the meeting a constable was sent on complaint of a minister to arrest Brother Woodruff for preaching to the people. Elder Woodruff said he had a license to preach as well as the rector, and if the constable would take a chair and sit beside him until the close of the meeting he would be at his service. He then gave a discourse on the first principles and at the close of the meeting opened the door for baptism. Several came forward among whom were four of the preachers and the constable, who said: "Mr. Woodruff, I would like to be baptized." He then went to the complaining rector and told him that if he wanted Mr. Woodruff arrested, he must serve the writ himself, for he had heard him preach the only true Gospel sermon he had ever heard. The rector then sent two clerks of the Church of England as spies, and they were both baptized. The ministers and rectors of the Church of England then sent a petition to the

Archbishop of Canterbury, to request Parliament to pass a law prohibiting the "Mormons" from preaching in the British Isles, declaring that they had baptized fifteen hundred persons, many of whom were members of the Church of England. The archbishop replied that if the petitioners had the worth of souls at heart as much as they valued ground where hares, foxes and hounds ran, they would not lose so many of their flock (Joseph Fielding Smith, *Church History and Modern Revelation*, 4 vols. [Salt Lake City: Council of the Twelve Apostles of The Church of Jesus Christ of Latter-day Saints, 1946–49], 4:52).

Wilford Woodruff

(A summary of an experience Wilford had while preaching in Hawcross.)

Opposition grew as the Church prospered in the area. While preaching in the village of Hawcross, Wilford Woodruff was surrounded by a hostile mob. When some of the villagers requested baptism, Wilford told them that if they had faith enough to be baptized, he had sufficient faith to administer the ordinance, in spite of the threatened physical violence. The small group walked down to a pond and was soon surrounded by a mob armed with stones. Wilford Woodruff reported, "I walked into the water with my mind stayed on God and baptized five persons while they were pelting my body with stones, one of which hit me on the head and came very near knocking me down" (Wilford Woodruff, "Elder Woodruff's Letter," *Times and Seasons* [March 1, 1841]: 329–30).

Brigham Young

In our travels, either in America or Europe, we have never before found a people, from whose minds we have had to remove a greater multiplicity of objections, or combination of obstacles, in order to excite an interest in the subject and prepare the heart for the reception of the word of God, than in the city of London (*History of the Church*, 4:222).

Heber C. Kimball

When I left them, my feelings were such as I cannot describe. As I walked down the street I was followed by numbers; the doors were crowded by the inmates of the houses to bid me farewell, who could only give vent to their grief in sobs and broken accents. While contemplating this scene I was constrained to take off my hat, for I felt as if the place was holy ground. The Spirit of the Lord rested down upon me and I was constrained to bless that whole region of country. I was followed by a great number to Clithero, a considerable distance from the villages, who could then hardly separate from me. My heart was like unto theirs, and I thought my head was a fountain of tears, for I wept several miles after I bid them adieu (*Life of Heber C. Kimball*, 187–88).

11

GATHERING TO NAUVOO

On May 1, 1839, the Prophet Joseph purchased a one hundred and thirty-five acre farm from Hugh White, lying near the Mississippi River. He purchased another larger farm from Isaac Galland, at Commerce, Illinois. He later renamed the place Nauvoo, a Hebrew word meaning "beautiful." Within four years, Nauvoo grew to become one of the largest and most prosperous communities in Illinois. It truly became a "beautiful" place and a testament to the Prophet Joseph Smith's inspired leadership.

Joseph Smith Jr.

(Referring to the lands he had purchased at Commerce.)

The place was literally a wilderness. The land was mostly covered with trees and bushes, and much of it was so wet that it was with the utmost difficulty that a footman could get through, and totally impossible for teams. Commerce was unhealthy, very few could live there; but believing that it might become a healthy place by the blessing of heaven to the saints, and no more eligible place presenting itself, I considered it wisdom to make an attempt to build up a city (as cited in B. H. Roberts, *A Comprehensive History of the Church,* 6 vols. [Salt Lake City: Deseret News Press, 1930], 2:9).

Joseph Smith III

(Joseph III was six years old when his family moved to Nauvoo in 1839.)

Father and his family left Quincy, May 9, arrived at Commerce the following day, and moved into a log house which is yet standing. This was known as the Hugh White residence . . .

I recall there was a spring nearby from which we obtained our drinking water. . . .

Standing close upon the bank of the river, which at this point ran almost due east, our little house occupied a very handsome site, and was the central habitation of a farm of one hundred and thirty-five acres . . .

The times were busy ones. The winter had not proved, for all its afflictions, too severe for the many Saints who came into the place to secure locations and to build shelters for their families. A period of great activity ensued, and history shows that among the buildings erected at the settlement called Commerce there were three frame houses, one of stone, and two of blocks [squared logs] (*The Memoirs of President Joseph Smith III*, ed. Mary Audentia Smith Anderson [Independence, Missouri: Price Publishing Co., 2001], 1453–54).

Charlotte Haven

(In a letter to her mother, she describes the intense poverty of the Saints when they arrived in Nauvoo.)

When we consider the short time since the Mormons came here, and their destitution after having had every vestige of property taken from them, and after having undergone great suffering and persecution, their husbands and sons in some instances murdered; when we remember that, driven from their homes in Missouri, with famine before them, five thousand men, women, and children crossed the Mississippi to this State in the winter of 1841 [1838–39], we cannot wonder that they have no fitter dwelling place and so few of the comforts of life (as cited in Richard Neitzel Holzapfel and Jeni Brogerg Holzapfel, *Women of Nauvoo* [Salt Lake City: Bookcraft, 1992], 39).

Charlotte Haven

(Describing her family's move to Nauvoo in the winter of 1843.)

Our stage much resembled an Eastern butcher's wagon, and we soon ascertained that the curtains on the sides were destitute of fastenings, for they flapped up and down, to and fro, admitting a bracing circulation of air at every gust, which seemed to come direct from Arctic regions. The driver, who occupied the seat before us, told us we must on no account stop talking, "for," says he, "people freeze to death on these prairies before they know it" (*Women of Nauvoo*, 23).

A Day of God's Power
(July 22, 1839)

Wilford Woodruff

While I was living in this cabin in the old barracks, we experienced a day of God's power with the Prophet Joseph. It was a very sickly time and Joseph had given up his home in Commerce to the sick and had a tent pitched in his dooryard and was living in that himself. The large number of Saints who had been driven out of Missouri were flocking into Commerce; but had no homes to go into and were living in wagons, in tents, and on the ground. Many, therefore, were sick through the exposure they were subjected to. Brother Joseph had waited on the sick until he was worn out and nearly sick himself.

On the morning of the 22nd of July, 1839, he arose reflecting upon the situation of the Saints of God in their persecutions and afflictions, and he called upon the Lord in prayer and the power of God rested upon him mightily, and as Jesus healed all the sick around Him in His day, so Joseph, the Prophet of God, healed all around on this occasion. He healed all in his house and dooryard, then, in company with Sidney Rigdon and several of the Twelve, he went through among the sick lying on the back of the river and he commanded them in a loud voice, in the name of Jesus Christ, to come up and be made whole, and they were all healed. When he had healed all that were sick on the east side of the river, they crossed the Mississippi River in a ferryboat to the west side, to Montrose where we were. The first house they went into was President Brigham Young's. He was sick on his bed at the time. The Prophet went into his house and healed him, and they all came out together. As they were passing by my door, Brother Joseph said: "Brother Woodruff, follow me." These were the only words spoken by any of the company from the time they left Brother Brigham's house till we crossed the public square and entered Brother Fordham's house. Brother Fordham had been dying for an hour and we expected each minute would be his last.

I felt the power of God that was overwhelming His Prophet.

When we entered the house, Brother Joseph walked up to Brother Fordham and took him by the right hand; in his left hand he held his hat.

He saw that Brother Fordham's eyes were glazed, and that he was speechless and unconscious.

After taking hold of his hand, he looked down into the dying man's face and said: "Brother Fordham, do you not know me?" At first he made no reply; but we could all see the effect of the Spirit of God resting upon him.

Elijah Fordham
(Courtesy of the Church Archives, The Church of Jesus Christ of Latter-day Saints)

He again said: "Elijah, do you not know me?"

With a low whisper, Brother Fordham answered, "Yes!"

The Prophet then said, "Have you not faith to be healed?"

The answer, which was a little plainer than before, was: "I am afraid it is too late. If you had come sooner, I think it might have been."

He had the appearance of a man awaking from sleep. It was the sleep of death. Joseph then said: "Do you not believe that Jesus is the Christ?"

"I do, Brother Joseph," was the response.

Then the Prophet of God spoke with a loud voice, as in the majesty of the Godhead: "Elijah, I command you, in the name of Jesus of Nazareth, to arise and be made whole!"

The words of the Prophet were not like the words of man, but like the voice of God. It seemed to me that the house shook from its foundation.

Elijah Fordham leaped from his bed like a man raised from the dead. A healthy color came to his face, and life was manifest in every act.

His feet were done up in Indian meal poultices. He kicked them off his feet, scattered the contents, and then called for his clothes and put them on. He asked for a bowl of bread and milk and ate it; then put on his hat and followed us into the street, to visit others who were sick.

The unbeliever may ask: "Was there not deception in this?"

If there is any deception in the mind of the unbeliever, there was certainly none with Elijah Fordham, the dying man, nor with those who were present with him, for in a few minutes more he would have been in the spirit world had he not been rescued. Through the blessing of God, he lived up till 1880, in which year he died in Utah while all who were with him on that occasion, with the exception of two, are in the spirit world. Among the number [present at the time of his healing] were Joseph and Hyrum Smith, Sidney Rigdon, Brigham Young, Heber C. Kimball, George A. Smith and Parley P. Pratt. Orson Pratt and Wilford Woodruff are the only two living who were present . . .

As soon as we left Brother Fordham's house, we went into the home of Joseph B. Noble, who was very low and dangerously sick.

When we entered the house, Brother Joseph took him by the hand and commanded him in the name of Jesus Christ to arise and be made whole. He did arise and was immediately healed.

While this was going on, the wicked mob in the place, led by one Kilburn, had become alarmed, and followed us into Brother Noble's house.

Before they arrived there, Brother Joseph had called upon Brother Fordham to offer prayer.

While he was praying the mob entered, with all the evil spirits accompanying them.

As soon as they entered, Brother Fordham, who was praying, fainted and sank to the floor.

When Joseph saw the mob in the house, he arose and had the room cleared of both that class of men and their attendant devils. Then Brother Fordham immediately revived and finished his prayer.

This shows what power evil spirits have upon the tabernacles of men. The Saints are only saved from the power of the devil by the power of God.

This case of Brother Noble's was the last one of healing upon that day. It was the greatest day for the manifestation of the power of God through the gift of healing since the organization of the Church.

When we left Brother Noble, Joseph went with those who accompanied him from the other side to the banks of the river to return home. While waiting for the ferryboat, a man of the world, knowing of the miracles which had been performed, came to him and asked him if he would not go and heal two twin children of his, about five months old, who were both lying sick nigh unto death.

They were some two miles from Montrose.

The Prophet said he could not go; but, after pausing some time, he said he would send some one to heal them; and he turned to me and said: "You go with the man and heal his children."

He took a red silk handkerchief out of his pocket and gave it to me, and told me to wipe their faces with the handkerchief when I administered to them, and they should be healed. He also said unto me: "As long as you will keep that handkerchief, it shall remain a league between you and me."

I went with the man and did as the Prophet commanded me, and the children were healed. I have possession of the handkerchief unto this day (Wilford Woodruff, *Leaves from My Journal* [Grantsville, Utah: LDS Archive Publishers, 1997], 99–104; spelling and punctuation standardized).

Heber C. Kimball

This was a day never to be forgotten by the Saints, nor by the wicked, for they saw the power of God manifest in the flesh (Heber C. Kimball, *Journal of Heber C. Kimball*, comp. R. B. Thompson [Nauvoo, Illinois: Robinson and Smith, 1840], 83).

John Lyman Smith

(John Smith's family came to Nauvoo when it was being settled by the Saints. At first, the only place the family could find to live was a stable made of logs. Everyone in the family except their mother soon came down with fever as a result of living in the swampy area.)

The Prophet Joseph Smith and his brother Hyrum visited us and administered to all of us, father being delirious from the effects of the fever. Their words comforted us greatly, as they said in the name of the Lord "you all shall be well again." Upon leaving the hovel, Joseph placed his slippers upon my father's feet and sprang upon his horse from the doorway and rode home barefoot. The next day Joseph removed father to his own house and nursed him until he recovered (*Stories About*

Joseph Smith, the Prophet: A Collection of Incidents Related by Friends Who Knew Him, comp. Edwin F. Parry [Salt Lake City: The Deseret News Press, 1934], 33–34).

Greeting New Immigrants in Nauvoo

A favorite pastime of the Prophet Joseph Smith was greeting arriving immigrants to Nauvoo, who would come up the Mississippi River via steamboat. For these early Saints, seeing the Prophet was a joyful end to their long journey and an experience they never forgot.

Mary Ann Stearns Winters

And oh! The anxiety of the Saints to see the Prophet Joseph Smith! Some thought they would be able to discern him in a multitude, and they all longed to behold him and grasp his hand. Brothers Joseph and Hyrum and a large company of people were a[t] the landing to meet us. Brother Pratt had introduced him to the company, and a general handshaking followed with the friends who had come to take them to their various homes and destinations. Then Brother Joseph came to the boat and into the cabin where our family were. After cordial greetings, he took a seat and taking the little boys, Parley and Nathan, upon his knees, seemed much affected . . . It was indeed a time of rejoicing, that two boat loads of Saints had arrived in one day. Brother Joseph arose saying, "Come, be more comfortable after your long journey." My mother was placed in a big chair, and Brother Hodge, with others of Brother Joseph's bodyguard, carried her up to the Mansion, Brother Pratt carrying the baby—the rest of us following along, listening to all that Brother Joseph had to say (Mary Ann Stearns Winters, *The Winters Book of Remembrance* [LDS Church Archives, The Church of Jesus Christ of Latter-day Saints, Salt Lake City, Utah], n.p.).

Robert Crookston

(A convert from England.)

As we approached the landing place to our great joy we saw the Prophet Joseph Smith there to welcome his people who had come so far. We were all so glad to see him and set our feet upon the promised land so to speak. It was the most thrilling experience of my life for I knew he was Prophet of the Lord (Robert Crookston, *Autobiography of Robert Crookston* [LDS Church Archives, The Church of Jesus Christ of Latter-day Saints, Salt Lake City, Utah], 65).

Priscilla Staines

(A convert from England.)

I felt impressed by the spirit that I should know him. As we neared the pier the prophet was standing among the crowd. At that moment, however, I recognized him according to the impression, and pointed him out (Edward W. Tullidge, *The Women of Mormondom* [New York: Tullidge & Crandall, 1877], 291).

Mary Alice Cannon Lambert

At Nauvoo, several of the leading brethren were there to meet the company . . . Among those brethren was the Prophet Joseph Smith. I knew him the instant my eyes rested upon him, and at that moment I received my testimony that he was a Prophet of God, for I never had such a feeling for mortal man as then thrilled my being . . . He was not pointed out to me. I knew him from all the other men, and, child that I was (I was only fourteen), I knew that I saw a Prophet of God.

Many, many times between the time I reached Nauvoo and his martyrdom, I heard him preach. The love the saints had for him was inexpressible. They would willingly have laid down their lives for him. If he was to talk, every task would be laid aside that they might listen to his words. He was not an ordinary man. Saints and sinners alike felt and recognized a power and influence which he carried with him. It was impossible to meet him and not be impressed by the strength of his personality and influence.

In May, 1844, he went to the stone shops where the men were working on the Nauvoo Temple and blessed them, each man by the power of his Priesthood. Brother Lambert (whom I afterward married) he gathered right in his arms and blessed, and it was ever his testimony that he was thrilled from head to foot by that blessing ("Joseph Smith, The Prophet," *Young Women's Journal* [December 1905]: 554).

Emmeline Blanche Wells

Journeying from my home in Massachusetts to Nauvoo, Illinois, with a company of Latter-day Saints . . . among them was the late Jacob Gates, who was accompanied by his wife. . . . Sister Gates talked a great deal about the Prophet Joseph . . . and when she saw that I was specially interested in him, promised me that she would introduce me to him on our arrival in Nauvoo. . . .

As we neared our destination . . . the elders were full of enthusiasm at the thought of seeing the Prophet again. But not once in all the conversation did I hear a description of his personal appearance. . . . I had not formed any idea of him except of his wonderful power. . . .

At last the boat reached the upper landing, and a crowd of people were coming toward the bank of the river. As we stepped ashore. . . . I could see one person who towered away and above all the others around him; in fact I did not see distinctly any others. His majestic bearing, so entirely different from any one I had ever seen (and I had seen many superior men) was more than a surprise. It was as if I beheld a vision; I seemed to be lifted off my feet, to be as it were walking in the air, and paying no heed whatever to those around me. I made my way through the crowd, then I saw this man whom I had noticed, because of his lofty appearance, shaking hands with all the people, men, women and children. Before I was aware of it he came to me, and when he took my hand, I was simply electrified,—thrilled through and through to the tips of my fingers, and every part of my body, as if some magic elixir had given me new life and vitality. I am sure that for a few minutes I was not conscious of motion. I think I stood still, I did not want to speak, or be spoken to. I was overwhelmed with indefinable emotion.

Sister Gates came to me and said, "I'll introduce you to the Prophet Joseph now, he is here."

I replied, "I don't want to be introduced to him."

She was astonished, and said curtly, "Why, you told me how desirous you were of meeting him."

I answered, "Yes, but I've seen him and he spoke to me."

"But he didn't know who you were!"

I replied, "I know that but it don't matter," and Sister Gates walked away without another word of explanation. I was in reality too full for utterance. I think had I been formally presented to the Prophet, I should have fallen down at his feet. . . . The one thought that filled my soul was, I have seen the Prophet of God, he has taken me by the hand, and this testimony has never left me in all the "perils by the way." . . . For many years, I felt it too sacred an experience even to mention ("Joseph Smith, The Prophet," 554–56).

Life in Nauvoo

After being driven from New York, Kirtland, Independence, and finally Far West, the Saints once again sought peace and safety in a place free from religious oppression. Though they often faced poverty, they remained optimistic and grateful for their new home, Nauvoo, the City Beautiful.

Joseph Smith Jr.

The name of our city (Nauvoo) is of Hebrew origin, and signifies a beautiful situation, or place, carrying with it, also, the idea of rest; and is truly descriptive of the most delightful location. It is situated on the east bank of the Mississippi river, at the head of the Des Moines Rapids, in Hancock county, bounded on the east by an extensive prairie of surpassing beauty, and on the north, west, and south, by the Mississippi (Joseph Smith, *History of The Church of Jesus Christ of Latter-day Saints,* 7 vols., ed. B. H. Roberts [Salt Lake City: Deseret Book, 1966], 4:268).

Joseph Smith Jr.

(The Illinois legislature granted Nauvoo a city charter that gave the Saints much latitude and authority. Among those in the legislature who voted in favor of the Nauvoo Charter was Abraham Lincoln.)

All the power there was in Illinois she gave to Nauvoo. . . .

The municipal court has all the power to issue and determine writs of habeas corpus within the limits of this city that the legislature can confer. This city has all the power the state courts have, and was given [it] by the same authority—the legislature. . . .

There is nothing but what we have power over, except where restricted by the constitution of the United States. "But," says the mob,

"What dangerous power!" Yes—dangerous, because they will protect the innocent and put down mobocrats. . . .

If these powers are dangerous, then the constitution of the United States and of this state are dangerous; but they are not dangerous to good men . . .

The lawyers themselves acknowledge that we have all power granted us in our charters that we could ask for—that we had more power than any other court in the state; for all other courts were restricted, while ours was not (*History of the Church*, 5:466–73).

Report of the Progress of the Church

(At a general conference of the Church in Nauvoo, the First Presidency read this report of the rise and progress of the city.)

It is with unfeigned pleasure that they have to make known the steady and rapid increase of the Church in this state . . . Peace and prosperity attend us; and we have favor in the sight of God and virtuous men. The time was, when we were looked upon as deceivers, and that "Mormonism" would soon pass away, come to naught, and be forgotten. But . . . it is now taking a deep hold in the hearts and affections of all those who are noble-minded enough to lay aside the prejudice of education, and investigate the subject with candor and honesty. . . . In the language of one of our own poets, we would say—

In Illinois we've found a safe retreat,
A home, a shelter from oppression dire;
Where we can worship God as we think right,
And mobbers come not to disturb our peace;
Where we can live and hope for better days,
Enjoy again our liberty, our rights:
That social intercourse which freedom grants,
And charity requires of man to man.
And long may charity pervade each breast,
And long may Illinois remain the scene
Of rich prosperity, by *peace secured.*

(*History of the Church*, 4:336–38; spelling standardized)

Abigail Pitkin

(Abigail penned this poem about life in Nauvoo in a letter to her friend Rebecca Raymond.)

I often thought I'd like to give
You an account of where we live.
What's our employ, what we possess,
How we appear, and how we dress.
In Nauvoo City we reside,
Where we in peace can now abide,
Our dwelling measures "Thirteen Feet,"
With walls rough-hewn and white-washed neat.

Our bed springs up against the wall
Because our room is rather small;
For we in building count the cost
Lest too much money should be lost,
For mobs you know have saucy grown
And will not let us have our own.
Our table measures just "Three feet,"
With falling leaves and varnished neat.

With chairs we're blessed with only two,
Missouri claims the remaining few.
Our glass above the table stands,
Cracked through the center by your hands,
Which oft reminds us of the scene
When it was decked with evergreen.
On shelves our dishes are ranged neat
By pegs supported, quite complete.

For old Missouri's wicked clan
Our cupboard kept and warming pan.
We have a heifer, very small,
At present gives no milk at all;
And fowls which throng our door,
But lack of corn will keep them poor.
Poor things, they'll have to make us meat
When we have nothing else to eat.

We have a bag to hold our flour,
Now nearly full stands near the door,
And many old trunks scattered round,
In which our cabin doth abound.
Our old red boxes join the ring,
Of them awhile I fain would sing.
Like trusty friends they've by us stood,
And from them we've derived much good.

We've many useful things around
That scarce will get a passing sound.
I'd not forget to name the sink
For that is useful, oft, I think.
On subjects long I must not dwell,
But shortly now the tale must tell
How we, like "Dorcas;" garments make
For which we goods or money take.

In building often we engage,
But that our foes doth much enrage.
Our homes to them seem very fair,
Which leads them on to act more rare.
In dress and manners we appear
Much as we did when you were here.
Our names we keep but rather would
Exchange for better if we could.

We've many friends and many foes,
Many wants and many woes,
But still I am content to be
A "Mormon," not a "Pharisee."
I still remain your friend, A.P.
And wish in faith we could agree.
May health and peace your steps attend,
And wisdom guide you to the end.

(Abigail Pitkin, "Letter from Abigail Pitkin to Rebecca Raymond" [n.p., n.d.]; as cited in E. Cecil McGavin, *Nauvoo, the Beautiful* [Salt Lake City: Bookcraft, 1972], 41–42)

Bathsheba Smith

We have had the garden plowed. It looks very well, but would [do] better if it did not rain so much. The worms trouble all the neighbors' gardens, but have not mine but little. A great many people have had more or less out of our garden, such as lettuce, onions, radishes and greens. . . . Our early potatoes are getting quite large. The corn is in tassel, cabbage looks well, vines rather poor, tomatoes in bloom, beets quite large. [We] will soon have peas (Bathsheba W. Smith, "Bathsheba W. Smith to George A. Smith, 15 June 1844," *George A. Smith Collection* [LDS Church Archives, The Church of Jesus Christ of Latter-day Saints, Salt Lake City, Utah]; as cited in Kenneth W. Godfrey, Audrey M. Godfrey, and Jill Mulvay Derr, *Women's Voices* [Salt Lake City: Deseret Book, 1982], 129–30; spelling, capitalization, and punctuation standardized).

Charlotte Haven

We are having beautiful sunsets these days, and from our parlor window we have an extensive western view, and later on in the night the heavens are all aglow with light from the prairie fires. Between the river and the Iowa bluff eight or ten miles west, ten to twenty fires are started, burning the refuse grass and straw preparatory to putting in spring crops. Often I sit up a long time after going to my room, watching these long lines of fire as they seem to meet all along the horizon. The sun is down and darkness is fast gathering, so I must close, with much love from your sister, Charlotte (*Women of Nauvoo,* 61; March 5, 1843).

12

Organization of the Relief Society

During the time of the construction of the Nauvoo Temple, the Saints were required to sacrifice their time, talents, and all they had to the building up of the house of the Lord. In response to this requirement, Sarah Granger Kimball organized a sewing group that provided the temple workers with much needed shirts. Eventually Sister Kimball's sewing group extended beyond sewing and included other charitable acts. The Prophet Joseph Smith approved of the efforts of the sisters and suggested that the group be organized under the priesthood.

On the afternoon of March 17, 1842, the Prophet Joseph met with twenty women in the room above his red brick store in Nauvoo. There, he organized the "Female Relief Society of Nauvoo," with Emma Smith as first president and Elizabeth Ann Whitney and Sarah M. Cleveland acting as counselors (Richard Neitzel Holazpfel, Jeni Brogerg Holzapfel, *Women of Nauvoo* [Salt Lake City: Bookcraft, 1992], 4).

Origin of the Relief Society

Sarah Granger Kimball

In the spring of 1842, a maiden lady (Miss Cook) was seamstress for me, and the subject of combining our efforts for assisting the Temple hands came up in conversation. She desired to be helpful but had no means to furnish. I told her I would furnish material if she would make some shirts for the workmen. It was then suggested that some of the neighbors might wish to combine means and efforts with ours, and we decided to invite a few to come and consult with us on the subject of forming a Ladies Society. The neighboring sisters met in my parlor and decided to organize. I was delegated to call on Sister Eliza R. Snow and ask her to write for us a constitution and by-laws and submit them to President Joseph Smith prior to our next Thursday meeting. She cheerfully responded, and when she read them to him he replied that the constitution and by-laws were the best he had ever seen. "But," he said, "this is not what you want. Tell the sisters their offering is accepted of the Lord, and He has something better for them than a written constitution. Invite them all to meet me and a few of the brethren in the Masonic Hall over my store next Thursday afternoon, and I will organize the sisters under the priesthood after a pattern of the priesthood." He further said, "The Church was never perfectly organized until the women were thus organized" ("Story of the Organization of the Relief Society," *The Relief Society Magazine* [March 1919]: 6:129).

Joseph Smith Jr.

(March 17, 1842)

I assisted in commencing the organization of "The Female Relief Society of Nauvoo" in the Lodge Room. Sister Emma Smith, President, and Sister[s] Elizabeth Ann Whitney and Sarah M. Cleveland, Counselors. I gave much instruction, read in the New Testament, and Book of Doctrine and Covenants, [D&C 25:1–8] concerning the Elect Lady, and showed that the elect meant to be elected to a certain work, etc., and that the revelation was then fulfilled by Sister Emma's election to the Presidency of the Society, she having previously been ordained to expound Scriptures. Emma was blessed, and her counselors were ordained by Elder John Taylor (Joseph Smith, *History of The Church of Jesus Christ of Latter-day Saints*, 7 vols., ed. B. H. Roberts [Salt Lake City: Deseret Book, 1966], 4:552–53).

Joseph Smith Jr.

You will receive instructions through the order of the Priesthood which God has established, through the medium of those appointed to lead, guide and direct the affairs of the Church in this last dispensation; and I now turn the key in your behalf in the name of the Lord, and this Society shall rejoice, and knowledge and intelligence shall flow down from this time henceforth; this is the beginning of better days to the poor and needy, who shall be made to rejoice and pour forth blessings on your heads (*History of the Church,* 4:607).

Ellen Douglas

(Writing to her parents June 2, 1842, regarding the early meetings and types of instruction received during this initial period of organization.)

There is now in this city a female charity society of which I am a member. We are in number eight or nine hundred. Joseph Smith's wife is the head of our society, and we meet on a Thursday at ten o'clock, where we receive instructions bother temporally and spiritually (Ellen Briggs Douglas, "Ellen Briggs Douglas to mother and father, 2 June 1844" [LDS Church Archives, The Church of Jesus Christ of Latter-day Saints, Salt Lake City, Utah]; as cited in *Women of Nauvoo,* 109).

Lucy Mack Smith

This institution is a good one. . . . We must cherish one another, watch over one another, comfort one another and gain instruction, that we may all sit down in heaven together (as cited in Loren Burton and Annette Burton, "Relief Society origin observed in Nauvoo," *Church News* [March 27, 1999]: 12).

Richard Neitzel Holazpfel

It is evident that those sisters assembled at this first meeting also shaped their own destiny as the discussion turned to a formal name. John Taylor suggested that the organization's name incorporate the term *Benevolent* instead of *Relief.* Emma disagreed and debated Joseph and John Taylor on the point, saying that she did "not wish to have it called after other societies in the world" (*Women of Nauvoo,* 108; see also "Relief Society Minutes" [LDS Church Archives, The Church of Jesus Christ of Latter-day Saints, Salt Lake City, Utah], March 17, 1842).

Boyd K. Packer

I hope the name, the Relief Society, will never be changed. It ties back to the very charter given to women by the Prophet. Its full, balanced program responds to every worthy need that is by nature a part of womanhood (Boyd K. Packer, "The Relief Society," *Ensign*, November 1978, 7).

Boyd K. Packer
(Courtesy of the Church Archives, The Church of Jesus Christ of Latter-day Saints)

Purpose and Mission of the Relief Society

Emma Smith

(Commenting on the purpose of the Relief Society.)

We are going to do something *extraordinary*. When a boat is stuck on the rapids with a multitude of Mormons on board, we shall consider that a loud call for *relief*. We expect extraordinary occasions and pressing calls ("A Record of the Organization, and Proceedings of the Female Relief Society of Nauvoo," [LDS Church Archives, The Church of Jesus Christ of Latter-day Saints, Salt Lake City, Utah], March 17, 1842; as cited in *Women of Nauvoo*, 4).

Joseph Smith Jr.

A society has lately been formed by the ladies of Nauvoo for the relief of the poor, the destitute, the widow and the orphan; and for the exercise of all benevolent purposes. . . .

There was a very numerous attendance at the organization of the society and also at their subsequent meetings of some of our most intelligent, humane, philanthropic, and respectable ladies; and we are well assured from a knowledge of those pure principles of benevolence that flow spontaneously from their humane, and philanthropic bosoms, that with the resources they will have at command they will fly to the relief of the stranger, they will pour in oil and wine to the wounded heart of the distressed; they will dry up the tear of the orphan, and make the widow's heart to rejoice ("Ladies' Relief Society," *Times and Seasons* [April 1, 1842]: 743).

Emmeline B. Wells

Emmeline Wells
(Courtesy of the Church Archives, The Church of Jesus Christ of Latter-day Saints)

Sister Emma was benevolent and hospitable; she drew around her a large circle of friends, who were like good comrades. She was motherly in her nature to young people, always had a houseful to entertain or be entertained. She was very high-spirited and the brethren and sisters paid her great respect. Emma was a great solace to her husband in all his persecutions and the severe ordeals through which he passed; she was always ready to encourage and comfort him, devoted to his interests, and was constantly by him whenever it was possible. She was a queen in her home, so to speak, and beloved by the people, who were many of them indebted to her for favors and kindness (Emmeline B. Wells, "LDS Women of the Past: Personal Impressions," *Women's Exponent* [February 1908]: 49).

Joseph Smith Jr.

This is a charitable Society, and according to your natures; it is natural for females to have feelings of charity and benevolence. You are now placed in a situation in which you can act according to those sympathies which God has planted in your bosoms.

If you live up to these principles, how great and glorious will be your reward in the celestial kingdom! If you live up to your privileges, the angels cannot be restrained from being your associates (*History of the Church*, 4:605).

Minutes of the Female Relief Society

(Regarding some of the goals of the Relief Society.)

The object of the Society [being to] . . . provoke the brethren to good works in looking to the wants of the poor—searching after objects of charity, and in administering to their wants—to assist by correcting the morals and strengthening the virtues of the community, and save the Elders the trouble of rebuking; that they may give their time to other duties, &c., in their public teaching ("A Record of the Organization and Proceedings of the Female Relief Society of Nauvoo," 7; as cited in "Relief Society of The Church of Jesus Christ of Latter-day Saints," *History of the Relief Society: 1842–1966* [Salt Lake City: The General Board of Relief Society, 1966], 18).

Joseph Smith Jr.

Let this Society teach women how to behave towards their husbands, to treat them with mildness and affection. When a man is borne down with trouble, when he is perplexed with care and difficulty, if he can meet a smile instead of an argument or a murmur—if he can meet with mildness, it will calm down his soul and soothe his feelings; when the mind is going to despair, it needs a solace of affection and kindness (*History of the Church*, 4:606–7).

Joseph Smith Jr.

[Joseph counseled the sisters] not [to] injure the character of anyone—if members of the society shall conduct [themselves] improperly, deal with them and keep all your doings within your own bosoms; and hold all characters sacred (as cited in *Women of Nauvoo*, 108).

Eliza R. Snow

As daughters of Zion, we should set an example for all the world, rather than confine ourselves to the course which had been heretofore pursued (as cited in *Women of Nauvoo*, 108).

Eliza R. Snow

(This poem about the society's goals was published in the Times and Seasons *just after its founding.)*

The Female Relief Society of Nauvoo

What Is It?

It is an Institution form'd to bless
The poor, the widow, and the fatherless—
To clothe the naked and the hungry feed,
And in the holy paths of virtue, lead.

To seek out sorrow, grief and mute despair,
And light the lamp of hope eternal there—
To try the strength of consolation's art
By breathing comfort to the mourning heart.

To chase the clouds that shade the aspect, where
Distress presides; and wake up pleasure there—
With open heart extend the friendly hand
To hail the stranger, from a distant land.

To stamp a vetoing impress on each move
That Virtue's present dictates disapprove—
To put the tattler's coinage, scandal, down,
And make corruption feel its with'ring frown.

To give instruction, where instruction's voice
Will guide the feet and make the heart rejoice—
To turn the wayward from their recklessness,
And lead them in the ways of happiness.

It is an *Order,* fitted and design'd
To meet the wants of body, and of mind—
To seek the wretched, in their long abode—
Supply their wants, and raise their hearts to God .
(Eliza R. Snow, "The Female Relief Society of Nauvoo,"
Times & Seasons [1 July 1842]: 846).

Blessings Flowing from the Relief Society

Joseph Smith Jr.

The Female Relief Society have taken a most active part in my welfare against my enemies, in petitioning to the governor in my behalf. These measures were all necessary. . . . If these measures had not been taken, more serious consequences would have resulted. I have come here to bless you. The Society have done well: their principles are to practice holiness. God loves you, and your prayers in my behalf shall avail much: let them not cease to ascend to God continually (*History of the Church,* 5:140–41).

George Albert Smith
(Courtesy of the Church Archives, The Church of Jesus Christ of Latter-day Saints)

George Albert Smith

You are . . . more blessed than any other women in all the world. You were the first women to have the franchise; the first women to have a voice in the work of a church. It was God that gave it to you and it came as a result of revelation to a Prophet of the Lord. Since that time, think what benefits the women of this world have enjoyed. Not only you belonging to the Church have enjoyed the blessing of equality, but when the Prophet Joseph Smith turned the key for the emancipation of womankind, it was turned for all the world, and from generation to generation the number of women who can enjoy the blessings of religious liberty and civil liberty has been increasing (George Albert Smith, "Address to Members of the Relief Society," *Relief Society Magazine* [December 1945]: 717).

John Taylor

We have here our Relief Societies. . . . I was in Nauvoo at the time the Relief Society was organized by the Prophet Joseph Smith, and I was present at the occasion . . .

With regard to those Societies, I will say, they have done a good work and are a great assistance to our bishops, as well as being peculiarly adapted to console, bless, and encourage those of their sisters who need their care, and also to visit the sick, as well as to counsel and instruct the younger women in the things pertaining to their calling as children and saints of the Most High. I am happy to say that we have a great many honorable and noble women engaged in these labors of love, and the Lord blesses them in their labors, and I bless them in the name of the Lord (*The Gospel Kingdom*, sel. G. Homer Durham, 1943, 273; as cited in *Teachings of the Presidents of the Church: John Taylor* [Salt Lake City: The Church of Jesus Christ of Latter-day Saints, 2001], 93).

13

Joseph Smith and Politics

Joseph Smith's Meeting with President Van Buren

As directed by revelation, the Prophet Joseph Smith, along with a number of the brethren, traveled to Washington D.C. in November 1839 to seek help from the federal government and redress for the loss of the Saints' property in Missouri (D&C 124). President Van Buren showed little interest in assisting the Saints. Joseph persisted, only to have President Van Buren deny his request again in February.

Clark V. Johnson

(Describing the Prophet's journey to Washington, D.C., and his heroism in stopping a runaway stagecoach.)

The major appeal to the U.S. Government occurred during the winter of 1839–40, when the Prophet led the delegation to Washington. That group consisted of Elias Higbee, Sidney Rigdon, Porter Rockwell, and Robert Foster. They left Nauvoo 29 October 1839. On 30 October they stopped in Quincy, where Sidney Rigdon became ill. In Quincy they met Robert D. Foster, who agreed to travel with them to help care for Sidney Rigdon. The party was delayed at Quincy because of Rigdon's illness and also because they contacted influential people in Quincy to obtain additional papers to aid them in presenting their cause before the U.S. government. When they reached Columbus, Ohio, Rigdon was still critically ill. At this time Joseph realized that the party had to travel faster to reach Washington, D.C., in time for their appointment with Congress and President Martin Van Buren, and they split up. Joseph Smith and Higbee immediately left for Washington, while Rigdon, Foster, and Rockwell remained until Rigdon's health improved. On 17 November Smith and Higbee boarded a stagecoach bound for Washington, D.C. During the journey, the stagecoach driver lost control of the horses. The Prophet calmed the other passengers and prevented a mother from throwing her infant out of the stage window in an attempt to save its life. Then he climbed up on the stage and brought the runaway team to a halt. Just before the team stopped, Elias had jumped off the stage to assist Joseph, and was "slightly injured." Joseph Smith was acknowledged a hero until it was learned that he was the Mormon Prophet, and there were no references made to his heroism before Congress (Clark V. Johnson, "Government Responses to Mormon Appeals, 1840–1846," *Regional Studies in LDS History: Illinois* [Provo, Utah: Brigham Young University, 1995], 185–86).

Joseph Smith Jr.

While on the mountains some distance from Washington, our coachman stepped into a public house to take his grog, when the horses took fright and ran down the hill at full speed. I persuaded my fellow travelers to be quiet and retain their seats, but had to hold one woman to prevent her throwing her infant out of the coach. The passengers were exceedingly agitated, but I used every persuasion to calm their feelings; and opening the door, I secured my hold on the side of the coach the best way I could, and succeeded in placing myself in the coachman's seat, and reining up the horses, after they had run some two or three miles, and neither coach, horses, or passengers received any injury. My course was spoken of in the highest terms of commendation, as being one of the most daring and heroic deeds, and no language could express the gratitude of the passengers, when they found themselves safe, and the horses quiet. There were some members of Congress with us, who proposed naming the incident to that body, believing they would reward such conduct by some public act; but on inquiring my name, to mention as the author of their safety, and finding it to be Joseph Smith the "Mormon Prophet," as they called me, I heard no more of their praise, gratitude, or reward (Joseph Smith, *History of The Church of Jesus Christ of Latter-day Saints,* 7 vols., ed. B. H. Roberts [Salt Lake City: Deseret Book, 1966], 4:23–24).

Joseph Smith Jr.

On Friday morning, 29th, we proceeded to the house of the President. We found a very large and splendid palace, surrounded with a splendid enclosure, decorated with all the fineries and elegancies of this world. We went to the door and requested to see the President, when we were immediately introduced into an upper apartment, where we met the President, and were introduced into his parlor, where we presented him with our letters of introduction. As soon as he had read one of them, he looked upon us with a kind of half frown, and said, "What can I do? I can do nothing for you! If I do anything, I shall come in contact with the whole state of Missouri."

But we were not to be intimidated; and demanded a hearing, and constitutional rights. Before we left him he promised to reconsider what he had said, and observed that he felt to sympathize with us, on account of our sufferings (*History of the Church*, 4:40).

Joseph Smith Jr.

I had an interview with Martin Van Buren, the President, who treated me very insolently, and it was with great reluctance he listened to our message, which, when he had heard, he said: "*Gentlemen, your cause is just, but I can do nothing for you*" (*History of the Church*, 4:80).

Parley P. Pratt

(Recounting a meeting with the Prophet Joseph Smith in Philadelphia, en route to Washington, D.C.)

While visiting with brother Joseph in Philadelphia, a very large church was opened for him to preach in, and about three thousand people assembled to hear him. Brother Rigdon spoke first, and dwelt on the Gospel, illustrating his doctrine by the Bible. When he was through, brother Joseph arose like a lion about to roar; and being full of the Holy Ghost, spoke in great power, bearing testimony of the visions he had seen, the ministering of angels which he had enjoyed; and how he had found the plates of the Book of Mormon, and translated them by the gift and power of God. He commenced by saying: "If nobody else had the courage to testify of so glorious a message from Heaven, and of the finding of so glorious a record, he felt to do it in justice to the people, and leave the event with God."

The entire congregation were astounded; electrified, as it were, and overwhelmed with the sense of the truth and power by which he spoke, and the wonders which he related. A lasting impression was made; many souls were gathered into the fold. And I bear witness, that he, by his faithful and powerful testimony, cleared his garments of their blood. Multitudes were baptized in Philadelphia and in the regions around; while, at the same time, branches were springing up in Pennsylvania, in Jersey, and in various directions (Parley P. Pratt, *The Autobiography of Parley P. Pratt, revised and enhanced,* ed. Scot Facer Proctor and Maurine Jensen Proctor [Salt Lake City: Deseret Book, 2000], 362).

Candidate for U.S. President

In addition to speaking with President Martin Van Buren, the Prophet Joseph Smith also held lengthy discussions with Josiah Quincy, mayor of Boston and communicated by letter with those running for the 1844 presidential election. He was so disappointed with the answers he received that he decided to run for that office himself.

On January 29, 1844, an informal political caucus was held in the mayor's office in Nauvoo, Illinois, and it was moved by Willard Richards and voted unanimously to "have an independent electoral ticket, and that Joseph Smith be a candidate for the next Presidency; and [to] use all honorable means in [their] power to secure his election" (*History of the Church,* 6:188).

Joseph Smith Jr.

We believe that governments were instituted by God for the benefit of man, and that he holds men accountable for their acts in relation to them, both in making laws and administering them for the good and safety of society (*History of the Church,* 2:247–48).

Joseph Smith Jr.

If it has been demonstrated that I have been willing to die for a "Mormon," I am bold to declare before Heaven that I am just as ready to die in defending the rights of a Presbyterian, a Baptist, or a good man of any other denomination; for the same principle which would trample upon the rights of the Latter-day Saints would trample upon the rights of the Roman Catholics, or of any other denomination who may be unpopular and too weak to defend themselves (*History of the Church*, 5:498).

Joseph Smith Jr.

It is our duty to concentrate all our influence to make popular that which is sound and good, and unpopular that which is unsound. 'Tis right, politically, for a man who has influence to use it, as well as for a man who has no influence to use his. From henceforth I will maintain all the influence I can get (*History of the Church*, 5:286).

Some Political Views of Joseph Smith

(As outlined in his platform, titled "General Smith's Views of the Powers and Policy of the Government of the United States.")

A. Joseph Smith advocated freeing all the slaves by 1850 and compensating the owners for the slaves. The money was to be derived from the sale of public lands.

B. The Prophet advocated congressional reform, including reducing the number and pay of congressmen. Pay them, he said, only two dollars a day except Sunday. "That's more than the farmer gets, and he lives honestly."

C. Joseph was a leader in the prison reform movement. He believed that prisons should become schools of correction and in these seminaries they should not only learn to become law abiding citizens but should participate in public work projects.

D. The Prophet further advocated that the president should be given power to suppress mobs. (The federal government, at this time, was powerless to intervene with state's rights.)

E. Joseph advocated political freedom for all members [of the

Church]. On one occasion he taught: "I am not come to tell you to vote this way, that way or the other. In relation to national matters, I want it to go abroad unto the whole world that every man should stand on his own merits. The Lord has not given me a revelation concerning politics. I have not asked Him for one" (*History of the Church,* 5:526). (*Church History in the Fulness of Times,* prep. Church Educational System [Salt Lake City: The Church of Jesus Christ of Latter-day Saints, 1989], 270–71)

John A. Widtsoe
(Courtesy of the Church Archives, The Church of Jesus Christ of Latter-day Saints)

John A. Widtsoe

This campaign document is an intelligent, comprehensive, forward-looking statement of policies, worthy of a trained statesman. Many of the Prophet's recommendations have been adopted in the progressive passage of the years. All of them are reasonable and sound. . . .

The political utterances and practices of Joseph Smith point to him as a statesman—one from whom the statesman of the day could win help. Looking back to his day, one cannot help marveling at the breadth of his vision and how sanely he dealt with the problems of the day. When he touched a matter, whatever its nature, Joseph Smith overtopped the crowd (John Andreas Widtsoe, *Joseph Smith: Seeker After Truth, Prophet of God* [Salt Lake City: Deseret News Press, 1951], 219–20).

Parley P. Pratt

(Parley was assigned to stop in New York for Joseph Smith's presidential candidacy. He wrote a pamphlet titled "A Dialogue between Joseph Smith and the Devil," attempting to illustrate the differences between Joseph Smith's character and the adversary's fake political philosophies. Written much like C. S.

Lewis's later Screwtape Letters, *Pratt's pamphlet ends with a humorous exchange.)*

MR. DEVIL.—Well, Mr. Smith, we have talked a long while, and are agreed at last—you are a noble and generous fellow, and would not bring a railing accusation against even a poor old devil, nor cheat him out of a cent. Come, it is a warm day, and I feel as though it is my treat; Let us go down to Mammy Brewer's cellar and take something to drink.

MR. SMITH.—Agreed, Mr. Devil; you appear very generous just now.

(They enter the cellar together.)

MR. DEVIL.—Good morning, Mrs. Brewer, I make you acquainted with my good friend, Mr. Smith, the Prophet.

LANDLADY.—Why, Mr. Devil, is that you? Sit down, you're tired; but you don't say that this is Mr. Smith, your mortal enemy? I am quite surprised. What will you have, gentlemen, for if you can drink together, I think all the world ought to be friends.

MR. DEVIL.—As we are both temperance men and ministers, I think perhaps a glass of spruce beer apiece will be all right; what say you Mr. Smith?

[MR.] SMITH.—As you please, your majesty.

(They take the beer.)

MR. DEVIL.—*(Holding up glass)* Come, Mr. Smith, your good health, I propose to offer a toast.

MR. SMITH.—Well, proceed.

MR. DEVIL.—Here's to my good friend, Joseph Smith, may all sorts of ill luck befall him, and may he never be suffered to enter my kingdom, either in time or eternity, for he would almost make me forget that I am a devil and make a gentleman of me, while he gently overthrows my government at the same time that he wins my friendship.

MR. SMITH.—Here's to his Satanic majesty; may he be driven from the earth, and be forced to put to sea in a stone canoe with an iron paddle, and may the canoe sink, and a shark swallow the canoe and its royal freight, and an alligator swallow the shark, and may the alligator be bound in the northwest corner of hell, the door be locked, the key lost, and a blind man hunting for it (Parley P. Pratt, "A Dialogue between Joseph Smith and the Devil," *New York Herald* [January 1, 1844]: 18–19).

Gracia N. Jones

One time when Emma prepared one of her specialty desserts, a kind of deep-fried scone served with sugar and cream, she was asked what it was called. She replied, "In an election year such as this is, they are called candidates, all puffed up and air in them" (Youngreen, *Reflections of Emma*, 104–5).

One might wonder if she was speaking of all politicians generally, or if she was perhaps teasing her husband, who was at the time a candidate for the U.S. presidency (Gracia N. Jones, *Priceless Gifts* [American Fork, Utah: Covenant Communications, Inc., 1998], 79).

Joseph Smith Jr.

The government of the Almighty has always been very dissimilar to the government of men, whether we refer to His religious government, or to the government of nations. The government of God has always tended to promote peace, unity, harmony, strength, and happiness; while that of man has been productive of confusion, disorder, weakness, and misery.

The greatest acts of the mighty men have been to depopulate nations and to overthrow kingdoms; and whilst they exalted themselves and became glorious, it has been at the expense of the lives of the innocent, the blood of the oppressed, the moans of the widow, and the tears of the orphan. . . .

It has been the design of Jehovah, from the commencement of the world, and is His purpose now, to regulate the affairs of the world in His own time, to stand as a head of the universe, and take the reins of government into His own hand. When that is done, judgment will be administered in righteousness; anarchy and confusion will be destroyed, and "nations will learn war no more." It is for want of this great governing principle that all this confusion has existed; "for it is not in man that walketh, to direct his steps;" this we have fully shown. . . . Other attempts to promote universal peace and happiness in the human family have proven abortive; every effort has failed; every plan and design [has] fallen to the ground; it needs the wisdom of God, the intelligence of God and the power of God to accomplish this. The world has had a fair trial for six thousand years; the Lord will try the seventh thousand Himself; "He whose right it is will possess the kingdom, and reign until

He has put all things under His feet;" iniquity will hide its hoary head, Satan will be bound, and the works of darkness destroyed; righteousness will be put to the line, and judgment to the plummet, and "he that fears the Lord will alone be exalted in that day" ("Sermons and Writings of the Prophet Joseph," *Contributor* [September 1882]: 353–55; punctuation and capitalization standardized).

Joseph Smith's Comments about the Constitution of the United States of America

Joseph Smith Jr.

The only fault I find with the Constitution is, it is not broad enough to cover the whole ground.

Although it provides that all men shall enjoy religious freedom, yet it does not provide the manner by which that freedom can be preserved, nor for the punishment of Government officers who refuse to protect the people in their religious rights, or punish those mobs, states, or communities who interfere with the rights of the people on account of their religion (*Teachings of the Prophet Joseph Smith*, ed. Joseph Fielding Smith [Salt Lake City: Deseret Book, 1976] 326–27).

Joseph Smith Jr.

The different states, and even Congress itself, have passed many laws diametrically contrary to the Constitution of the United States (*Teachings of the Prophet Joseph Smith*, 279).

Joseph Smith Jr.

The Constitution of the United States is a glorious standard; it is founded in the wisdom of God. It is a heavenly banner; it is to all those who are privileged with the sweets of liberty, like the cooling shades and refreshing waters of a great rock in a thirsty and weary land. It is like a great tree under whose branches men from every clime can be shielded from the burning rays of the sun (*Teachings of the Prophet Joseph Smith*, 147).

Joseph Smith Jr.

(The first known statement of Joseph Smith concerning the fact that the Constitution will hang by a thread was given July 19, 1840, while he was speaking of the redemption of Zion.)

Even this nation will be on the verge of crumbling to pieces and tumbling to the ground and when the Constitution is on the brink of ruin this people will be the staff upon which the nation shall lean and they shall bear the Constitution away from the very verge of destruction (Joseph Smith, *Joseph Smith Papers* [LDS Church Archives, The Church of Jesus Christ of Latter-day Saints, Salt Lake City, Utah], Box 1, March 10, 1844; as cited in Michael Stewart, "I Have a Question," *Ensign*, June 1976, 65).

Eliza R. Snow

I heard the Prophet Joseph Smith say . . . that the time would come when this nation would so far depart from its original purity, its glory, and its love of freedom and protection of civil and religious rights, that the constitution of our country would hang as it were by a thread. He said, also, that this people, the sons of Zion, would rise up and save the constitution, and bear it off triumphantly (Edward W. Tullidge, *The Women of Mormondom* [New York: Tullidge & Crandall, 1877], 401).

14

Orson Hyde's Mission to Palestine

One hundred and eighteen years before both the 1948 War of Independence in Palestine and the recognition of the state of Israel; eighty-seven years before General Allenby entered Jaffa Gate in 1917, marking the end of the Ottoman rule in Israel; eighty-seven years before the Balfour Declaration was penned, announcing Britain's support for a Jewish state; and thirty years before Benjamin Zev (Theodor) Herzl's birth in 1860—the Prophet Joseph Smith declared that the predicted time when the Jewish people would return to Jerusalem was soon to be fulfilled. Thus, over sixty years before the 1897 Zionist movement, Joseph Smith became one of the first Christian advocates of the Jewish return.

In August 1833, Joseph Smith received a revelation commanding him to "seek diligently to turn . . . the hearts of the Jews unto the prophets" (D&C 98:16–17). On March 27, 1836, Joseph Smith offered a dedicatory prayer for the Latter-day Saint Kirtland Ohio Temple and implored, mid-prayer:

> Now these words, O Lord, we have spoken before thee, concerning the revelations and commandments which thou hast given unto us, who are identified with the Gentiles. But thou knowest that thou hast a great love for the children of Jacob, who have been scattered upon the mountains for a long time, in a cloudy and dark day. We therefore ask thee to have mercy upon the children of Jacob, that Jerusalem, from this hour, may begin to be redeemed; And the yoke of bondage may begin to be broken off from the house of David; And the children of Judah may begin to return to

> the lands which thou didst give to Abraham, their father. (D&C 109:60–64)

In an 1843 conference of the Church, Joseph Smith noted, "Judah must return, Jerusalem must be rebuilt, and the temple, and water come out from under the temple, and the waters of the Dead Sea be healed. It will take some time to rebuild the walls of the city and the temple, &c.; and all this must be done" (*Teachings of the Prophet Joseph Smith*, ed. Joseph Fielding Smith [Salt Lake City: Deseret Book, 1976], 286).

In the midst of all these pronouncements, in 1832, Joseph Smith confirmed a man named Orson Hyde as a new member of the LDS Church and said to him, "In due time thou shalt go to Jerusalem, the land of thy fathers, and be a watchman unto the house of Israel; and by thy hands shall the Most High do a great work, which shall prepare the way and greatly facilitate the gathering together of that people" (Joseph Smith, *History of The Church of Jesus Christ of Latter-day Saints*, 7 vols., ed. B. H. Roberts [Salt Lake City: Deseret Book, 1980], 4:375). In speaking of the mission Orson Hyde was called to serve in Palestine, B. H. Roberts observed that "it was in fulfillment of this prediction upon his head that he had been called upon this mission to Jerusalem, to dedicate the land of Palestine by apostolic authority, preparatory to the return of the Jews and other of the tribes of Israel to that land of promise. This mission he fully accomplished" (*History of the Church*, 4: xxxi).

In 1839 the Twelve traveled to England to preach the gospel. Suffering from malaria, Orson Hyde was unable to accompany them on this mission. However, in the early part of 1841, in response to a vision and a call from God, Orson Hyde journeyed to the Holy Land. Elder John E. Page was called to accompany him, but after a short time, Elder Page returned to Nauvoo and Elder Hyde continued on his own. After a brief interlude with the Twelve in Great Britain, Elder Hyde traveled on to Jerusalem to dedicate the land of Palestine for the return of the twelve tribes of Israel.

Orson Hyde

(While living in a rented cabin with his wife and two small daughters, Orson was recovering from an illness. Lying in bed one night in a wakeful, contemplative mood, the darkness suddenly dispersed into a scene of light. Transfixed for six thrilling hours, Orson watched as a series of specific cities came into his view.)

Orson Hyde
(Courtesy of the Church Archives, The Church of Jesus Christ of Latter-day Saints)

In the early part of March, 1840, I retired to my bed one night as usual; and while meditating and contemplating the field of my future labors, the vision of the Lord, like clouds of light, burst into my view (Joel 2:28). The cities of London, Amsterdam, Constantinople and Jerusalem, all appeared in succession before me, and the Spirit said unto me, "Here are many of the children of Abraham whom I will gather to the land that I gave to their fathers; and here also is the field of your labors. Take, therefore, proper credentials from my people, your brethren, and also from the Governor of your state, with the seal of authority thereon, and go ye forth to the cities which have been shown you, and declare these words unto Judah, and say, 'blow ye the trumpet in the land; cry, gather together, and say, assemble yourselves, and let us go into the defensed cities. Set up the standard towards Zion—retire, stay not, for I will bring evil from the north and a great destruction. The lion is come up from his thicket, and the destroyer of the Gentiles is on his way—he is gone forth from his place to make thy land desolate, and thy cities shall be laid waste, without an inhabitant.['] Speak ye comfortably to Jerusalem, and cry unto her, that her warfare is accomplished—that her iniquity is pardoned, for she hath received of the Lord's hand doubly for all her sins. Let your warning voice be heard among the Gentiles as you pass; and call yet upon them in my name for aid and for assistance. With you it mattereth not whether it be little or much; but to me it belongeth to show favor unto them who show favor unto you." The vision continued open about six hours, that I did not close my eyes in sleep. In this time many things were shown unto me which I have never written; neither shall I write them until they are fulfilled in Jerusalem (*History of the Church*, 4:375–76).

Conference Minutes

(April 1840)

Elder Orson Hyde addressed the conference and stated that it had some years previous been prophesied of him, that he had a great work to perform among the Jews; and that he had recently been moved upon by the spirit of the Lord to visit that people, and gather up all the information he could from them respecting their movements, expectations &c. and communicate the same to this church and to this nation at large. Stated that he intended to visit the Jews in New York, London, Amsterdam, and then visit Constantinople and the Holy Land.

It was then unanimously resolved that Elder Hyde proceed in his mission, and that his letter of recommendation be signed by the President and Clerk of the conference ("April 1840 General Conference Minutes," *Times and Seasons* [April 6, 1840]: 92).

Joseph Smith

(Orson began his mission on April 16, 1840. By September he had traveled only as far as Cincinnati, Ohio, where he found a letter waiting for him from Joseph Smith.)

I am happy that your mission swells "larger and larger." . . . Although it appears great at present, yet you have but just begun to realize the greatness, the extent and glory of the same. . . . Those engaged in seeking the outcasts of Israel, and the dispersed of Judah, cannot fail to enjoy the Spirit of the Lord and have the choicest blessings of Heaven rest upon them in copious effusions. . . . You are in the pathway to eternal fame, and immortal glory; and inasmuch as you feel interested for the covenant people of the Lord, the God of their fathers shall bless you. Do not be discouraged on account of the greatness of the work; only be humble and faithful (*History of the Church*, 4:128–29).

Orson Hyde's Journey

As he left the shores of America, Orson wrote "I have . . . a good and kind-hearted wife, and two lovely little girls, whose last embraces will long be remembered . . . I should not see them again for years, if ever." What reason would cause him to leave them and his native land for such a mission? He wrote, "The vision of the Lord, with floods of light and glory burst upon me; and the voice of the Most High bade me arise and go, trusting in him. . . . Knowing that the Lord has spoken to me, I am not only willing to go to Jerusalem, but to die there if necessary. Paul once said, 'behold I go bound in spirit to Jerusalem not knowing the things that befall me there' [Acts 20:22]; and so say I" (Orson Hyde, "Communications," *Millennial Star* [April 12, 1841]: 307–8).

While journeying to Israel, Orson Hyde wrote four letters to report on his progress. These eyewitness accounts preserve in vivid detail many of his harrowing experiences. In them, he described that he arrived in England on March 3, 1841 and remained in London until June 20, using his time to visit with Jewish leaders. He wrote a letter of introduction to Rev. Dr. Solomon Hirschell, President Rabbi of the Hebrew Society in London, explaining the call given him by the Prophet Joseph Smith. Of the letter, Elder Hyde said that it is probably one of the first recorded statements in this dispensation relative to a special mission of dedication for the eventual gathering of Israel ("Orson Hyde: Olive Branch of Israel," *The New Era* [April 1979]: 14). A portion of the letter reads:

> About nine years ago, a young man with whom I had a short acquaintance, and one, too, in whom dwelt much wisdom and knowledge, in whose bosom the Almighty had deposited many secrets, laid his hand upon my head and pronounced these remarkable words—"In due time thou shalt go to Jerusalem, the land of thy fathers, and be a watchman unto the house of Israel; and by thy hands shall the Most High do a great work, which shall prepare the way and greatly facilitate the gathering together of that people." ("Orson Hyde: Olive Branch of Israel," 14)

He also assured the Rabbi and the Jewish people of their glorious destiny, saying:

> When I look at the condition of your fathers in the days of David and Solomon, and contrast that with the present condition of their descendants, I am led to exclaim, "How are the mighty fallen!" Then they possessed a kingdom—a land flowing with milk and honey . . . But now, no kingdom—no country . . . The time has arrived when the day-star of your freedom already begins to dispel the dark and gloomy clouds which have separated you from the favor of your God. Ere long it will be said to you, "Arise, shine, for thy light has come, and the glory of the Lord has risen upon thee" [Isaiah 60:1]. (*History of the Church*, 4:376–78)

En route, Orson made stops in London, Amsterdam, and Constantinople to converse with Jewish leaders.

Howard H. Barron

Upon arriving in Jaffa, Orson penned a letter on October 20 to Parley P. Pratt. "My journey has been long and tedious, and consequently expensive. If I get back to England with money enough to buy my dinner, I shall think myself well off." Orson reported a near fatal journey between Smyrna and Beirut; the trip normally took four days, so the voyagers put in seven days' supplies, thinking that would be ample; however, the trip ended up stretching out into nineteen days. Orson nearly starved to death:

> A number of days I ate snails gathered from the rocks, while our vessel was becalmed in the midst of several small and uninhabitable islands, but the greatest difficulty was, I could not get enough of them. I was so weak and exhausted that I could not go on shore after the slight exertion of drawing on my boots. (Howard H. Barron, *Orson Hyde* [Bountiful, Utah: Horizon Publishers and Distributors, 1978], 122)

As Elder Hyde made immense sacrifices for the Lord's work, he was blessed with remarkable outpourings of the Spirit. One night, while on a ship en route to Jaffa, a vision opened before his eyes.

> On my passage from Beyroote to this place (Jaffa) night before last, at one o'clock, as I was meditating on the deck

> of the vessel as she was beating down against a sultry wind, a very bright glittering sword appeared in the heavens, about six feet in length, with a beautiful hilt, as plain and complete as any cut you ever saw. And what is still more remarkable, an arm with a perfect hand stretched itself out, and took hold on the hilt of the sword.—The appearance really made my hair rise, and the flesh, as it were, crawl on my bones. The Arabs made a wonderful outcry at the sight. Oh, "Allah! Allah! Allah!" was their exclamation all over the vessel. (Orson Hyde, "Extract of a Letter from Elder Hyde," *Millennial Star* [January 1842]: 144)

He took this to be one of the signs in the heavens that had been promised him.

Arrival in Jerusalem

Orson Hyde

(In a letter to Parley P. Pratt.)

I have only time to say that I have seen Jerusalem precisely according to the vision which I had. I saw no one with me in the vision; and although Elder Page was appointed to accompany me there, yet I found myself there alone (*History of the Church,* 4:455).

Joseph Fielding Smith

Elder John E. Page was . . . appointed to go with [Elder Hyde], but lost the spirit of his mission before he reached the eastern border of the United States, and failed to cross the water, leaving Elder Hyde to make the journey alone (Joseph Fielding Smith, *Essentials in Church History* [Salt Lake City: Deseret Book, 1979], 258).

Orson Hyde

Is that city which I now look down upon really Jerusalem, whose sins and iniquities swelled the Savior's heart with grief, and drew so many tears from his pitying eye? Is that small enclosure in the valley of Kedron, where the boughs of those lonely olives are waving their green foliage so gracefully in the soft and gentle breeze, really the garden of Gethsemane, where powers infernal poured the flood of hell's dark gloom around the princely head of the immortal Redeemer? . . .

"My natural eyes, for the first time beheld" Jerusalem; and as I gazed upon it and its environs, the mountains and hills by which it is surrounded, and considered, that this is the stage upon which so many scenes of wonders have been acted . . . a storm of commingled emotions suddenly arose in my breast, the force of which was only spent in a profuse shower of tears.

I entered the city at the west gate. . . .

Jerusalem at this time contains about twenty thousand inhabitants; about seven thousand are Jews, and the remainder mostly Turks and Arabs. It is enclosed by a strong wall from five to ten feet thick. On those sides which are most accessible, and consequently most exposed to an attack, the wall is thickest, and well mounted with cannon; it is from twelve to thirty feet in height. . . . As I stood upon this almost sacred spot and gazed upon the surrounding scenery, and contemplated the history of the past in connection with the prophetic future, I was lost in wonder and admiration, and felt almost ready to ask myself—Is it a reality that I am here gazing upon this scene of wonders? or am I carried away in the fanciful reveries of a night vision? . . . The fact that I entered the garden and plucked a branch from an olive, and now have that branch to look upon, demonstrates that all was real (Orson Hyde, "A Sketch of the Travels and Ministry of Elder Orson Hyde," *Times and Seasons* [July 15, 1842]: 17, 849–51).

Orson Hyde's Prayer on the Mount of Olives

Orson Hyde

On Sunday morning, October 24, a good while before day, I arose from sleep, and went out of the city as soon as the gates were opened, crossed the brook Kedron, and went upon the Mount of Olives, and there, in solemn silence, with pen, ink, and paper, just as I saw in the vision, offered up the following prayer to Him who lives forever and ever (*History of the Church*, 4:456).

In his dedicatory prayer for Israel, Orson Hyde petitioned God for five important blessings. First, that God, who covenanted with Abraham, and who renewed that covenant with Isaac and Jacob, would remember their seed who are still looking forward for the fulfillment of those promises, and that God would remember the seed of Abraham and "let not their enemies prevail against them."

Second, that God would "remove the barrenness and sterility of this land," so that the curse of the land should depart and that once again there should be an abundance there.

Third, that the Jews would be "incline[d] . . . to gather in upon this land," and that Gentile nations would assist them. "Let Thy great kindness," he implored, "conquer and subdue the unbelief of Thy people. Do thou take from them their stony heart, and give them a heart of flesh; and may the Sun [sic] of Thy favor dispel the cold mists of darkness which have beclouded their atmosphere."

Fourth, that God would "raise up Jerusalem as its capital, and constitute her people a distinct nation and government" and that the city would be allowed to be rebuilt and a great temple to be reared.

And Fifth, he prayed for a stranger who had assisted him in his journey by giving him the purse of two hundred dollars in gold in Philadelphia.

He prayed for his family, for the persecutions against the Latter-day Saints in America to cease, for the First Presidency of the LDS Church to be blessed, and for Zion, with all her assemblies, to be remembered. (*History of the Church*, 4:457).

Orson Hyde's Prayer

O Thou! who art from everlasting to everlasting, eternally and unchangeably the same, even the God who rules in the heavens above, and controls the destinies of men on the earth, wilt Thou not condescend, through thine infinite goodness and royal favor, to listen to the prayer of Thy servant which he this day offers up unto Thee in the name of Thy holy child Jesus, upon this land, where the Son of Righteousness set in blood, and thine Anointed One expired. . . .

Now, O Lord! Thy servant has been obedient to the heavenly vision which Thou gavest him in his native land; and under the shadow of Thine outstretched arm, he has safely arrived in this place to dedicate and consecrate this land unto Thee, for the gathering together of

Judah's scattered remnants, according to the predictions of the holy Prophets—for the building up of Jerusalem again after it has been trodden down by the Gentiles so long, and for rearing a Temple in honor of Thy name. Everlasting thanks be ascribed unto Thee, O Father, Lord of heaven and earth, that Thou hast preserved Thy servant from the dangers of the seas, and from the plague and pestilence which have caused the land to mourn. The violence of man has also been restrained, and Thy providential care by night and by day has been exercised over Thine unworthy servant. Accept, therefore, O Lord, the tribute of a grateful heart for all past favors, and be pleased to continue Thy kindness and mercy towards a needy worm of the dust. . . .

Incline [Thy people] to gather in upon this land according to Thy word. Let them come like clouds and like doves to their windows. Let the large ships of the nations bring them from the distant isles; and let kings become their nursing fathers, and queens with motherly fondness wipe the tear of sorrow from their eye.

Thou, O Lord, did once move upon the heart of Cyrus to show favor unto Jerusalem and her children. Do Thou now also be pleased to inspire the hearts of kings and the powers of the earth to look with a friendly eye towards this place, and with a desire to see Thy righteous purposes executed in relation thereto. Let them know that it is Thy good pleasure to restore the kingdom unto Israel—raise up Jerusalem as its capital, and constitute her people a distinct nation and government, with David Thy servant, even a descendant from the loins of ancient David to be their king.

Let that nation or that people who shall take an active part in behalf of Abraham's children, and in the raising up of Jerusalem, find favor in Thy sight. Let not their enemies prevail against them, neither let pestilence or famine overcome them, but let the glory of Israel overshadow them, and the power of the Highest protect them (*History of the Church*, 4:456–57).

When he finished petitioning the Lord on behalf of Israel, he memorialized the event in true Old Covenant fashion: "On the top of Mount Olives I erected a pile of stones as a witness according to ancient custom. On what was anciently called Mount Zion, where the Temple stood, I erected another" (*History of the Church*, 4:459).

[Note: A complete text of Orson Hyde's prayer can be found in *Orson Hyde*, 137–40; or *History of the Church*, 4:456–59.]

Orson Hyde's Return to Nauvoo

On December 7, 1842, Orson Hyde arrived back in Nauvoo and was reunited with his wife, children, and the Saints. He had fulfilled one of the longest and most perilous missions in the history of the Church, covering 20,000 miles. The day following his return, Orson, accompanied by Marinda, called on the Prophet Joseph Smith at his home. The first Sunday after his arrival, December 11, 1842, he gave a public lecture at the Prophet Joseph's home on his mission to Palestine.

After nearly three years of travel, Orson Hyde returned home, having successfully and faithfully performed his calling from the Lord.

Announcement of Elder Hyde's Return

Elder Hyde has by the grace of God been the first proclaimer of the fullness of the Gospel both on the continent of Europe and in far off Asia, among the nations of the East, in Germany, Turkey (Constantinople), Egypt, and Jerusalem. He has reared as it were the ensign of the latter-day glory, and sounded the trump of truth, calling upon the people of those regions to awake from their thousand years' slumber, and to make ready for their returning Lord . . . and we humbly trust that his labors will be a lasting blessing to Jew and Gentile (*History of the Church*, 4:495).

1 Kings 8:41–43

(Some have felt that this portion of the dedicatory prayer offered by Solomon on the temple he built was, in part, fulfilled by the 1840–42 mission of Orson Hyde to Palestine.)

Moreover concerning a stranger, that *is* not of thy people Israel, but cometh out of a far country for thy name's sake;

(For they shall hear of thy great name, and of thy strong hand, and of thy stretched out arm;) when he shall come and pray toward this house;

Hear thou in heaven thy dwelling place, and do according to all that the stranger calleth to thee for: that all people of the earth may know thy name, to fear thee, as *do* thy people Israel; and that they may know that this house, which I have builded, is called by thy name.

Dedication of the Orson Hyde Memorial Park

On October 24, 1979, one-hundred and thirty-eight years after Orson Hyde's prayer was offered for the building up of Jerusalem and the gathering of Abraham's posterity, President Spencer W. Kimball dedicated a five-and-one-quarter acre landscaped garden in Jerusalem, designated as the Orson Hyde Memorial Garden, in honor of Orson Hyde's prayer. This park is situated across the Kidron Valley from the City of Jerusalem and offers a breathtaking view of the Old City. A heroic-sized plaque in the garden, inscribed in English and Hebrew, once contained excerpts from Orson Hyde's prayer. Unfortunately, due to vandalism, it has since been removed.

President Kimball also noted that much of Orson Hyde's prayer has been fulfilled: "The land has become abundantly fruitful again, with flocks and orchards and fields. The scattered children of Abraham have returned in great numbers to build up this land as a refuge, and the city of Jerusalem has flourished" ("News of the Church," *Ensign*, December 1979, 67–68).

In the dedicatory prayer offered for the garden park in 1979, President Kimball pled:

> Father, bless these grounds . . . that they may radiate the loveliness and give pleasure to those who visit here . . .
>
> Protect this garden from the ravages of war and storm and depredation of every kind. Let it be a haven where all may meditate upon the glory which thou hast shed upon Jerusalem in ages past, and of the greater glory yet to be.
>
> Let those who come here feel of thy Spirit and influence, and the spirit of the holy prophets who have traversed this beautiful land.
>
> We acknowledge, Father, that through Thy power much that he spoke in Thy name has already come to pass. The land has become abundantly fruitful again, with flocks and orchards and fields. The scattered children of Abraham have returned in great numbers to build up this land as a refuge,

Spencer W. Kimball
(Courtesy of the Church Archives, The Church of Jesus Christ of Latter-day Saints)

and the city of Jerusalem has flourished. And we know that in Thine own time all else Thou hast prophesied for this city and land and people shall surely come to pass.

We pray for Abraham's children, both those by blood and those who by faithfulness are truly His through adoption. Extend Thy special care to them; draw them unto Thee and put in them a heart which is eager to fulfill righteousness. ("News of the Church," 68)

15

The Nauvoo Temple

Upon the arrival of the Saints at the city of Nauvoo, they were commanded to sacrifice time, talent, and material goods to build a house to the Lord. As they followed the Lord's command to build His house, great eternal blessings were showered upon them.

Brief Chronology of the Nauvoo Temple

January 19, 1841: Joseph Smith receives a revelation commanding that the temple be built (D&C 124:25–44).

April 6, 1841: The cornerstones are laid under the direction of Joseph Smith (Joseph Smith, *History of The Church of Jesus Christ of Latter-day Saints,* 7 vols., ed. by B. H. Roberts [Salt Lake City: Deseret Book, 1966], 4:326–31).

November 8, 1841: Basement and baptismal font are dedicated, under the direction of Brigham Young (*History of the Church,* 4:446–47).

November 21, 1841: The first baptisms are performed.

May 24, 1845: The capstone is laid on the southeast corner by Brigham Young; the southeast corner was also known as "Joseph's corner" (*History of the Church,* 7:417–18).

November 30, 1845: The attic rooms are dedicated for ordinance work; Brigham Young gives the prayer in the presence of those who have already received their endowments from Joseph Smith and who will now administer the same ordinances to others (*History of the Church,* 7:534–35).

December 10, 1845–February 7, 1846: Endowments are given in the Nauvoo Temple.

January 7, 1846: The sealing altar is dedicated by Brigham Young. The altar was located in Room 1, which was also Brigham Young's temple office, in the southeast corner of the attic (*History of the Church,* 7:566).

The Nauvoo Temple
(Courtesy of the Church Archives, The Church of Jesus Christ of Latter-day Saints)

February 8, 1846: The temple is dedicated, as far as completed, by Brigham Young before he left Nauvoo for the West (*History of the Church,* 7:580). Henry Bigler was present and left an account, saying: "The Twelve met in the southeast corner, room No. 1, the upper story in the temple, kneeling round the altar and dedicating the building to the most high and asked His blessings upon our intended move to the west, also asking Him to enable them someday to finish the lower part of the building and dedicated it to Him and to preserve the temple as a monument to Joseph Smith. The Twelve, then left" (Henry W. Bigler, "Autobiography," *Writings of Early Latter-day Saints and Their Contemporaries, a Database Collection,* comp. Milton V. Backman [Provo, Utah: BYU Religious Studies Center, 1996], 14).

April 30, 1847: A private dedication is held for the completed temple, by those who, at the risk of their lives, remained to finish the temple; the dedicatory prayer was given by Joseph Young, senior president of the Seventy, whom Brigham Young had left in charge of the men working to finish the temple for dedication (Brigham Young, *Manuscript History of Brigham Young,* ed. Elden J. Watson [Salt Lake City: E. J. Watson, 1971], 147–48).

May 1–3, 1847: The public dedication of the temple is held, under the direction of Orson Hyde, senior Apostle living in Nauvoo.

October 9, 1848. The interior of the temple is burned by an arsonist.

May 27, 1850: A tornado topples two walls, leaving the rest of the temple unstable; stones are then removed, by townspeople, to use in constructing businesses and homes in Nauvoo.

February 20, 1937: The abandoned Nauvoo Temple site is purchased by The Church of Jesus Christ of Latter-day Saints.

April 4, 1999: President Gordon B. Hinckley announces plans to rebuild the Nauvoo Temple.

October 24, 1999: The Nauvoo Temple groundbreaking and site dedication is held.

November 5, 2000: The cornerstone ceremony, patterned after the original four-corner dedication, is held.

September 21, 2001: The Angel Moroni statue is placed atop the bell tower.

June 27, 2002: The Nauvoo Temple is dedicated by President Gordon B. Hinckley.

Introduction of Vicarious Temple Work for Deceased Ancestors

In the Nauvoo Temple, the Lord introduced proxy baptisms for deceased loved ones, for the first time in this dispensation.

Joseph Smith

(August 15, 1840)

I first mentioned the doctrine in public when preaching the funeral sermon of Brother Seymour Brunson; and have since then given general instructions in the Church on the subject. The Saints have the privilege of being baptized for those of their relatives who are dead, whom they believe would have embraced the Gospel, if they had been privileged with hearing it, and who have received the Gospel in the spirit, through the instrumentality of those who have been commissioned to preach to them while in prison (*History of the Church,* 4:231).

Simon Baker

I was present at a discourse that the prophet Joseph delivered on baptism for the dead 15 August 1840. He read the greater part of the 15th chapter of Corinthians and remarked that the Gospel of Jesus Christ brought glad tidings of great joy . . . He also said the apostle [Paul] was talking to a people who understood baptism for the dead, for it was practiced among them. He went on to say that people could now act for their friends who had departed this life, and that the plan of salvation was calculated to save all who were willing to obey the requirements of the law of God (Simon Baker, *Journal History* [LDS Church Archives, The Church of Jesus Christ of Latter-day Saints, Salt Lake City, Utah], August 15, 1840).

Brigham Young

When he [Joseph Smith] had first received the knowledge by the spirit of revelation how the dead could be officiated for, there are brethren and sisters here, I can see quite a number here who were in Nauvoo, and you recollect that when this doctrine was first revealed, and in hurrying in the administration of baptism for the dead, that sisters were baptized for their male friends, were baptized for their fathers, their grandfathers, their mothers and their grandmothers, etc. I just mention this so that you will come to [an] understanding, that as we knew nothing about this matter at first, the old Saints recollect, there was little by little given, and the subject was made plain, but little was given at once. Consequently, in the first place people were baptized for their friends and no record was kept. Joseph afterwards kept a record, etc. (in *Journal of Discourses*, 26 vols. [London: Latter-day Saints' Book Depot, 1854–86], 16:165).

Restoration of the Temple Endowment

In answer to Joseph Smith's humble prayer in the Sacred Grove, the Lord promised to restore the true gospel to the earth. In fulfillment of this promise, the Lord continued to restore lost ordinances and blessings as they existed anciently. While the Nauvoo Temple was under construction, the temple endowment was first introduced on May 5, 1842, in the upper room of Joseph Smith's red brick store.

Joseph Smith Jr.

(May 5, 1842)

I spent the day in the upper part of the store ... in council with General James Adams, of Springfield, Patriarch Hyrum Smith, Bishops Newel K. Whitney and George Miller, and President Brigham Young and Elders Heber C. Kimball and Willard Richards, instructing them in the principles and order of the Priesthood, attending to washings, anointings, endowments and the communication of keys pertaining to the Aaronic Priesthood, and so on to the highest order of the Melchizedek Priesthood, setting forth the order pertaining to the Ancient of Days, and all those plans and principles by which any one is enabled to secure the fullness of those blessings which have been prepared for the Church of the First Born, and come up and abide in the presence of the Eloheim in the eternal worlds (*History of the Church*, 5:1–2).

Mary Ann Stearns Winters

When the [Nauvoo] Temple was far enough completed to begin giving endowments my Pa and Ma were of the first company to receive those blessings. Each had a special and individual invitation to attend those services and it was the first time for women to receive such blessings in a Temple in this dispensation—though some had received endowments in other places previous to this time (Mary Ann Stearns Winters, *Winters Book of Remembrance* [LDS Church Archives, The Church of Jesus Christ of Latter-day Saints, Salt Lake City, Utah], n.p.).

Construction of the Nauvoo Temple *(1845–46)*

Joseph Smith III

The structure was of splendid material. The stones were of limestone formation and were obtained from some of the quarries nearby, one being located along the river above the city and another below. I saw the big carts under which these stones were swung by heavy chains, and the ox teams dragging them along the roads between the quarries and the Temple block. I stood by the workmen when with hammers and chisels they fashioned and polished the massive pieces which formed the outer wall from cellar to roof. I watched the pillars grow from their moon-shaped pedestals to their star-and sun- crowned capitals, and the roof from its eaves to the gilded angle that swung at the top of the spire (*The Memoirs of President Joseph Smith III*, ed. Mary Audentia Smith Anderson [Independence, Missouri: Price Publishing Company, 2001], 177–78).

Truman O. Angell

I had steady employment upon the [Nauvoo] Temple, having been appointed superintendent of joiner work under Architect William Weeks, and God gave me wisdom to carry out the architect's designs which gained me the goodwill and esteem of the brethren.

Persecutions have been so frequent that I scarce think of it. But I will say that I suffered much—in common with the rest of my brethren—during the persecutions in which the Prophet and Patriarch lost their lives.

The [Nauvoo] Temple was, at this writing, October 28, 1845, enclosed, and the inside work progressing very rapidly. The attic was finished up complete and made ready for endowments, while the lower rooms, basement and lower hall were going on. I received my endowments in the aforesaid attic, together with Polly, my wife, and afterward our sealing and second anointings, which far excelled any previous enjoyments of my life up to that time. At the time when the first encampment of the brethren—the Twelve and others—left Nauvoo, William Weeks, the architect, was taken away with them.

This left me to bring out the design and finishing of the lower hall which was fully in my charge from then on to its completion, and was dedicated by a few of us, Brother Orson Hyde taking charge, he having come back from the encampment of the Twelve for that purpose (Truman O. Angell, "Autobiography," *Writings of Early Latter-day Saints*, 200).

William Adams

The [Nauvoo] Temple was built by tithing and other donations of the Saints and the Committee had much difficulty to furnish the workmen means to live upon so that their families had many times to be [stinted] for food.

I had worked on the [Nauvoo] Temple four weeks and had received no pay, so very little tithing had been received at the Temple door. By selling and trading some of our clothing and other things that we could best do without I was enabled to buy shorts from Bro. Newell Knight who owned a small grist mill on the bank of the Mississippi river, run by the current of the stream. This might be considered hard fare to those who had been brought up to have the finest of flour. We were satisfied to have enough of that and not complain, as it was the desire of my heart to serve God and keep His commandments in adversity and prosperity.

The Prophet was very anxious to have the Temple finished so the Saints could receive their endowments, and encourage[d] the workmen to not slack in their hands and the saints to come forward and pay their tithing so the hands could be steadily employed (William Adams, *Autobiography of William Adams* [L. Tom Perry Special Collections,

Harold B. Lee Library, Brigham Young University, Provo, Utah], 11; punctuation standardized).

William Farrington Cahoon

During this time, the Prophet Joseph had purchased a small location for the Saints to gather, which he laid off in squares and named Nauvoo. I remained in Montrose until the spring of 1842. I then moved to Nauvoo and commenced working on the temple of the Lord as a carpenter and joiner. The Lord prospered me in my labors so that I was enabled to build a small house for a home among the Saints. I was appointed timekeeper of the carpenters and joiners who worked on the [Nauvoo] temple (William Farrington Cahoon, "Autobiography of William Farrington Cahoon," *Writings of Early Latter-day Saints,* 87).

Ezra T. Benson

(Grandfather of President Ezra Taft Benson.)

The remainder of the summer and fall I worked on the [Nauvoo] Temple and stood guard at night; also worked at many places by the day to procure provisions for my family.

When the Twelve commenced to give endowments in the Temple, which was about the tenth of December 1845, I was called and my wives, Pamelia and Adeline, to go into the Temple of the Lord to receive our endowments, which privilege we were very grateful to our Heavenly Father for, after which Bro. Brigham Young requested me to labor in the Temple to assist in giving endowments to others, and I remained there till within three or four days of our ceasing to give endowments and of our leaving for the wilderness (Ezra T. Benson, "An Autobiography," *The Instructor* [May 1945]: 215).

Joseph Grafton Hovey

(May 24, 1845)

The capstone of the [Nauvoo] temple was laid in its place this morning, a little past six o'clock. A goodly number of Saints had the honor and the glory to witness the completion. The morning was clear, cool, and beautiful. The Saints felt glorious. The band on top of the walls played charmingly. When the stone was placed there was a united shout,

"Hosanna to God, Amen, and Amen," three times. This not only gave joy on earth but filled the heavens with gladness. A hymn composed for the occasion was sung. The first verse of the hymn is as follows:

Have you heard the revelation
Of this latter dispensation
Which is unto every nation
Oh, prepare to meet thy God

Chorus
We are a band of brethren
And we've reared the Lord a temple
And the capstone now is finished
And will sound the news abroad.

Brother Brigham remarked that Saturday is a Jewish Sabbath and that God finished his work on that day and that we may go and do likewise if we had a mind to. Therefore, the Saints did go home and keep this day in rejoicing in the Lord (Joseph Grafton Hovey, "Autobiography of Joseph Grafton Hovey," *Writings of Early Latter-day Saints*, 29).

Administering Temple Ordinances to the Saints

Sadly, the Nauvoo Temple was opened for the blessing of the Saints on December 10, 1845. Ironically, the Saints were feverishly working to complete the temple, while simultaneously building wagons to begin the trek west. They earnestly desired to receive their temple blessings before leaving Nauvoo, and from December 10, 1845 to February 12, 1846, 5,615 Saints were endowed in the Nauvoo Temple.

William Hyde

The Endowments were commenced in the [Nauvoo] Temple on the 9th of December, 1845, and were closed about the 8th of February, 1846. January 5, I was called upon to assist in the ordinance of the endowments, and from this time until the 8th of February I remained in the Temple the most of the time (William Hyde, *Private Journal of William Hyde* [L. Tom Perry Special Collections, Harold B. Lee Library,

Brigham Young University, Provo, Utah], 16).

Brigham Young

(The following entries from President Brigham Young's journal illustrate how eager the Saints were to receive the temple ordinances.)

This morning there was an immense crowd at the reception room waiting for admission.... One hundred twenty-one persons received ordinances (*History of the Church*, 7:565).

Brigham Young

Such has been the anxiety manifested by the saints to receive the ordinances [of the Temple], and such the anxiety on our part to administer to them, that I have given myself up entirely to the work of the Lord in the Temple night and day, not taking more than four hours sleep, upon an average, per day, and going home but once a week.

Elder Heber C. Kimball and the others of the Twelve Apostles were in constant attendance but in consequence of close application some of them had to leave the Temple to rest and recruit their health (*History of the Church*, 7:567).

Brigham Young

(He had announced that it was time for the Twelve and the Saints to leave Nauvoo. The Saints wept and remained at the temple, so great was their desire to receive temple blessings.)

Tuesday, 3.—Notwithstanding that I had announced that we would not attend to the administration of the ordinances, the House of the Lord was thronged all day, the anxiety being so great to receive, as if the brethren would have us stay here and continue the endowments until our way would be hedged up, and our enemies would intercept us. But I informed the brethren that this was not wise, and that we should build more Temples, and have further opportunities to receive the blessings of the Lord, as soon as the saints were prepared to receive them. In this Temple we have been abundantly rewarded, if we receive no more. I also informed the brethren that I was going to get my wagons started and be off. I walked some distance from the Temple supposing the crowd would disperse, but on returning I found the house filled to overflowing.

Looking upon the multitude and knowing their anxiety, as they were thirsting and hungering for the word, we continued at work diligently in the House of the Lord.

Two hundred and ninety-five persons received ordinances (*History of the Church*, 7:579).

Destruction of the Nauvoo Temple

Joseph Smith III

It was there in that little room over the store that I was sleeping on the night of October 8, 1848, when the Temple burned. I was aroused by someone shouting, "Fire!" . . . The light from the conflagration was . . . great and it shone through the front windows . . . Hastily dressing, I went down to the Mansion House, and found that the Major had already been aroused and gone to the fire. I did not follow, thinking it wiser for someone to stay about the place. . . .

That night the whole interior of the Temple burned out. The inner surfaces of the bare walls which were left standing were ruined by the intense heat and many pieces of outside masonry shared the same fate. . . .

I was over every foot of this building while it was being formed, and after it was enclosed I often visited it in company with many who came to view it, both before and after the exodus of the Saints. And when, on the night I have mentioned, it was set on fire through the work of an incendiary ruffian, I saw it burn, sense[d] to some extent the gravity of its loss to the city, and witnessed some of the scenes by which the people expressed their grief over its passing (*The Memoirs of President Joseph Smith III*, 177–78; spelling standardized).

Joseph Smith III

Not long after that night of gloom a fierce storm raged over the city and some parts of the south wall of the ruin fell. This so weakened the remaining portions on the north that before long they followed suit. The walls kept falling from time to time, bit by bit, until there remained standing only the southwest corner—one of the stairway towers near the main entrance. Finally, the city council deemed it advisable, for the safety of the public, to raze this portion. This was done and the demolition was complete, so much so that indeed, so far as the existence of that particular building was concerned, "not one stone was left upon another," from the angel at the top of the spire with the brave trumpet in his hand, to the heavy foundation stones below.

During the years which followed there was a gradual spoliation of the ruins of the Temple, to which I was witness. The place became a veritable quarry and provided the materials with which many homes, wine cellars, and saloons in the town were built. At last the time came when the last stone was upturned from its resting-place and taken away, and little remained to indicate the spot where once the magnificent and stately edifice had reared its proud head (*The Memoirs of President Joseph Smith III*, 178).

REDEDICATION OF THE NAUVOO TEMPLE

Gordon B. Hinckley

(These excerpts come from President Hinckley's dedicatory prayer, given June 27, 2002, for the newly built Nauvoo Illinois Temple.)

Almighty God, we come unto Thee in solemn and reverent prayer in the name of Thy Beloved Son, our Redeemer, even the Lord Jesus Christ.

On this same site in the year 1841, Thy people, under the direction of the Prophet Joseph Smith, and in obedience to revelation from Thee, began construction of a temple to the Most High. They spared nothing in their efforts. They used the best materials, and with great skill and in a spirit of consecration, they labored through the years. Even when their Prophet and Patriarch were murdered by the ruthless mob in Carthage, the work on this structure continued. So did persecution against them. Denied the protection of the law and left to the mercy of the mob, they knew they would be forced to abandon their homes, their farms, and their city. Nonetheless, they determined to complete the temple.

They did so, and in that holy house ordinances dealing with the things of eternity, as revealed from Thee, were administered to thousands. They then left Nauvoo in bitter winter weather, many of them crossing the Mississippi on the ice, bound for a place of asylum somewhere in the West.

Thou knowest, dear Father, of the travails of those who made that long journey. Many died and were buried along that trail of tears. Great was their suffering, tremendous their courage.

We thank Thee that those harsh days are now long past. We thank Thee for this season in which we live, with the many blessings of peace and prosperity which we enjoy at Thy hands. Thy Spirit has brooded over us and moved upon us, and in obedience to its prompting we have now reconstructed on this hallowed ground the temple that once stood here. Through the tithes of Thy people and the generosity of faithful Saints there has been brought together all of the elements and the necessary skills to create this magnificent structure.

And now, acting in the authority of the divine priesthood which comes from Thee, and in the name of Jesus Christ, our Lord, we dedicate and consecrate unto Thee and unto Him this the Nauvoo Illinois Temple of The Church of Jesus Christ of Latter-day Saints. . .

We pray that Thou wilt accept of this our offering. The hearts of the children have literally turned to those fathers who worked on the original building. They have done so with love and a wonderful spirit of consecrated effort.

Now, Beloved Father, this is Thy house, the gift of Thy thankful Saints. We pray that Thou wilt visit it. Hallow it with Thy presence and that of Thy Beloved Son. Let Thy Holy Spirit dwell here at all times. May Thy work be accomplished here, and Thine eternal purposes brought to pass in behalf of Thy children, both the living and the dead. May our hearts reach to Thee as we serve within these walls. May all who are baptized in behalf of those beyond the veil of death know that they are doing something necessary under Thine eternal plan. May those who are here endowed understand and realize the magnitude of the blessings that come of this sacred ordinance. Seal upon them the covenants which they make with Thee. Open their eyes to a clear perception of Thy divine purposes. As they move into the beautiful celestial room, may their minds be brought to an understanding of Thy glorious plan for the salvation and exaltation of Thy children.

May those who gather at the altars in the sealing rooms, whether in their own behalf or in behalf of their forebears, comprehend by the power of the Spirit Thy divine will concerning the eternity of the family—fathers, mothers, and children, joined together in an everlasting union. May they receive a vision of Thine infinite "plan of happiness" which Thou hast designed for Thy faithful sons and daughters.

May all who come within these hallowed walls be worthy to enter into Thy presence. Save this structure from desecration of any kind. May it stand immaculate with "holiness to the Lord." Strike down the evil hand of any who may seek to injure or destroy. Preserve this Thy house from the storms of nature and destructive elements of all kinds. . . .

Father dear, bless this land that those who govern shall never trample the rights of the people as was once done in Nauvoo. May liberty and peace be maintained under the banner of the Constitution, which Thou hast caused to be established "for the rights and protection of all flesh" (D&C 101:77). Bless this city of Nauvoo, which came to be known as the City of Joseph. May it shine with a renewed luster as the home of a Temple of God. May this sacred house stand as a memorial to him who lived here and was buried here, Joseph Smith, the great prophet of this dispensation, and his brother Hyrum, whom he loved.

We love Thee, Father. We love Thy Beloved Son. Smile with favor upon us. Strengthen our resolve to walk acceptably before Thee at all times. Increase our dedication to Thy will. Keep ever bright in our memories the solemn covenants into which we have entered with Thee. May Thy blessings attend us, and all who seek to live Thy commandments.

Praise be to Thee, Thou great Elohim, Thou who dwellest in the heavens and governeth the universe. Thou art our Father and our God, to whom we may come in prayer. To Thee we lift our voices in adoration and worship.

Increase our love for Thine Only Begotten Son, our Redeemer who has snatched us from the jaws of death and opened before us the wonders of eternity. Accept this our prayer, we ask Thee in His holy name, even the name of Jesus Christ. Amen (Gordon B. Hinckley, "'This magnificent structure,'" *Church News* [June 29, 2002]: 5).

16

Persecution in Nauvoo

Although the Saints did their best to establish a haven of peace in Nauvoo, persecution continued to haunt them. Once again, the Saints were oppressed because of their faith. At first, the majority of the persecution came from old Missouri conflicts, but the harassment in Illinois continued to escalate until Joseph Smith was forced into hiding in order to protect himself from those seeking to kidnap or kill him.

Wilford Woodruff

(Describing the severe trials experienced by Joseph Smith during this time.)

President Joseph Smith has been much persecuted of late by being hunted and sought for by sheriffs and officers from Missouri and Illinois, by the orders of Governors Reynolds and Carlin, under pretence of taking him to Missouri to try him for being accessory to the shooting of ex-Gov. Boggs. But it is no more or less than the spirit of persecution.

But though Joseph has been deprived of the privilege of appearing openly and deprived of the society of his own family, because sheriffs are hunting him to destroy him without cause, yet the Lord is with him as he was upon the Isle of Patmos with John. Joseph has presented the Church of late with some glorious principles from the Lord, concerning baptism for the dead and other interesting subjects [see D&C 127 and 128]. He has appeared occasionally in the midst of the Saints which has been a great comfort to the Saints (Wilford Woodruff, *Wilford Woodruff's Journal,* 9 vols., ed. Scott G. Kenney [Midvale, Utah: Signature Books, 1983], 2:187; capitalization and punctuation standardized).

Brigham Young

The anti-"Mormons" had public meetings, which were very numerously attended, where they passed resolutions of the most violent and inflammatory kind, threatening to drive, expel and exterminate the "Mormons" from the state, at the same time accusing them of every evil in the vocabulary of crime (as cited in Joseph Smith, *History of The Church of Jesus Christ of Latter-day Saints,* 7 vols., ed. by B. H. Roberts [Salt Lake City: Deseret Book, 1932], 7:60).

Joseph Smith III

This kind of persecution was not confined to "Mormons" alone; whoever was an advocate for law and order or dared to speak or act in defense of the rights of the persecuted, was liable to receive similar treatment, and they were contemptuously called "Jack Mormons."

Christopher E. Yates, a farmer living in the eastern part of Hancock County, was one who suffered much loss because of his friendship for the abused. He was a New Yorker and a very prosperous man. Nevertheless, because of his outspoken defense of the rights of the Saints to occupy their farms and to possess unmolested other property, his own grain was ruined, his stock killed or stolen, and his fine barn burned. This treatment did not change his opinion one iota or his determination to express it, though he was compelled to move off his farm. He came into the city, where he bought the property occupied before the exodus by Uncle John Smith and his son George A. . . .

Mr. Edmunds was a fearless man, of Quaker parentage. He came from western New York, with his wife, and purchased the Orson Hyde property just across the street to the north of us . . . Mr. Edmunds was always outspoken in his opposition to "mobocracy," and was always ready to defend those who needed an advocate. He was materially helpful to my mother in preventing the spoliation of the properties left her and her children at the death of my father . . .

Some months after he came to the city, a rather important suit was heard before a Justice by the name of Chapman. This suit was hotly contested and a clash occurred between the two groups of citizens who took sides in the matter. Some bitter denunciations were hurled against those men dubbed "Jack Mormons," in the course of which a rabid anti-Mormon threatened to kill Mr. Edmunds.

I was standing not far away when this occurred, and noticed that Mr. Edmunds showed not the slightest sign of fear. Instead he answered:

"You will do no such thing. You will not kill me or anyone else, for you are too cowardly. I am here to do my duty as a man and a decent citizen, and I do not propose to be frightened from it by being called hard names or by threats from a mere bully!"

I had seen many personal quarrels by that time and heard so many threats that did not result in blows from either fist or knife or in injury from pistol shots, that I had come to believe that men who talked too loudly about injuring others were seldom the ones courageous enough to really kill in cold blood. I admired Mr. Edmunds, whom I then knew only by sight and name, for his fearless answer to his antagonist. Later, when I came to know him better, I came to respect him as highly for his manliness and justice, for he stood squarely and unwaveringly to prevent injustice being done to many of the families of outgoing Saints (*The Memoirs of President Joseph Smith III*, ed. Mary Audentia Smith Anderson [Independence, Missouri: Price Publishing Company, 2001], 336, 367–68).

B. H. Roberts

Wild rumors abounded also as to what the Missourians intended to do; and some of the letters from Missouri that fell into the hands of President Smith, through friends of his, threatened Illinois with invasion, and for a time it would seem that a border war was inevitable (B. H. Roberts, *A Comprehensive History of The Church of Jesus Christ of Latter-day Saints*, 6 vols. [Provo, Utah: Brigham Young University Press, 1965], 2:198).

Sheriff Reynolds

(Reynolds was a Missouri sheriff who continually harassed the Prophet Joseph Smith.)

If Illinois, by her own authority, cannot capture the prophet, it will be but a small matter to raise volunteers enough here to raze the city of Nauvoo to the ground; if Illinois fails to deliver up Jo Smith, there will be something serious between the two states (*History of the Church*, 5:539; punctuation standardized).

Governor Thomas Ford

(Governor Ford believed the falsehoods being spread about Joseph Smith, and he wrote negatively about the Prophet.)

[Joseph Smith is] a man who, though ignorant and coarse, had some great natural parts which fitted him for temporary success, but which were so obscured and counteracted by the inherent corruption and vices of his nature, that he never could succeed in establishing a system of policy which looked to permanent success in the future. . . .

It must not be supposed that the pretended prophet practiced the tricks of a common imposter; that he was a dark and gloomy person, with a long beard, a grave and severe aspect, and a reserved and saintly carriage of his person; on the contrary, he was full of levity, even to boyish romping; dressed like a dandy, and at times drank like a sailor and swore like a pirate. He could, as occasion required, be exceedingly meek in his deportment; and then again rough and boisterous as a highway robber; being always able to satisfy his followers of the propriety of his conduct. He always quailed before power, and was arrogant to weakness. At times he could put on the air of a penitent, as if feeling the deepest humiliation of his sin, and suffering unutterable anguish, and indulging in the most gloomy foreboding of eternal woe. At such times he would call for the prayers of the brethren in his behalf, with a wild and fearful energy and earnestness. He was full six feet high, strongly built, and uncommonly well muscled. No doubt he was as much indebted for his influence over an ignorant people, to the superiority of his physical vigor, as to his greater cunning and intellect (as cited in *Comprehensive History of the Church,* 2:347).

Conspiracies in Nauvoo

For a time, traitors within the church at Nauvoo were more dangerous to the Prophet than persecutors from without.

Joseph Smith Jr.

My enemies were determined to get me into their power and take my life, and thereby thought they would accomplish the overthrow of "Mormonism." And to enable them to effect this, they had secured the services of some of my most confidential friends, whom I did not suspect, and who were living in Nauvoo, to deliver me into their hands so that their religious organizations upon their own principles might stand; for they feared that "Mormonism" would destroy their present religious creeds, organizations, and orthodox systems. They did not design to try me, but hang me, or take my life anyhow (*History of the Church*, 6:164).

George Laub

(George heard Joseph speak to the Saints for the last time and recorded the Prophet's testimony.)

The enemy is seeking my life and are laying plans to kill me, but if they kill me they kill an innocent man. This I will call on God, angels and men to witness. . . . But I have laid the foundation of the work of what the Lord has gave me to do, therefore have no longer lease of my life. I have accomplished my work that was given me and others can build on the same ("George Laub's Nauvoo Journal," ed. Eugene England, *Brigham Young University Studies* [Winter 1978]: 160; spelling standardized).

Joseph Smith Jr.

(As quoted by Wilford Woodruff.)

I have been informed by two gentlemen that a conspiracy is got up in this place for the purpose of taking the life of President Joseph Smith, his family, and all the Smith family, and the heads of the Church. One of the gentlemen will give his name to the public, and the other wishes it to be hid for the present: they will both testify to it on oath, and make an affidavit upon it. The names of the persons revealed at the head of the conspiracy are as follows:—Chancey L. Higbee, Dr. Robert D. Foster, Mr. Joseph H. Jackson, William and Wilson Law. And the lies that C. L. Higbee has hatched up as a foundation to work upon are—he says that I had men's heads cut off in Missouri, and that I had a sword run through the hearts of the people that I wanted to kill and put out of the way. I won't swear out a warrant against them, for I don't fear any of them: they would not scare off an old setting hen. I intend to publish all the iniquity that I know of them. If I am guilty, I am ready to bear it. There is sometimes honor among enemies. I am willing to do anything for the good of the people. I will give the name of one of the gentlemen who have divulged the plot: his name is M. G. Eaton. He will swear to it: he is a bold fellow. Joseph H. Jackson said a Smith should not be alive in two weeks,—not over two months anyhow. Concerning the character of these men, I will say nothing about it now; but if I hear anything more from them on this subject, I will tell what I know about them (*History of the Church*, 6:272).

Joseph Smith Jr.

Renegade "Mormon" dissenters are running through the world and spreading various foul and libelous reports against us, thinking thereby to gain the friendship of the world, because they know that we are not of the world, and that the world hates us; therefore they [the world] make a tool of these fellows [the dissenters]: and by them try to do all the injury they can, and after that they hate them worse than they do us, because they find them to be base traitors and sycophants.

Such characters God hates; we cannot love them. The world hates them, and we sometimes think that the devil ought to be ashamed of them (*History of the Church*, 3:230).

Joseph Smith Jr.

My life is more in danger from some little dough-head of a fool in this city than from all my numerous and inveterate enemies abroad. I am exposed to far greater danger from traitors among ourselves than from enemies without, . . . and if I can escape from the ungrateful treachery of assassins, I can live as Caesar might have lived, were it not for a right-hand Brutus. I have had pretended friends betray me. All the enemies upon the face of the earth may roar and exert all their power to bring about my death, but they can accomplish nothing, unless some who are among us and enjoy our society, have been with us in our councils, participated in our confidence, taken us by the hand, called us brother, saluted us with a kiss, join with our enemies, turn our virtues into faults, and, by falsehood and deceit, stir up their wrath and indignation against us, and bring their united vengeance upon our heads. All the hue-and-cry of the chief priests and elders against the Savior, could not bring down the wrath of the Jewish nation upon His head, and thereby cause the crucifixion of the Son of God, until Judas said unto them, "Whomsoever I shall kiss, he is the man; hold him fast." Judas was one of the Twelve Apostles, even their treasurer, and dipt with their Master in the dish, and through his treachery, the crucifixion was brought about; and *we have a Judas in our midst* (*History of the Church*, 6:152).

William M. Allred

Another time when I heard him preaching he said if he should tell the people all the Lord had revealed to him, some would seek his life. Even as good a man as old Father C—, here on the stand, he added, (pointing back to him) would seek his life (William M. Allred, "Recollections of the Prophet Joseph Smith," *Writings of Early Latter-day Saints and Their Contemporaries, a Database Collection*, comp. Milton V. Backman [Provo, Utah: BYU Religious Studies Center, 1996], 471).

Benjamin F. Johnson

(Writing to George F. Gibbs, 1903.)

Benjamin F. Johnson
(Courtesy of the Church Archives, The Church of Jesus Christ of Latter-day Saints)

Criticism had already commenced by those near him in authority with regard to his teachings and his doing. And we began now, in a degree, to understand the meaning of what he had so often publicly said, that "should he teach and practice the principles that the Lord had revealed to him, and now requested of him, that those then nearest him in the stand would become his enemies and the first to seek his life;" which they soon did, just as he had foretold. And to show you that under conditions then existing that the Prophet did not really desire longer to live, and that you may see how my mind was in a degree prepared for after results, I will briefly relate an incident that occurred at his last visit to us at Ramus.

After he had at evening preached with great animation to a large congregation, and had blessed nineteen children, he turned to me and said, "Benjamin, I am tired, let us go home," which only a block distant, we soon reached; and entering we found a warm fire with a large chair in front, and my wife sitting near with her babe, our eldest, upon her lap, and approaching her, I said, "Now, Melissa, see what we have lost by your not going to meeting; Brother Joseph has blessed all the children in the place but ours, and it is left out in the cold." But the Prophet at once said, "You shall lose nothing," and he proceeded to bless our first born, and then, with a deep drawn breath as a sigh of weariness, he sank down heavily in his chair, and said, "Oh! I do get so tired and weary, that at times I almost yearn for my rest," and then proceeded briefly to recount to us some of the most stirring events of his life's labors, suffering and sacrifices, and then he said, "I am getting tired and would like to go to my rest." His words and tone thrilled and shocked me, and like an arrow pierced my hopes that he would long remain with us, and I said, as with a heart full of tears, "Oh! Joseph, what could we, as a people, do without you? and what would become of the great Latter-day work if you should leave us?" He saw and was touched by my emotions, and in reply he said, "Benjamin, I should not be far away from you, and if on the other side of the veil I should still be working with you, and with a power greatly increased, to roll on this kingdom." And such was the tone, earnestness and pathos of his words to me then, that they can never be fully recalled but with emotion.

And now before fully returning to the council and subject in connection with the above, I will relate a dream told to us in council by the Prophet but a short time before his death, which was as follows: "I dreamed that by the Laws, Marks, Higbys, and Fosters, I was bound, both hand and foot, and cast into a deep well, soon after which I heard screams of terror and cries of 'Oh! Brother Joseph, save us, save us!' This cry continued until, with my elbows and toes, I had worked my way to the top, and looking out, I saw all of those who had bound me within the folds of a terrible serpent, that was preparing to swallow them, and I told them that as they had bound me, I could render them no assistance."

This dream made upon my mind an impression never forgotten, and just as he related it, so it was fulfilled in his death; for those were the men that opened the way for his assassination (E. Dale LeBaron, "Benjamin Franklin Johnson: Colonizer, Public Servant, and Church

Leader" [master's thesis, Brigham Young University, 1966], 332–33; punctuation standardized).

Benjamin F. Johnson

The days of tribulation were now fast approaching, for just as the Prophet so often told us, so it came to pass; and those he had called around him as a cordon of safety and strength were worse than a rope of sand, and were now forging his fetters. William Law was his first counselor; Wilson Law, Major General of the Legion; Wm. Marks, President of the Stake; the Higbys, his confidential attorneys, and Dr. Foster, his financial business agent. All of these and many others entered into secret covenant so much worse than Judas, that they would have the Prophet's life, just in fulfillment of what he had said so often publicly. With all their power, they began to make a party strong enough to destroy the Prophet.

At one of the meetings in the presence of the Quorum of the Twelve and others who were encircled around him, he arose, gave a review of his life and sufferings, and of the testimonies he had borne, and said that the Lord had now accepted his labors and sacrifices, and did not require him longer to carry the responsibilities and burden and bearing of this kingdom. Turning to those around him, including the twelve, he said, "And in the name of the Lord Jesus Christ I now place it upon my brethren of this council, and I shake my skirts clear of all responsibility from this time forth," springing from the floor and shaking his skirt at the same time (Benjamin F. Johnson, *My Life's Review* [Mesa, Arizona: 21st Century Printing, 1992], 99–100).

Sarah Stoddard

(She was the mother of fourteen-year-old Charles, who was asked by the Prophet to serve as a house boy at William Law's residence.)

Charles had another faith-promoting experience last night.

Early this morning, even while the darkness still hemmed out the light of the day, Mr. Law, after he had been drinking and planning with his associates through the night, got Charles out of bed to clean and oil his gun. He said he was going to shoot the Prophet, only William Law called him "old Joe Smith." Poor Charles was frightened beyond description, but Mr. Law stood over him and prodded him with his foot when Charles hesitated through fright and anxiety. Finally, when Mr. Law was satisfied with the way the gun was working, he put one bullet in. (He boasted he could kill the Prophet with one shot.) He sent Charles to bring the Prophet.

He ran as fast as he could and delivered the message, but he begged the Prophet not to go to Mr. Law's as Mr. Law was drunk and Charles was afraid he would carry through on his threat to shoot the Prophet in cold blood.

As they walked the few blocks from the Mansion House to the Law residence, the Prophet assured Charles that no harm would come to him that day. Charles was frightened, and he said that it kept racing through his mind, "I am the one that cleaned the gun that is going to be used to kill the Prophet," until he was sick with fear. The Prophet in a final attempt to calm my dear son uttered the fateful words, "Mr. Law may someday kill me, Charles, but it won't be today."

As they approached their destination, Mr. Law came staggering out of the house shouting out what he intended to do.

The Prophet said kindly and unafraid, "You sent for me, Mr. Law?" to which Mr. Law replied with oaths that now he was doing the whole a favor by disposing of the Prophet with one shot.

Calmly the Prophet unbuttoned his shirt and bared his chest, then said, "I'm ready now, Mr. Law." Charles said at this point he nearly fainted. Sick fear strangled him until he was speechless and paralyzed, unable to move a muscle.

Mr. Law paced a few steps, turned, aimed, and pressed the trigger. There was complete silence. Then the air rang with profanity, and Mr. Law turned on Charles, accusing him of fixing the gun so it would not go off and threatening to kill even Charles—my innocent, frightened, but faithful son.

The Prophet, to divert Mr. Law's blame of Charles, suggested that a can be placed on a fence post for Mr. Law to take a practice shot. Relieved, Charles ran for a can and laid it on its side on the post. Mr. Law paced back, took aim, and fired. His "one shot" streaked through the exact center of the can.

Even Mr. Law was quiet, as if stunned.

The Prophet buttoned up his shirt, gave Charles a meaningful look, and then said, "If you are finished with me now, Mr. Law, I have other things needing to be done. Good morning" (Sarah Stoddard, *Diary of Sarah Stoddard, April 1844* [n.p., n.d.]; as cited in Robert H. Daines, "The Doctrine of Christ," *Speeches* [Provo, Utah: BYU Publications and Graphics, 2001], 43–44).

Dallin H. Oaks

Dallin H. Oaks
(Courtesy of the Church Archives, The Church of Jesus Christ of Latter-day Saints)

In the spring of 1844, some men were plotting against the Prophet Joseph Smith. One of the leaders, William Law, held a secret meeting at his home in Nauvoo. Among those invited were nineteen-year-old Dennison Lott Harris and his friend, Robert Scott. Dennison's father, Emer Harris, who is my second great-grandfather, was also invited. He sought counsel from the Prophet Joseph Smith, who told him not to attend the meeting but to have the young men attend. The Prophet instructed them to pay close attention and report what was said.

The spokesmen at this first meeting denounced Joseph Smith as a fallen prophet and stated their determination to destroy him. When the Prophet heard this, he asked the young men to attend the second meeting. They did so, and reported the plotting.

A third meeting was to be held a week later. Again the Prophet asked them to attend, but he told them this would be their last meeting. "Be careful to remain silent and not to make any covenants or promises with them," he counseled. He also cautioned them on the great danger of their mission. Although he thought it unlikely, it was possible they would be killed. Then, the Prophet Joseph Smith blessed Dennison and Robert by the power of the priesthood, promising them that if their lives were taken, their reward would be great.

In the strength of this priesthood blessing, they attended the third meeting and listened to the murderous plans. Then, when each person was required to take an oath to join the plot and keep it secret, they bravely refused. After everyone else had sworn secrecy, the whole group turned on Dennison and Robert, threatening to kill them unless they took the oath also. Because any refusal threatened the secrecy of their plans, about half of the plotters proposed to kill these two immediately. Knives were drawn, and angry men began to force them down into a basement to kill them.

Other plotters shouted to wait. Parents probably knew where they were. If they didn't return, an alarm would be sounded and a search could reveal the boys' deaths and the secret plans. During a long argument, two lives hung in the balance. Finally, the group decided to threaten to kill the young men if they ever revealed anything that had occurred and then to release them. This was done. Despite this threat, and because they had followed the Prophet's counsel not to make any promises to the conspirators, Dennison and Robert promptly reported everything to the Prophet Joseph Smith.

For their own protection, the Prophet had these courageous young men promise him that they would never reveal this experience, not even to their fathers, for at least twenty years. A few months later, the Prophet Joseph Smith was murdered (Dallin H. Oaks, "Priesthood Blessings," *Ensign,* May 1987, 38–39; see also "Verbal Statement of Bishop Dennison L. Harris" [LDS Church Archives, The Church of Jesus Christ of Latter-day Saints, Salt Lake City, Utah], May 15, 1881).

Joseph Smith Jr.

(In the privacy of his home, Joseph wondered if William Law and William Marks were among the group seeking to betray him. His suspicion was later proven correct.)

What can be the matter with these men? . . . Is it that the wicked flee when no man pursueth, that hit pigeons always flutter, that drowning men clutch at straws, or that *President Law and Marks are absolutely traitors to the church,* and my remarks should produce such excitement in their midst? Can it be possible that the "traitor" whom Porter Rockwell reports to me as being in correspondence with my Missouri enemies is one of my quorum [the First Presidency]? (*Comprehensive History of the Church,* 2:222; italics added).

B. H. Roberts

(One evening William Law came to Joseph Smith's home on the pretense of wanting to talk to him, intending to betray him into the hands of a mob in an attempt to kidnap the Prophet. The attempt failed, and one of the mob later commented on the incident.

If Law could have succeeded in getting an introduction for us to Joe Smith, damn him, we would have gagged him and nabbed him; and, damn him, all hell could not have rescued him from our hands (History of the Church, 6:501).

George A. Smith

(Discovering the dishonesty of William Law.)

In Nauvoo we had another shower of dust around the Prophet. There was a man by the name of William Law, who was a Counselor to Joseph Smith, and a man of great gravity. He preached a great deal on the stand in Nauvoo, and told the people they must be punctual and pay their debts; and he repeated it over and over again. Sunday after Sunday he preached *punctuality*, PUNCTUALITY, PUNCTUALITY.

I was then on a mission in England; but when I got home, I would hear, Sunday after Sunday, these addresses. Thinks I, this is a very righteous fellow; it will be perfectly safe to deal with him; and everybody thought so.

The first time I suspected but what he was as straight as a loon's leg, at least in relation to his trading, was one day in his mill. Brother Willard Richards and myself met Bishop Smoot, and he offered to bet a barrel of salt that the Doctor was heavier than I was. We went into Law's mill to be weighed. I was weighed on the scales where he weighed wheat *into* the mill.

To my surprise, I did not weigh as much by twelve pounds as usual. I thought this was a curiosity. I saw there was another pair of scales on the other side of the mill where they weighed out flour. I weighed the Doctor twice, and he weighed me twice on both scales; and I found that if I had been a bag of flour, I should have weighed twelve pounds *too much;* and, if I had been a bag of wheat, I should not have weighed *enough* by twelve pounds.

The Doctor and myself soon discovered that the gain by this villainous fraud would supply the mill with wood and hands to tend it.

Brother Joseph and I saw brother Law come out of his house one day, and brother Joseph said to me, referring to Law, "George, do you know that there is the meanest man in this town?"

"Yes," I said, "I know he is, but did not know you thought so."

"How did you find it out?"

"He has two sets of weights in his mill." He also told me something about Law's visit to certain disreputable houses in St. Louis, and gave me to understand that he knew something about Law's hypocrisy and dishonesty in dealing, as well as myself.

I only tell this circumstance because he pulled the leading string in putting Joseph Smith to death. When he comes forth, he may expect to find his white robe dyed in the blood of innocence, and he may expect in all time to come to have that stigma upon him (in *Journal of Discourses*, 26 vols. [London: Latter-day Saints' Book Depot, 1854–86], 7:116; spelling and punctuation standardized).

Joseph Smith Jr.

(On June 13, 1844, Joseph attended a meeting in the Seventies' Hall on Parley Street. At the meeting, he related a dream about the treachery of several of the Saints.)

I thought I was riding out in my carriage, and my guardian angel was along with me. We went past the Temple, and had not gone much further before we espied two large snakes so fast locked together that neither of them had any power. I inquired of my guide what I was to understand by that. He answered, "Those snakes represent Dr. Foster and Chauncey L. Higbee. They are your enemies and desire to destroy you; but you see they are so fast locked together that they have no power of themselves to hurt you. I then thought I was riding up Mulholland Street, but my guardian angel was not along with me. On arriving at the prairie, I was overtaken and seized by William and Wilson Law and others, saying, "Ah! Ah! we have got you at last! We will secure you and put you in a safe place!" and, without any ceremony dragged me out of my carriage, tied my hands behind me, and threw me into a deep, dry pit, where I remained in a perfectly helpless condition, and they went away. While struggling to get out, I heard Wilson Law screaming for help hard by. I managed to unloose myself so as to make a spring, when I caught hold of some grass which grew at the edge of the pit.

I looked out of the pit and saw Wilson Law at a little [distance] attacked by ferocious wild beasts, and heard him cry out, "Oh! Brother Joseph, come and save me!" I replied, "I cannot, for you have put me into this deep pit." On looking out another way, I saw William Law with outstretched tongue, blue in the face, and the green poison forced out of his mouth, caused by the coiling of a large snake around his body. It had also grabbed him by the arm, a little above the elbow, ready to devour him. He cried out in the intensity of his agony, "Oh, Brother Joseph, Brother Joseph, come and save me, or I die!" I also replied to him, "I cannot, William; I would willingly, but you have tied me and put me in this pit, and I am powerless to help you or liberate myself." In a short time after my guide came and said aloud, "Joseph, Joseph, what are you doing there?" I replied, "My enemies fell upon me, bound me and threw me in." He then took me by the hand, drew me out of the pit, set me free, and we went away rejoicing (*History of the Church*, 6:461–62).

Joseph Smith III

(Recalling an incident when individuals plotted to harm Joseph Smith during a sham battle of the Nauvoo Legion.)

Another remembrance . . . is that Colonel Brower, a one-armed man who had been an army officer, had been secured to teach the use of the sword to those who chose to learn. A sham battle had been arranged on a parade day. Considerable excitement existed in the city from a rumor that an arrangement had been made by some persons at enmity with Father to take advantage of the excitement prevalent in the military maneuvers and assassinate him. One of the brethren in the Church was appointed, with a number of his comrades, to have special watch care over Father on that day. It was expected that this Colonel Brower was by some means implicated; so John P. Green, Hosea Stout, and another were especially careful not to lose sight of Colonel Brower (from *Journal History*, April 1910 and October 1910, and "The Memoirs of President Joseph Smith" from *The Saints' Herald*, November 13, 1934; December 11, 18, and 25, 1934; January 1, 8, 22, and 29, 1935; and February 5 and 12, 1935; see also Joseph Smith III, *Memories of Old Nauvoo*, sel. and ed. by Paul V. Ludy, [Bates City, Missouri: Paul V. Ludy and Associates, 2001], 9–10).

MOB ATROCITIES AGAINST THE SAINTS IN NAUVOO

Joseph Smith III

(Recalling how Orrin Porter Rockwell, one of Joseph Smith's closest friends, escaped a mob.)

One incident connected with [Porter Rockwell] stands out clearly in memory. At some time subsequent to Father's death a man named Frank Worrell was killed . . . An attempt was made to make Porter Rockwell responsible for the crime, and a warrant was issued for his arrest. . . .

[A number of men, many of whom were members of the mob, were gathered on the sidewalk, just outside a hotel.] While they were still there, a carriage drove up to the door, a lady got out and tripped by the guards and up the stairs. She remained there a short while (the carriage waiting), and then came down the steps, passed through the cordon of officers, entered the carriage, and was driven rapidly away.

Image the chagrin of the officers later when they learned that this "lady" was Porter Rockwell, for whom they also had a warrant. I was within twenty feet of the carriage when he got out, and stood near it when he got in again; by some intuition or through some glance he gave me, I knew who it was, although the officers were completely fooled (*The Memoirs of President Joseph Smith III*, 111).

General A. W. Doniphan

(A friend to Joseph Smith and the Saints, Doniphan was a lawyer who greatly assisted the Saints in the lawsuits they faced as a result of false charges brought against them during their stay in Jackson, Daviess, and Caldwell Counties. Doniphan was hired as the attorney to represent Porter Rockwell when Rockwell was falsely accused of attempting to assassinate Governor Boggs. While visiting with Doniphan, Joseph Smith III asked him if he thought Rockwell was guilty of the crime. Doniphan's response follows.)

No, indeed! There was not one scintilla of evidence to connect him with it in any way, or to prove he ever had knowledge of it. The only thing they had against him was that he was a member of the Latter Day Saints Church, or, as stated by the prosecution, "a Mormon." He was honorably acquitted, and I took him home with me for supper. Afterward we had a talk, and I advised him to leave the State at once and to get to his friends in Illinois as soon as he could, for feeling there still ran high.

At first he objected to this procedure, saying he had done no wrong, had been raised in the town, it was his home, he belonged there, and saw no reason why he should leave. But I counseled him to go. I told him that Mr. Smith, the President of his church, had sent word to me to see that he had a fair trial, which I had done, and now he was fully acquitted, and I thought it best for him to leave and that at once, not staying even another night, for I felt if he did he would surely be killed for his enemies would not let him alone.

So he agreed to go, and did. I gave him a ten-dollar gold piece as we parted, to help him bear his expenses in getting to his friends (*The Memoirs of President Joseph Smith III*, 111–12).

Joseph Smith III

Mother [Emma Smith] was given warning upon one occasion that if she did not move out of her house in three days, it would be burned over her head. I well remember the night with which that given period closed. It was warm, and some of us children were to sleep on the floor in the lower room of Mother's apartments, with the south door left open for comfort. Mother cautioned us to be quiet but said if anything unusual occurred to be sure and let her know, as she would be just overhead, upstairs.

In spite of some childish qualms on our part, evening prayers were said, each in simple fashion commending ourselves to God and his keeping. We lay down in quietness and finally went to sleep. In the morning the house was found to be still over our heads and intact, but on the north side were discovered the remains of some fire material piled against the wall. A fire had been started and a portion of the siding was scorched, but it had not caught sufficiently to set the house on fire; hence we escaped (*The Memoirs of President Joseph Smith III*, 144).

Brigham Young

(Harassment and persecution did not end with the death of Joseph Smith. Brigham Young described an incident following the Martyrdom, when a group attempted to kidnap him.)

I was in my room in the Temple; it was in the south-east corner of the upper story. I learned that a posse was lurking around the Temple, and that the United States Marshal was waiting for me to come down, whereupon I knelt down and asked my Father in heaven, in the name of Jesus, to guide and protect me that I might live to prove advantageous to the Saints. Just as I arose from my knees and sat down in my chair, there came a rap at my door. I said, "Come in," and brother George D. Grant, who was then engaged driving my carriage and doing chores for me, entered the room. Said he, "Brother Young, do you know that a posse and the United States Marshal are here?" I told him I had heard so. On entering the room Brother Grant left the door open. Nothing came into my mind what to do, until looking directly across the hall I saw brother William Miller leaning against the wall. As I stepped towards the door I beckoned to him; he came. Said I to him, "Brother William, the Marshal is here for me; will you go and do just as I tell you? If you will, I will serve them a trick." I knew that Brother Miller was an excellent man, perfectly reliable and capable of carrying out my project. Said I, "Here, take my cloak;" but it happened to be Brother Heber C. Kimball's; our cloaks were alike in color, fashion and size. I threw it around his shoulders, and told him to wear my hat and accompany brother George D. Grant. He did so. I said to brother Grant, "George, you step into the carriage and look towards Brother Miller, and say to him, as though you were addressing me, 'Are you ready to ride?' You can do this, and they will suppose brother Miller to be me, and proceed accordingly," which they did.

Just as brother Miller was entering the carriage, the Marshal stepped up to him, and, placing his hand upon his shoulder, said, "You are my prisoner." Brother William entered the carriage and said to the Marshal, "I am going to the Mansion House, won't you ride with me?" They both went to the Mansion House. There were my sons Joseph A., Brigham, jun., and brother Heber C. Kimball's boys, and others who were looking on, and all seemed at once to understand and partake of the joke. They followed the carriage to the Mansion House and gathered around brother Miller, with tears in their eyes, saying, "Father, or

President Young, where are you going?" Brother Miller looked at them kindly, but made no reply; and the Marshal really thought he had got "Brother Brigham."

Lawyer Edmonds, who was then staying at the Mansion House, appreciating the joke, volunteered to brother Miller to go to Carthage with him and see him safe through. When they arrived within two or three miles of Carthage, the Marshal with his posse stopped. They arose in their carriages, buggies and wagons, and, like a tribe of Indians going into battle, or as if they were a pack of demons, yelling and shouting, they exclaimed, "We've got him! we've got him! we've got him!" When they reached Carthage the Marshal took the supposed Brigham into an upper room of the hotel, and placed a guard over him, at the same time telling those around that he had got him. Brother Miller remained in the room until they bid him come to supper. While there, parties came in, one after the other, and asked for Brigham. Brother Miller was pointed out to them. So it continued, until an apostate Mormon, by the name of Thatcher, who had lived in Nauvoo, came in, sat down and asked the landlord where Brigham Young was. The landlord, pointing across the table to brother Miller, said, "That is Mr. Young." Thatcher replied, "Where? I can't see any one that looks like Brigham." The landlord told him it was that fat, fleshy man eating. "Oh, h___!" exclaimed Thatcher, "that's not Brigham; that is William Miller, one of my old neighbors." Upon hearing this the landlord went, and, tapping the Sheriff on the shoulder, took him a few steps to one side, and said, "You have made a mistake, that is not Brigham Young; it is William Miller, of Nauvoo." The Marshal, very much astonished, exclaimed, "Good heavens! and *he* passed for Brigham." He then took brother Miller into a room, and, turning to him, said, "What in h___ is the reason you did not tell me your name?" Brother Miller replied, "You have not asked me my name." "Well," said the Sheriff, with another oath, "What is your name?" "My name," he replied, "is William Miller." Said the Marshal, "I thought your name was Brigham Young. Do you say this for a fact?" "Certainly I do," said brother Miller. "Then," said the Marshal, "why did you not tell me this

Brigham Young
(Courtesy of the Church Archives, The Church of Jesus Christ of Latter-day Saints)

before?" "I was under no obligations to tell you," replied brother Miller, "as you did not ask me." Then the Marshal, in a rage, walked out of the room, followed by brother Miller, who walked off in company with Lawyer Edmonds, Sheriff Backenstos, and others, who took him across lots to a place of safety; and this is the real pith of the story of "Bogus" Brigham, as far as I can recollect (in *Journal of Discourses*, 14:218–19; spelling standardized).

Nauvoo after the Saints Were Driven Out

Thomas Cottam

(On visiting Nauvoo in 1846.)

I found Nauvoo, but oh, how desolate! The houses uninhabited, the once beautiful gardens full of weeds; peach and apple trees broken, and fences down; instead of peace and happiness there was ruin and desolation; but cease my soul, mourn not over the desolation of this place. I look forward for more happy and glorious days (The Church of Jesus Christ of Latter-day Saints, *Nauvoo the Beautiful* [Salt Lake City: The Church of Jesus Christ of Latter-day Saints, 1972], 249).

Charles Lanman

(An essayist and journalist, Lanman visited Nauvoo in 1846.)

The "Mormon" City occupies an elevated position, and, as approached from the south, appears capable of containing a hundred thousand souls. But its gloomy streets bring a most melancholy disappointment. Where lately resided no less than 25,000 people, there are not to be seen more than about 500; and these, in mind, body, and purse, seem to be perfectly wretched. In a walk of about ten minutes, I counted several hundred chimneys, which were all at least that number of families had left behind them as memorials of their folly and the wickedness of their persecutors. When their city was in its glory, every dwelling was surrounded with a garden . . . but now all the fences are in ruin, and lately crowded streets actually rank with vegetation. Of the houses left standing, not more than one out of ten was occupied, excepting by the spider and the toad. Hardly a window retained a whole pane of glass, and the doors were broken, and open, and hingeless.

Not a single laughing voice did I hear in the whole place, and the lines of suffering and care, seemed to be imprinted on the faces of the very children who met me in the way. I saw not a single one of those numerous domestic animals, which add so much to the comforts of human life; and I heard not a single song even from the robin and the wren, which are always so sure to build their nests about the habitations of man. Aye, the very sunshine and the pleasant passing breeze, seemed to speak of sin, sorrow, and utter desolation (*Nauvoo the Beautiful*, 250).

Thomas L. Kane

Thomas L. Kane
(Courtesy of the Church Archives, The Church of Jesus Christ of Latter-day Saints)

I have seen the site of Nauvoo before it was a city, and in nearly all the stages of progress, from the planning of the first colony to this time. I have been present at some of the most exciting scenes that have occurred within its limits, and I had a desire to see it as it now is, shorn of its glory and in other hands. The change has been very great. A few months ago, I rode through it . . . and there was the appearance of business and activity in every direction. The Temple, the greatest and chief ornament of Nauvoo, was then, on Sundays, crowded to suffocation. Everywhere . . . there were signs of enjoyment and contentment.

Now, how changed the scene. The streets are deserted—the houses are empty, the hum and bustle of the city has passed away—the faces and voices lately seen and heard are gone. All is changed, and a gloomy depression, as appalling as the low whispers of the death-chamber, is palpable to every sense (*Nauvoo the Beautiful*, 254).

Thomas L. Kane

A few years ago, . . . ascending the Upper Mississippi, in the autumn, when its waters were low, I was compelled to travel by land past the region of the Rapids. . . .

I was descending the last hill-side upon my journey, when a landscape in delightful contrast broke upon my view. Half encircled by a bend of the river, a beautiful city lay glittering in the fresh morning sun; its bright new dwellings, set in cool green gardens, ranging up around a stately dome-shaped hill, which was crowned by a noble edifice, whose high tapering spire was radiant with white and gold. The city appeared to cover several miles, and beyond it, in the background, there rolled off a fair country, chequered by the careful lines of fruitful husbandry. The unmistakable marks of industry, enterprise, and educated wealth everywhere, made the scene one of singular and most striking beauty. . . .

[Later, after the Saints had been driven from the place, Kane again visited and describes what he saw.] The town lay as in a dream, under some deadening spell of loneliness, from which I almost feared to wake it, for plainly it had not slept long. There was no grass growing up in the paved ways; rains had not entirely washed away the prints of dusty footsteps.

Yet I went about unchecked. I went into empty workshops, ropewalks and smithies. The spinner's wheel was idle; the carpenter had gone from his work-bench and shavings, his unfinished sash and casing. Fresh bark was in the tanner's vat, and the fresh-chopped lightwood stood piled against the baker's oven. The blacksmith's shop was cold; but his coal heap and lading pool, and crooked water horn were all there, as if he had just gone off for a holiday. No work-people anywhere looked to know my errand.

If I went into the gardens, clinking the wicket-latch loudly after me, to pull the marigolds, heartsease, and lady-slippers, and draw a drink with the water-sodden well-bucket and its noisy chain . . . no one called out to me from any opened window, or dog sprang forward to bark an alarm.

I could have supposed the people hidden in the houses, but the doors were unfastened; and when at last I timidly entered them, I found dead ashes white upon the hearths, and had to tread a tip-toe, as if walking down the aisle of a country church, to avoid rousing irreverent echoes from the naked floors. On the outskirts of the town was the city graveyard; but there was no record of plague there . . . Some of the mounds were not long sodded. . . . Fields upon fields of heavy-headed yellow grain lay rotting ungathered upon the ground. No one was there to take in their rich harvest.

As far as the eye could reach they stretched away—they sleeping, too, in the hazy air of autumn. Only two portions of the city seemed to suggest the import of this mysterious solitude. On the southern suburb, the houses looking out upon the country showed, by their splintered wood-work and walls battered to the foundation, that they had lately been the mark of a destructive cannonade. And in and around the splendid Temple, which had been the chief object of my admiration, armed men were barracked, surrounded by their stacks of musketry and pieces of heavy ordnance. These challenged me to render an account of myself, and why I had had the temerity to cross the water without a written permit from a leader of their band.

Though these men were generally more or less under the influence of ardent spirits, after I had explained myself as a passing stranger, they seemed anxious to gain my good opinion. They told the story of the Dead City: that it had been a notable manufacturing and commercial mart, sheltering over twenty thousand persons; that they had waged war with its inhabitants for several years, and had been finally successful only a few days before my visit, in an action fought in front of the ruined suburb; after which they had driven them forth at the point of the sword. The defense, they said, had been obstinate, but gave way on the third day's bombardment. They boasted greatly of their prowess, especially in this battle, as they called it; but I discovered they were not of one mind as to certain of the exploits that had distinguished it, one of which, as I remember, was, that they had slain a father and his son, a boy of fifteen, not long residents of the fated city, whom they admitted to have borne a character without reproach.

They also conducted me inside the massive sculptured walls of the curious Temple . . .

They permitted me also to ascend into the steeple, to see where it had been lightning-struck the Sabbath before; and to look out, east and south, on wasted farms like those I had seen near the city, extending till they were lost in the distance. Here, in the face of pure day, close to the scar of the divine wrath left by the thunderbolt, were fragments of food, cruises of liquor, and broken drinking vessels . . .

It was after nightfall when I was ready to cross the river on my return. The wind had freshened since the sunset, and the water beating roughly into my little boat, I edged higher up the stream than the point I had left in the morning, and landed where a faint glimmering light invited me to steer.

Here, among the dock and rushes, sheltered only by the darkness, without roof between them and the sky, I came upon a crowd of several hundred human beings, whom my movements roused from uneasy slumber on the ground.

Passing these on my way to the light, I found it . . . shone flickeringly on the emaciated features of a man in the last stage of a bilious, remittent fever. . . . He rested on a partially ripped open old straw mattress, with a hair sofa cushion under his head for a pillow. . . . [Some friends] had furnished the apothecary he needed; a toothless old baldhead, whose manner had the repulsive dullness of a man familiar with death scenes. He, so long as I remained, mumbled in his patient's ear a monotonous and melancholy prayer, between the pauses of which I heard the hiccup and sobbing of two little girls, who were sitting upon a piece of drift wood outside.

Dreadful, indeed, was the suffering of these forsaken beings; bowed and cramped by cold and sunburn, alternating as each weary day and night dragged on, they were, almost all of them, the crippled victims of disease. . . .

These were Mormons, in Lee County, Iowa, in the fourth week of the month of September, in the year of our Lord 1846. The city—it was Nauvoo, Ill. The Mormons were the owners of that city, and the smiling country around. And those who had stopped their ploughs, who had silenced their hammers, their axes, their shuttles, and their workshop wheels; those who had put out their fires, who had eaten their food, spoiled their orchards, and trampled under foot their thousands of acres of unharvested bread; these were the keepers of their dwellings, the carousers in their Temple, whose drunken riot insulted the ears of their dying. . . .

They were, all told, not more than six hundred and forty persons who were thus lying on the river flats. But the Mormons in Nauvoo and its dependencies had been numbered the year before at over twenty thousand. Where were they? They had last been seen, carrying in mournful train their sick and wounded, halt and blind, to disappear behind the western horizon, pursuing the phantom of another home (in *Journal of Discourses,* 13:115–18).

17

The Martyrdom

In his final years of life, the Prophet Joseph Smith was unremittingly hounded by his enemies. Beginning in 1842, Joseph repeatedly revealed that there were organized groups plotting to take his life. As hostile feelings towards the Church intensified, an anti-Mormon group launched a newspaper, called the *Nauvoo Expositor,* aimed at demeaning the Prophet and other Church leaders. In 1844, the *Nauvoo Expositor* was declared a public nuisance for inciting a spirit of mobocracy against the Saints. As mayor, Joseph Smith ordered its destruction. He was arrested and charged with destruction of public property. With Governor Thomas Ford's assurance of his protection, Joseph Smith willingly submitted himself to the authorities to stand trial, even though he realized he would not come out of Carthage Jail alive. On June 27, 1844, Governor Ford broke his promise of protection and left town, leaving Joseph, his brother Hyrum, Willard Richards, and John Taylor to face an armed mob bent on the destruction of these brethren. Joseph and Hyrum sealed their testimonies with their blood, and the Saints everywhere lamented and mourned the loss of their beloved Prophet.

The Lord Promised to Protect Joseph Smith until His Mission Was Completed

Joseph Smith Sr.
(Courtesy of the Church Archives, The Church of Jesus Christ of Latter-day Saints)

Joseph Smith Sr.

(From a blessing given by Joseph Smith Sr., on his deathbed, to his son Joseph Smith Jr.)

"Joseph, my son, you are called to a high and holy calling. You are even called to do the work of the Lord. Hold out faithful and you shall be blest and your children after you. You shall even live to finish your work." At this Joseph cried out, weeping, "Oh! my father, shall I?" "Yes," said his father, "you shall live to lay out the plan of all the work which God has given you to do. This is my dying blessing upon your head in the name of Jesus. I also confirm your former blessing upon your head; for it shall be fulfilled. Even so. Amen" (Lucy Mack Smith, *History of Joseph Smith By His Mother* [Salt Lake City: Bookcraft, 1958], 309–10).

Joseph Smith Jr.

(The Prophet made numerous statements about what he knew concerning his life and its divine preservation.)

August 31, 1842: Inasmuch as the Lord Almighty has preserved me until today, He will continue to preserve me . . . until I have fully accomplished my mission (*Teachings of the Prophet Joseph Smith,* ed. Joseph Fielding Smith [Salt Lake City: Deseret Book Company, 1976], 258).

January 22, 1843: I understand my mission and business. God Almighty is my shield; and what can man do if God is my friend? I shall not be sacrificed until my time comes; then I shall be offered freely (*Teachings of the Prophet Joseph Smith,* 274).

October 15, 1843: I prophesy [that] they [my enemies] never will have power to kill me till my work is accomplished, and I am ready to die (*Teachings of the Prophet Joseph Smith,* 328).

April 7, 1844: I cannot lie down until all my work is finished (*Teachings of the Prophet Joseph Smith,* 361).

Joseph Prophesied of His Own Death

D&C 5:22

(In March 1829, the Lord declared the following to Joseph Smith.)

Be firm in keeping the commandments wherewith I have commanded you; and if you do this, behold I grant unto you eternal life, even if you should be slain.

D&C 6:30

(One month later, in April 1829, the Lord gave the following warning.)

And even if they do unto you even as they have done unto me, blessed are ye, for you shall dwell with me in glory.

Joseph Smith Jr.

April 1844: Brethren, I have desired to live to see this temple [Nauvoo] built. I shall never live to see it, but you will (as recorded by Wilford Woodruff, *Discourses of Wilford Woodruff*, ed. G. Homer Durham [Salt Lake City: Bookcraft, 1969], 72).

June 22, 1844: I told Stephen Markham that if I and Hyrum were ever taken again we should be massacred, or I was not a prophet of God (*Teachings of the Prophet Joseph Smith*, 376–77).

June 23, 1844: [After fleeing from their enemies, the Prophet and his brother courageously decided to give themselves up to the authorities, resulting in their martyrdom at Carthage Jail.] Hyrum Smith said to Joseph: "Let us go back and give ourselves up, and see the thing out." Joseph replied: "If you go back I will go with you, but we shall be butchered" (*Teachings of the Prophet Joseph Smith*, 377–78).

June 24, 1844: I am going like a lamb to the slaughter . . . and it shall be said of me, "He was murdered in cold blood!" (*Teachings of the Prophet Joseph Smith*, 379).

Brigham Young

I heard Joseph say many a time, "I shall not live until I am forty years of age" (*Discourses of Brigham Young,* ed. John A. Widtsoe [Salt Lake City: Deseret Book, 1978], 467).

B. H. Roberts

(Speaking of the Prophet and the Relief Society.)

As he had [the] opportunity, he was going to instruct the ladies of this Society . . . He did not know that he should have many opportunities of teaching them, as they were going to be left to themselves; they would not long have him to instruct them; that the Church would not have his instructions long, and the world would not be troubled with him a great while, and would not have his teachings [in person]. . . .

According to his prayers, God had appointed him elsewhere (Joseph Smith, *History of The Church of Jesus Christ of Latter-day Saints,* 7 vols., ed. B. H. Roberts [Salt Lake City: Deseret Book, 1966], 4:604).

Orson Hyde

We were in council with Brother Joseph almost every day for weeks, says Brother Joseph in one of those councils there is something going to happen; I don't know what it is, but the Lord bids me to hasten and give you your endowment before the temple is finished. He conducted us through every ordinance of the holy priesthood, and when he had gone through with all the ordinances he rejoiced very much, and says, now if they kill me you have got all the keys, and all the ordinances and you can confer them upon others, and the hosts of Satan will not be able to tear down the kingdom, as fast as you will be able to build it up ("Trial of Elder Rigdon," *Times and Seasons* [September 15, 1844]: 651).

George Q. Cannon

(Describing Joseph's exchange with the mob at Carthage, June 25, 1844.)

Several officers of the mob militia . . . gazed upon him [Joseph] with much curiosity, and he asked them if he appeared like a desperate character. They replied that his outward appearance seemed to indicate exactly the opposite, but they could not tell what was in his heart.

To this Joseph responded:

George Q. Cannon
(Courtesy of the Church Archives, The Church of Jesus Christ of Latter-day Saints)

"Very true, gentlemen, you cannot see what is in my heart, and you are therefore unable to judge me or my intentions; but I can see what is in your hearts, and will tell you what I see. I can see you thirst for blood, and nothing but my blood will satisfy you. It is not for crime of any description that I and my brethren are thus continually persecuted and harassed by our enemies, but there are other motives . . . and inasmuch as you and the people thirst for blood, I prophesy, in the name of the Lord, that you shall witness scenes of blood and sorrow to your entire satisfaction. Your souls shall be perfectly satiated with blood, and many of you who are now present shall have an opportunity to face the cannon's mouth from sources you think not of; and those people that desire this great evil upon me and my brethren, shall be filled with regret and sorrow because of the scenes of desolation and distress that await them. They shall seek for peace, and shall not be able to find it. Gentlemen, you will find what I have told you to be true" (George Q. Cannon, *Life of Joseph Smith, The Prophet* [Salt Lake City: Deseret Book, 1986], 509).

Joseph Smith Jr.

(Before his martyrdom, Joseph Smith delivered all the priesthood keys he had received to the Twelve.)

Some important scene is near to take place. It may be that my enemies will kill me, and in case they should, and the keys and power which rest on me not be imparted to you, they will be lost from the earth; but if I can only succeed in placing them upon your heads, then let me fall a victim to murderous hands if God will suffer it, and I can go with all pleasure and satisfaction, knowing that my work is done, and the foundation laid on which the kingdom of God is to be reared (Ronald K. Esplin, "Joseph Smith's Mission and Timetable: 'God Will Protect Me until My Work is Done,'" *The Prophet Joseph: Essays on the Life and Mission of Joseph Smith*, ed. Larry C. Porter and Susan Easton Black [Salt Lake City: Deseret Book, 1988], 319; capitalization standardized).

Stephen Markham

(Recorded June 20, 1856)

The first conversation I had with the Prophet on the following subjects was the night the guard came to take him a writ. We walked together towards the river and sat down. I asked him how this thing was going to come out. He replied if the brethren would let him manage the business, there should be no blood shed, but if not it would be the hardest blow the Church ever had or would receive, that if he and Hyrum were ever taken again they would be massacred or he was not a Prophet of God. He said he wanted to save Hyrum to avenge his blood. He said that Hyrum was determined not to leave him, but die with him (Stephen Markham, "Stephen Markham's Personal Account of Events Leading to the Death of Joseph Smith," *Wilford Woodruff's Papers* [LDS Church Archives, The Church of Jesus Christ of Latter-day Saints, Salt Lake City, Utah], n.p.).

Nauvoo Expositor Incident

William Law and several of his associates brought a printing press into Nauvoo and commenced publishing a paper called the *Nauvoo Expositor* that denounced Church doctrine, called for repeal of the Nauvoo City Charter, and defamed, humiliated, and destroyed the reputations of the members of the community who supported the Saints. In 1844, Joseph Smith, mayor of Nauvoo, declared the paper a public nuisance and ordered it destroyed.

William Adams

Mobocrats and bad men from Missouri were busy stirring up the citizens of Nauvoo and the border county of Hancock, also a few apostates in Nauvoo joined with them, viz; William Law, Doctor [Robert P.] Foster, Chauncy Higbee and others. Their object was to kidnap the Prophet and take him to Missouri under the pretend of law, so that they might kill him. The above name[d] apostates commenced printing a newspaper in Nauvoo called the *Expositor*, defaming the character of the prominent men of the city, publishing lie, and traducing their families. The city council declared it a nuisance, and ordered it to be abetted, which was done by the marshal and police of the city. I was there and saw it

A page from the *Nauvoo Expositor*
(Courtesy of the Church Archives, The Church of Jesus Christ of Latter-day Saints)

destroyed. I was an eyewitness, and took an active part to protect the city from any attack of the mob (William Adams, "Autobiography of William Adams," *Writings of Early Latter-day Saints and Their Contemporaries, a Database Collection*, comp. Milton V. Backman [Provo, Utah: BYU Religious Studies Center, 1996], 11; spelling standardized).

Prospectus of the Nauvoo Expositor

The *Nauvoo Expositor* will be issued on Friday of each week, on an imperial sheet, with a new press and materials of the best quality, and rendered worthy of the patronage of a discerning and enlightened public.

The *Expositor* will be devoted to a general diffusion of useful knowledge, and its columns open for the admission of all courteous communications of a religious, moral, social, literary, or political character without taking a decided stand in favor of either of the great political parties in the country. A part of its columns will be devoted to a few primary objects, which the publishers deem of vital importance to the public welfare. Their particular locality gives them a knowledge of the many *gross abuses exercised under the "pretended" authorities of the Charter of the City of Nauvoo,* by the legislative authorities of said city and the *insupportable oppression* of the *Ministerial powers in carrying out the unjust, illegal and unconstitutional ordinances of the same.* The publishers therefore deem it a sacred duty they owe to their country and their fellow-citizens to advocate through the columns of the *Expositor* THE UNCONIDTIONAL REPEAL OF THE NAUVOO CITY CHARTER, to restrain and correct the abuses of the UNIT POWER, to ward off the iron rod which is held over the devoted heads of the citizens of Nauvoo and the surrounding country, to advocate unmitigated DISOBEDIENCE TO POLITICAL REVELATIONS, and to censure and decry gross moral imperfections wherever found, either in the plebeian, patrician or SELF-CONSTITUTED MONARCH—to advocate the pure principles of morality, the pure principles of truth, designed not to destroy, but strengthen the main-spring of God's moral government—to advocate and exercise the freedom of speech in Nauvoo, independent of the ordinances abridging the same—*to give free toleration to every man's religious sentiment,* and sustain ALL in worshipping their God according to the monitions of their own consciences, as guaranteed by the Constitution of our country, and to oppose with uncompromising hostility any UNION OF CHURCH AND STATE, or any preliminary step tending to the same—to sustain ALL *however humble,* in their equal and constitutional rights, and oppose the sacrifice of the liberty, the property and the happiness of the MANY, to the *pride* and *ambition* of the FEW; in a word, to give a full, candid and succinct statement of FACTS AS THEY REALLY

EXIST IN THE CITY OF NAUVOO *fearless of whose particular case the facts may apply*—being governed by the laws of editorial courtesy, and the inherent dignity which is inseparable from honorable minds, at the same time exercising their own judgment in cases of flagrant abuses of moral delinquencies,—to use such terms and names as they deem proper, when the object is of such high importance that the end will justify the means. In this great and indispensable work, we confidently look to an enlightened public to aid us in our laudable effort (*History of the Church*, 6:443–44).

Joseph Smith Jr.

Can it be supposed that after all the indignities to which we have been subjected outside, that this people could suffer a set of worthless vagabonds to come into our city, and right under our own eyes and protection, vilify and calumniate not only ourselves, but the character of our wives and daughters, as was impudently and unblushingly done in that infamous and filthy sheet? (*History of the Church*, 6:581).

John Taylor

[Joseph] stated that no man was a stronger advocate for the liberty of the speech and of the press than himself; yet, when this noble gift is utterly prostituted and abused, as in the present instance, it loses all claim to our respect, and becomes as great an agent of evil as it can possibly be for good; and notwithstanding the apparent advantage we should give our enemies by this act, yet it behooved us, as men, to act independent of all secondary influences, to perform the part of men of enlarged minds, and boldly and fearlessly to discharge the duties devolving upon us by declaring as a nuisance, and removing this filthy, libelous, and seditious sheet from our midst (John Taylor, *The Martyrdom*, ed. Mark H. Taylor [Salt Lake City: Deseret Book, 1999], 32).

John Taylor

(Recalling the following about the newspaper.)

[It was] no sooner put in circulation, than the indignation of the whole community was aroused; so much so, that they threatened its annihilation; and I do not believe that in any other city in the United

States, if the same charges had been made against the citizens, it would have been permitted to remain one day (*The Martyrdom*, 15).

Nathan Cheney

The city council declared [the press] to be a nuisance and ordered the city marshal to destroy it. The marshal called on eighteen or twenty men to assist him, the marshal went to the building and took the press and papers into the street and burned the papers, and broke the press (Nathan Cheney, "Nathan Cheney to Charles Beebe, 28–29 Jun 1844" [LDS Church Archives, The Church of Jesus Christ of Latter-day Saints, Salt Lake City, Utah] n.p.; see also *History of the Church*, 6:432).

The City Council

(The council passed the following resolution.)

Resolved, by the City Council of the city of Nauvoo, that the printing-office from whence issues the *Nauvoo Expositor* is a public nuisance and also all of said *Nauvoo Expositors* which may be or exist in said establishment; and the Mayor is instructed to cause said printing establishment and papers to be removed without delay, in such manner as he shall direct. . . .

[The mayor promptly issued the following order to the marshall of the city:]

You are here commanded to destroy the printing press from whence issues the *Nauvoo Expositor*, and pi the type of said printing establishment in the street, and burn all the *Expositors* and libelous handbills found in said establishment; and if resistance be offered to your execution of this order by the owners or others, demolish the house; and if anyone threatens you or the Mayor or the officers of the city, arrest those who threaten you, and fail not to execute this order without delay, and make due return hereon.

By order of the City Council,
Joseph Smith. Mayor (*History of the Church*, 6:448).

Charles Foster

(In a letter to Thomas Sharp, the editor of the Warsaw Signal *and the man who organized the anti-Mormon party in 1841.)*

Mr. Sharp:—I hasten to inform you of the UNPARRALLELED OUTRAGE, perpetrated upon our rights and interests by the ***ruthless, lawless, ruffian band of*** *MORMON MOBOCRATS*, at the dictation of that UNPRINCIPLED wretch Joe Smith.

We were privately informed that the CITY COUNCIL, which had been in *extra session* for two days past, had enacted an ordinance in relation to libels, providing that any thing that *had* been published, or any thing that *might* be published *tending* to disparage the character of the officers of the city should be **regarded as LAWLESS.** They also declared the "Nauvoo Expositor" a "*nuisance*" and directed the police of city to proceed immediately to the office of the Expositor, and **DESTROY the PRESS and also the MATERIALS**, by THROWING them into the STREET!!!!

If any resistance were made, the officers were directed to demolish the building, and property of all who were concerned in publishing said paper; and also take all into custody who might refuse to obey the authorities of the City.

Accordingly, a company consisting of some 200 men, armed and equipped, with MUSKETS, SWORDS, PISTOLS, BOWIE-KNIVES, SLEDGE HAMMERS, etc., assisted by a crowd of several hundred minions, who volunteered their services on the occasion, marched to the building, and breaking open the doors with a SLEDGE HAMMER, commenced the work of destruction and desperation.

They tumbled the press and materials into the street and set *fire to them, and demolished the machinery with a sledge hammer, and injured the building very materially.* We made no resistance; but . . . leave it for the public, to avenge this climax of insult and injury (Charles Foster, *The Warsaw Signal* [June 12, 1844]: 2; punctuation standardized).

Thomas Sharp

(The editor of the Warsaw Signal *published a one-paragraph response concerning Foster's letter, on June 12.)*

Thomas Sharp
(Courtesy of the Church Archives, The Church of Jesus Christ of Latter-day Saints)

We have only to state, that this is sufficient! War and extermination is inevitable! CITIZENS ARISE, ONE and ALL!!!—Can you *stand* by, and suffer such INFERNAL DEVILS! to ROB men of their property and RIGHTS, without avenging them. We have no time for comment, every man will make his own. LET IT BE MADE WITH POWDER AND BALL!!! (Thomas Sharp, *The Warsaw Signal* [June 12, 1844]: 2).

Joseph Smith's Farewell to Nauvoo En Route to Carthage Jail

Joseph Smith Jr.

If I do not go there [Carthage], the result will be the destruction of this city and its inhabitants; and I cannot think of my dear brothers and sisters and their children suffering the scenes of Missouri again in Nauvoo; no, it is better for your brother, Joseph, to die for his brothers and sisters, for I am willing to die for them. My work is finished (Dan Jones, "The Martyrdom of Joseph Smith and His Brother, Hyrum," trans. Ronald D. Dennis, *BYU Studies* [Winter 1984]: 85).

Eunice B. Snow

I remember hearing the Prophet the last time he spoke in Nauvoo. . . . He said, "I go like a lamb to the slaughter," referring to the great shadow, which seemed even then to hover over his life and to foreshadow his impending doom.

On the last day which he spent in Nauvoo, he passed our house with his brother, Hyrum, both riding. My mother and I were standing in the dooryard, and as he passed, he bowed with uplifted hat to my mother. Hyrum seemed like one in a dream, sad and despondent, taking no notice of any one. They were on their way to the Carthage jail, and it was the last time I saw the Prophet alive (Eunice B. Snow, "A Sketch of the Life of Eunice Billings Snow," *Women's Exponent* [September 1910]: 22).

Joseph Smith Jr.

(En route to Carthage, he paused to look at the unfinished Nauvoo Temple and declare the following.)

This is the loveliest place and the best people under the heavens; little do they know the trials that await them (*History of the Church*, 6:554).

Events at Carthage Jail

Col. J. W. Woods

(This statement was published in a newspaper in Ottawa, Iowa, June 26, 1844.)

I had an interview with Joe Smith after the Governor announced his intention of going to Nauvoo . . . In this interview Joe Smith proved himself a prophet, for he said to me, on parting that he should not live to see another day, so fully was he impressed with the belief that he would be murdered, all of which proved true (Col. J. W. Woods, "The Mormon Prophet," *Daily Democrat* [May 10, 1885]: n.p.).

Frank Worrell

(One of Joseph's jailers, an avowed enemy to the Prophet, said the following to Stephen Markham.)

We have had too much trouble to bring Old Joe here to let him ever escape alive, and unless you want to die with him you had better leave before sundown; and you are not a damned bit better than him for taking his part, and you'll see that I can prophesy better than Old Joe, for neither he nor his brother, nor anyone who will remain with them will see the sun set today (*History of the Church*, 6:602).

Joseph Smith Jr.

(The Prophet wrote a letter to Governor Ford, seeking protection by requesting to accompany the governor when he traveled to Nauvoo. Governor Ford did indeed go to Nauvoo, but he did not take the Prophet with him. Joseph was left at the mercy of the mobs. Joseph's request follows.)

And furthermore, again, let me say, Governor Ford, I shall look to you for our protection. I believe you are talking of going to Nauvoo; if you go, sir, I wish to go along. I refuse not to answer any law, but I do not consider myself safe here (*Teachings of the Prophet Joseph Smith*, 390).

Governor Ford

(Responding to the Prophet's request.)

I am in hopes that you will be acquitted; but if I go, I will certainly take you along. I do not, however, apprehend danger. I think you are perfectly safe, either here or anywhere else. I cannot, however, interfere with the law. I am placed in peculiar circumstances and seem to be blamed by all parties (*Teachings of the Prophet Joseph Smith*, 390).

Stephen Markham

I went to jail and told Joseph that they intended to kill him. He made an observation like this: "Be not afraid." Nothing more particular passed through the day. The next morning I went out again and found that the Governor was going to the City of Nauvoo with about one hundred men. I went and told Joseph that I did not consider them safe as the Governor had gone, leaving the Carthage Grays to guard the jail, and dismissing the rest of the troops. Before leaving I went to the Governor and got a permit written and signed by his own hand, giving me leave to go in and out of the jail when I pleased. Before starting he pledged his word on the honor of the State that nothing would molest the prisoners. I told the Governor that I did not consider the Carthage Grays a safe guard, saying that I considered he should leave another guard. It was at this time that he pledged his honor, and faith of the State, that no measure would be taken but according to law. . . .

Doctor Richards was taken sick. Then Bro. Joseph said to me, "Bro Markham, as you have a pass to go out and in, you will need to go out and get the Doctor a pipe and tobacco to settle his stomach." I went out and got a pipe from Sheriff Backenstos and bought some tobacco in a store close by and was returning. John Eagle was in the store and threw out considerable threats against the Mormons, and in particular against me. When proceeding to the jail, I was assailed by a man by the name of Stewart. He called to me, "Old man, you have got to leave the town in five minutes." I replied, "I shall not do it. Neither can you drive me. You can kill me, but you cannot drive me." Then he turned and charged upon me with his bayonet, and I parried it off with my left hand and knocked him down with my right. He hollowed and all the Carthage Grays rallied round me with their guns and bayonets, and told me I had got to leave the town forthwith or I would be a dead man in a short time, making passes at me with their bayonets. I parried them off with my left and knocked them down to the amount of ten or twelve with my right. Then they got so close that I had no chance, Eagle in the gang urging them on. Hamilton, the Inn keeper, came out and said I had better go home as I would only get killed if I remained. He said, "You can do the prisoners no good and I will bring you your horse." I told him I was not going home and not to bring him. He cried and brought my horse up, and they forced me on him with the points of their bayonets until the blood filled my shoes. Then they formed a hollow square round me and marched me to the timber ("Stephen Markham's Personal Account of Events Leading to the Death of Joseph Smith," n.p.; spelling standardized).

John Taylor

I was sitting at one of the front windows of the jail, when I saw a number of men, with painted faces, coming around the corner of the jail, and aiming towards the stairs. The other brethren had seen the same, for, as I went to the door, I found Brother Hyrum Smith and Dr. Richards already leaning against it. . . . While in this position, the mob, who had come upstairs, and tried to open the door, probably thought it was locked, and fired a ball through the keyhole; at this Dr. Richards and Brother Hyrum leaped back from the door, with their faces towards it; almost instantly another ball passed through the panel of the door, and struck Brother Hyrum on the left side of the nose, entering his face and head. At the same instant, another ball from the outside entered his back, passing through his body and striking his watch. . . . Immediately, when the balls struck him, he fell flat on his back, crying as he fell, "I am a dead man!" He never moved afterwards.

I shall never forget the deep feeling of sympathy and regard manifested in the countenance of Brother Joseph as he drew nigh to Hyrum, and, leaning over him, exclaimed, "Oh! my poor, dear brother Hyrum!" He, however, instantly arose, and with a firm, quick step, and a determined expression of countenance, approached the door, and pulling the six-shooter left by Brother [Cyrus] Wheelock from his pocket, opened the door slightly, and snapped the pistol six successive times; only three of the barrels, however, were discharged. . . . While I was engaged in parrying the guns, Brother Joseph said, "That's right, Brother Taylor, parry them off as well as you can." These were the last words I ever heard him speak on earth (*History of the Church*, 7:102–3).

Willard Richards

(Elder Richards was a friend of the Prophet and a member of the Quorum of the Twelve. He was in Carthage Jail when the Prophet was martyred. His account begins as the mob arrived at the jail just after 5 P.M. on the afternoon of June 27, 1844.)

A shower of musket balls were thrown up the stairway against the door of the prison in the second story, followed by many rapid footsteps. . . .

A ball was sent through the door, which passed between us, and showed that our enemies were desperadoes . . .

Joseph Smith, Mr. Taylor and myself sprang back to the front part of the room, and General Hyrum Smith retreated two-thirds across the chamber directly in front of and facing the door.

Willard Richards
(Courtesy of the Church Archives, The Church of Jesus Christ of Latter-day Saints

A ball was sent through the door which hit Hyrum on the side of his nose, when he fell backwards, extended at length, without moving his feet.

From the holes in his vest . . . it appears evident that a ball must have been thrown from without, through the window, which entered his back on the right side, and passing through, lodged against his watch, which was in his right vest pocket, completely pulverizing the crystal and face, tearing off the hands and mashing the whole body of the watch. At the same instant the ball from the door entered his nose.

As he struck the floor he exclaimed emphatically, "I am a dead man." Joseph looked towards him and responded, "Oh, dear brother Hyrum!" and opening the door two or three inches with his left hand, discharged one barrel of a six shooter (pistol) at random in the entry, from whence a ball [from the musket of one of the mob members, had] grazed Hyrum's breast, and entering his throat passed into his head, while other muskets were aimed at him and some balls hit him.

Joseph continued snapping his revolver round the casing of the door into the space as before . . . while Mr. Taylor with a walking stick stood by his side and knocked down the bayonets and muskets which were constantly discharging through the doorway . . .

When the revolver failed, we had no more firearms, and expected an immediate rush of the mob, and the doorway full of muskets, half way in the room, and no hope but instant death from within.

Mr. Taylor rushed into the window, which is some fifteen or twenty feet from the ground. When his body was nearly on a balance, a ball from the door within entered his leg, and a ball from without struck his watch . . . in his vest pocket near the left breast, and smashed it into "pie," leaving the hands standing at 5 o'clock, 16 minutes, and 26 seconds, the force of which ball threw him back on the floor, and he rolled under the bed which stood by his side . . .

Joseph attempted, as the last resort, to leap [from] the same window from whence Mr. Taylor fell, when two balls pierced him from the door, and one entered his right breast from without, and he fell outward, exclaiming, "Oh Lord, my God!" . . . He fell on his left side a dead man (*History of the Church*, 6:619–20).

[Note: Elder John Taylor was shot four times but recovered from his wounds. In fulfillment of a prophecy that the Prophet had made more than a year before, Elder Willard Richards received no wounds. Elder Richards recalled that in this prophecy the Prophet had told him "that the time would come that the balls would fly around him like hail, and he should see his friends fall on the right and on the left, but that there should not be a hole in his garment" (*History of the Church*, 6:619).]

Mrs. J. C. Metlen

(Mrs. Metlen was the daughter of George W. Stigall, who was deputy sheriff of Hancock County and who was living with his family in the old jail at the time the mob attacked and killed Joseph and Hyram Smith. She was seven years old at the time and retained a vivid memory of the events of that historic day.)

Mr. Stigall was out of town on some business connected with his office and the jail and its occupants were left in charge of his wife and sixteen year old son, Henry Stigall. Henry was carrying the tray of dishes from the rooms of the Smiths to the kitchen when the uproar began, and he was so startled, he dropped the tray, dishes and all, and ran to see what was the trouble. The mother was baking pies in the kitchen and just as she stooped to look into the oven, a bullet whizzed over her stopping body and buried itself in the wall opposite. Terribly frightened, she took her two little girls and hastened across to a residence that stood on the south side of the square. The battle at the jail was swift. The men of the mob accomplished their errand and were gone quicker than it takes to tell it (*Carthage Republican* [March 5, 1913]: 5; original at Hancock County Historical Society).

Eliza Clayton

I went with my sister Lucy to the jail; we found the doors and windows open and everything in confusion, as though the people had left in great haste. We went upstairs to the room in which the Prophet and his brother had been shot. Everything seemed upset. There were some Church books on the table and portraits of Joseph and Hyrum's families on the mantle piece, blood in pools on the floor and spattered on the walls, at sight of which we were overcome with grief and bust into tears (Eliza Clayton, "Reminiscences of Nauvoo," *Voices from the Past: Diaries, Journals, and Autobiographies*, ed. Leonard J. Arrington [Provo, Utah: Brigham Young University Press, 1980], 15).

Willard Richards

(This letter describes the deaths of Joseph and Hyrum and promises that the Saints will not retaliate against the citizens of Carthage.)

Transcription: CARTHAGE JAIL, 8:05 o'clock, p. m., June 27th, 1844.

Joseph and Hyrum are dead. Taylor wounded, not very badly. I am well. Our guard was forced, as we believe, by a band of Missourians from 100 to 200. The job was done in an instant, and the party fled towards Nauvoo instantly. This is as I believe it. The citizens here are afraid of the Mormons attacking them; I promise them no.

Willard Richards.

John Taylor.

N.B.—The citizens promise us protection. Alarm guns have been fired (*History of the Church*, 6:621–22).

John Taylor

These servants of God have gone to heaven by fire—the fire of an ungodly mob. Like the Prophets of ancient days they lived as long as the world would receive them; and this is one furnace in which the saints were to be tried, to have their leaders cut off from their midst, and not be permitted to avenge their blood (*History of the Church*, 7:173).

John Taylor

Governor Ford is certainly a man who performed mighty wonders. He not only compelled two innocent men, by virtue of his office as Governor of Illinois, to go before two different magistrates on the same charge, contrary to the Constitution and laws of the state; to surrender themselves into the custody of a mob magistrate (not the one who issued the writ); go to prison under a military guard on an illegal mittimus, granted contrary to law, without any examination; put in a criminal cell without having been examined for crime; brought them out of prison contrary to law; thrust them back again under the most solemn and sacred pledges of his personal faith, and the faith of the state, for their protection; guarded them with men whom he knew to be treacherous, and to have resolved on the death of the prisoners, until they were murdered in cold blood, and then professed to be "thunderstruck"! (*History of the Church,* 7:2).

William W. Phelps

(On the morning of June 27, Joseph Smith related a dream he had the night before. It was a premonition of his death and the deaths of his brothers Hyrum and Samuel.)

In June 1844 when Joseph Smith went to Carthage and delivered himself up to Gov. Ford I accompanied him, and while on the way thither he related to me and his Brother Hyrum the following dream. He said, "While I was at Jordan's in Iowa the other night I dreamed that myself and my brother Hyrum went on board a large steamboat lying in a small bay near the great ocean. Shortly after we went on board their was an alarm of fire, and I discovered that the boat had been anchored some distance from the shore out in the bay, and that an escape from the fire in the confusion appeared hazardous. But as delay was folly, I and Hyrum jumped overboard and tried our faith at walking upon the water. At first we sank in the water nearly to our knees, but as we proceeded we increased in faith and were soon able to walk upon the water.

"Looking towards the burning boat in the east, we saw that it was drifting towards the wharf and the town with a great flame and clouds of smoke, and as if by whirlwind the town was taking fire too, so that the scene of destruction and horrors of the frightened inhabitants was terrible. We proceeded on the bosom of the mighty deep and were soon out of sight of land. The ocean was still, the rays of the sun were bright, and we forgot all the troubles of our Mother Earth.

William W. Phelps
(Courtesy of the Church Archives, The Church of Jesus Christ of Latter-day Saints)

"Just at that moment I heard the sound of a human voice, and turning round saw my brother Samuel H. approaching towards us from the east. We stopped and he came up. After a moment's conversation he informed me that he had been lonesome and had made up his mind to go with me across the mighty deep.

"We all started again and in a short time were blessed with the first sight of a city, whose silver steeples and towers were more beautiful than any that I had ever seen or heard of on earth. It stood, as it were, upon the western shore of the mighty deep we [were] walking on, and its order and glory seemed far beyond the wisdom of man. While we were gazing upon the perfection of the city, a small boat launched off from the port and almost as quick as thought came to us. In an instant they took us on board and saluted, with welcome and with music, such as is not of earth.

"The next scene on landing was more than I can describe. The greetings and the music from a thousand towers, and the light of God himself at the return of three of his sons, soothed my soul into [such] quiet and joy that I felt as if I were truly in heaven. I gazed upon the splendor. I greeted my friends.

"I awoke, and lo, it was a dream.

"While I meditated upon such a marvelous scene, I fell asleep again, and behold, I stood near the shore of the burning boat, and there was great consternation among the officers, crew, and passengers of the flaming craft, as there seemed to be much ammunition or powder on board. The alarm was given that the fire was near the magazine, and in a moment suddenly it blew up with a great noise and sank in the deep water with all on board. I then turned to the country east among the bushy openings and saw William and Wilson Law endeavoring to escape from the wild beasts of the forest, but two lions rushed out of a thicket and devoured them. I awoke again."

I will say that Joseph never told this dream again, as he was martyred about two days after. I relate from recollection as nearly as I can (William W. Phelps, *Joseph Smith's Last Dream* [LDS Church Archives, The Church of Jesus Christ of Latter-day Saints, Salt Lake City, Utah]; as cited in Mark L. McConkie, *Remembering Joseph* [Salt Lake City: Deseret Book, 2003], 390–91).

[Note: Samuel Smith rode to Carthage to save his brothers but arrived just moments after they had been murdered. He retrieved his brothers' bodies and returned to Nauvoo. He was suffering from a recent injury at the time and died three weeks later, on July 30, 1844. Thus, Mother Smith lost three sons, just as Joseph understood from his dream.]

Aftermath of the Martyrdom

Mary Alice Cannon Lambert

I well remember the night of the Prophet's death. The spirit of unrest was upon all, man and animal, in the city of Nauvoo. Why, we did not know, but we could not rest. My father was on guard. No one in the house had slept, the dogs were noisy, and even the chickens were awake.

About 3 o'clock the news of the martyrdom was brought to us, and we realized what had kept us awake. And oh, the mourning in the land! The grief felt was beyond expression—men, women and children, we were all stunned by the blow (Mary Alice Cannon Lambert, "Joseph Smith, The Prophet," *Young Women's Journal* [December 1905]: 554).

Mary Ann Stearns Winters

I cannot remember of meeting but twice in the Sunday School when those awful days came that terminated in the martyrdom of Brother Joseph and Hyrum Smith, and oh, the horror and gloom and heartaches and trials of those days. The very atmosphere was so oppressive that it seemed difficult to breathe. Everything seemed to stand still and with such an awful stillness and everyone seemed looking to another for some help, and to know what to do in their awful extremity. Many imagined that Brother Joseph's life could not be taken and the shock to them was doubly great, and all were looking for a message from somewhere, and it came in due time. Our Prophet and Patriarch were gone, and the weight of the Church rested on the body of the Church, and right bravely and unflinchingly did they hold it for the time being, faithfully trusting in the promise that God's kingdom had come to stay, and would not be broken up, though the headlight was obscured and the darkness was profound.

Brother Pratt on his mission in the eastern states was impressed by the Holy Spirit to return home to Nauvoo and while on the canal boat, heard the sad news of the tragedy that had been enacted, and tells of the oppression and gloom that pervaded his heart though so far away from the scene of sorrow, and before he was aware of what had transpired. He hastened onward, and a few days later, just as the sun appeared over the eastern prairies, he, coming from that direction, opened the door and walked into the dining room unannounced and unlooked for, the surprise being like an electric shock, and truly he brought the sunlight of the Holy Spirit with him—faith, hope, courage and strength—cheer to press onward undaunted. The burden seemed lifted, for he came with the power of the Holy Priesthood, and the light of revelation that had been given him for the occasion, and the hearts of the faithful turned from their sorrow to the upholding and sustaining of the work that our beloved Prophet and Patriarch had laid down their lives as a sacrifice for. Each day as he met in council with Brothers Richards and Taylor, he brought us fresh words of encouragement, and soon Brother Brigham, Brother Kimball and the others arrived, each filled with the spirit of their calling and were a mighty phalanx in the cause of righteousness, and though the gloom could be plainly felt, the rod of iron was there, and the majority took strong hold and walked firmly on even unto the end of their days on earth (Mary Ann Stearns Winters, *An Autobiographical Sketch of the Life of the Late Mary Ann Stearns Winters* [LDS Church Archives, The Church of Jesus Christ of Latter-day Saints, Salt Lake City, Utah], n.p.; grammar standardized).

Zina Young
(Courtesy of the Church Archives, The Church of Jesus Christ of Latter-day Saints)

Zina D. Huntington Young

It was June 27th, 1844, . . . and it was rumored that Joseph was expected in from Carthage. I did not know to the contrary until I saw the Governor and his guards descending the hill by the temple, a short distance from my house. Their swords glistened in the sun, and their appearance startled me, though I knew not what it foreboded. I exclaimed to a neighbor who was with me, "What is the trouble! It seems to me that the trees and the grass are in mourning!" A fearful silence pervaded the city, and after the shades of night gathered around us it was thick darkness. The lightnings flashed, the cattle bellowed, the dogs barked, and the elements wailed. What a terrible night that was to the saints, yet we knew nothing of the dark tragedy which had been enacted by the assassins at Carthage.

The morning dawned; the sad news came; but as yet I had not heard of the terrible event. I started to go to Mother Smith's, on an errand. As I approached I saw men gathered around the door of the mansion. A few rods from the house I met Jesse P. Harmon. "Have you heard the news?" he asked. "What news?" I inquired. "Joseph and Hyrum are dead!" Had I believed it, I could not have walked any farther. I hastened to my brother Dimick. He was sitting in his house, mourning and weeping aloud as only strong men can weep. All was confirmed in a moment. My pen cannot utter my grief nor describe my horror. But after awhile a change came, as though the released spirits of the departed sought to comfort us in that hour of dreadful bereavement.

> "The healer was there, pouring balm on my heart,
> And wiping the tears from my eyes;
> He was binding the chain that was broken in twain,
> And fastening it firm in the skies."

(as cited in Edward W. Tullidge, *The Women of Mormondom* [New York: Tullidge and Crandall, 1877], 325–26)

William Adams

I belonged to Captain Folshawa['s] Company of Col. Theodore Turley's regiment of infantry, Nauvoo Legion, drilled and stood guard and performed the duty of a soldier while the city was under martial law. Was close to the frame building where the prophet preached his great and last sermon, heard Governor Ford on the 27th of June make a speech accusing the Mormons of being disloyal to the government of the United States, and many other lies that I was aware of. At the same hour that Ford was haranguing the Saints of Nauvoo, the mob was assassinating the Prophet in Carthage Jail. News of the murder of Joseph was not received until the next morning, the 28th of June, it being stopped by the governor for fear that the Mormons would take his life in revenge for the murder of the Prophet. The bodies of Joseph and Hyrum were brought to Nauvoo the morning after the murder.

I am not able to describe the sorrow and lamentation of the Saints in beholding the dead bodies of the Prophet and Patriarch, butchered in cold blood by assassins and murdered under the promise of protection by the governor of the state of Illinois. The curse of God must have followed him, for I saw him at the legislature in Springfield, the capital of Illinois, not as a member, but having come from Peoria where he resided, and he had not influence enough to get a door keeper elected. He looked like a poor rejected creature, and [a] short time afterward he died a pauper and was buried by public expense in Peoria ("Autobiography of William Adams," 12).

Benjamin Ashby

Not dreaming of the tragedy that had been enacted that afternoon, I went to bed but at the dawn of morning the sad tale was brought to our ears and the grief and sorrow of a whole people cannot be pictured in language; for days, a man, woman or child could not be met but they were in tears for the loss of their beloved leader. Soon the wagons containing the two brothers arrived in the city and passed down to the Mansion House where we visited and viewed their marred features as they lay in the hallowments of the grave (Benjamin Ashby, "Autobiography of Benjamin Ashby," *Writings of Early Latter-day Saints*, 10).

Lewis Barney

As soon as this [the martyrdom of the Prophet] was done the whole country was deserted; men, women and children fled for their lives, not taking time to shut their doors after them. Stores were left standing open and there was gloom cast over the country, so much that strangers passing through the country spoke of it. As I was out looking, I met a stranger. He ask me what was the matter. That everything looks so gloomy and lonesome. I told him that last evening (27th of June, 1844) Joseph Smith the Prophet and his brother Hyrum were murdered at Carthage Illinois, and the people here all fled and left the country and when the blood of a prophet is shed it has a tendency to cast a gloom over the country.

The whole Church of Jesus Christ of Latter-day Saints were bathed in tears and mourning for the loss of the Prophet and the Patriarch. The mob supposed if Joseph was out of the way it would put an end to Mormonism as they called it. So things were more peaceable for about a year. But the Saints under the Presidency of Brigham Young increased their diligence in pushing forward the Temple that was under course of erection, and were more united than before the death of the Prophet. So the mob again commenced their depredations, by driving the Saints that lived in settlements outside of Nauvoo from their houses and setting them on fire and destroying their crops and killing their stock. This went on about a week (Lewis Barney, "Autobiography of Lewis Barney," *Writings of Early Latter-day Saints,* 24).

Gilbert Belnap

The afternoon previous to the martyrdom, we hurried to Nauvoo to announce the coming of the Prophet as was agreed by the governor [Thomas Ford]. But with him came not the beloved Prophet which soon convinced the people that treachery of the foulest kind was at work. This cowardly, would-be-great man tried his best to intimidate the people. It was with difficulty, however, that some few could be restrained from making sad havoc among his troops. . . .

On his return to Carthage, he met George D. Grant bearing the sad news of the slaughter at the jail, whereupon the cowardly curse arrested Grant and took him back to Carthage in order to give himself time to escape. Thus, the distance of eighteen miles was traveled over three times before the sorrowful news of the Prophet's death reached his friends.

In the afternoon of June [28th], the mournful procession arrived bearing the mangled bodies of the Prophet and the Patriarch and Elder John Taylor. Although the latter still survived, he mingled his with the best blood of the century. Willard Richards escaped without a hole in his garment. Their bodies were placed in a commodious position and the assembled thousands of Saints gazed in mournful silence on the faces of the illustrious dead (Gilbert Belnap, "Autobiography of Gilbert Belnap," *Writings of Early Latter-day Saints,* 36–37; spelling standardized).

Ezra T. Benson

(The grandfather of Ezra Taft Benson, Ezra T. was campaigning for Joseph Smith's election to the presidency of the United States when he heard the news of the Prophet's martyrdom.)

About the first of May we started and commenced our important labors, traveling through the different towns and cities, preaching the gospel and presenting Bro. Joseph before the people as being the most suitable man for president. Delegates were appointed throughout the state of New Jersey in different districts to meet in Trenton in August to hold a convention and I had made calculations to be on the ground according to appointment, and make a speech to the delegates, and all who might be present, and to attend to all other business necessary in a convention of that kind that nothing should be neglected on my part for I had the promise from the Prophet before I started that I should be blessed and his last words were, taking me by the hand, "You are blessed and shall be blessed abundantly, go in peace and return in safety."

But, oh, how soon the change; for no sooner had we commenced our labors and made our arrangements than the news came out that our Prophet was martyred in Carthage Jail. The question arose by Bro. Pack, "Who will now lead the Church?" I told him I did not know, but I knew who would lead me and that would be the Twelve Apostles. Our next business was to get home to our families and I was without means. I appointed several meetings throughout Jersey and took up collections among the Gentiles and some few Saints and soon procured means sufficient to take us home. I was very thankful to reach home once more, notwithstanding it was a time of great distress and grief on account of Joseph Smith's death (Ezra T. Benson, "Autobiography," *Writings of Early Latter-day Saints,* 214; spelling standardized).

Henry Bigler

In July of 1844, I went to Ripley the county seat of Jackson for it was to this place I had my papers [the *Times and Seasons*] sent . . . There was a report that Joseph and Hyrum Smith were killed but I did not believe it because I had heard years before of Joseph's death. But as soon as I was informed that my [people] were in mourning I believed the Prophet was dead. I hastened to the office with breathless anxiety to learn the truth about it. When I read the death of the Prophet and his brother Hyrum I felt as though I wanted to go through and tear [everything] in pieces. . . .

Afterwards I felt more like crying than fighting. The elders out on missions were advised through the same papers by the Twelve at Nauvoo not to preach unless they were invited to do so and even in that to do as they advised to preach or to let it alone (Henry Bigler, "Henry Bigler's Journal Book A," *Writings of Early Latter-day Saints,* 10–11).

William Draper

In the spring of 1843, I moved with my family and located in a place called Green Plain, in the vicinity of Warsaw in Hancock County, with the notorious Levi Williams for one of my neighbors.

I there bought a farm on good terms and went to improving; built me a good house and a small grist mill and put about twenty acres of land in a good state of cultivation, with a good fence around it; and was on good terms with my neighbors, although the most of them were gentiles. But they professed to be much pleased with my enterprise in the place, and all went on well with me, until some time in June 1844. Then there was frequent reports about Joseph from Nauvoo, that produced some little excitement, for priests and lawyers and apostates had combined together to again make trouble. The men in the neighborhood where I lived organized to go to Nauvoo and [assassinate] Joseph. They came and invited me to go with them to take Joseph, but I refused. They wanted to know if I would go if the Governor order me to go. I said no, I would not go if the devil himself ordered me to go against Joseph, for his people were my people and where he goes I will go also.

This appeared to vex them a little, although we had always been on good terms as neighbors, and they then said, "Then you will have to leave, for you can't live here although we like you as a neighbor." So they left me and soon started for Nauvoo, with old Colonel [Levi] Williams as there leader, which resulted in the martyrdom of Joseph the Prophet and Hyrum the Patriarch, Owen Brchers Brasher [sic] and [Willard Richards] and John Taylor, the present President of The Church of Jesus Christ of Latter-day Saints; this was done in Carthage Jail, June the 27th, 1844. Then the desperadoes came back to Green Plain without having the black thoroughly washed from their necks and faces and they never could get it from their character or consciences, but they did not interfere with me any more, until about the 20th of October 1845, although they engaged in a little town called Lima that was settled mostly with Saints, in burning houses and plundering and sometimes killed our brethren. And one day, there came an armed force of about sixty men. They set fire to my hay and grain that was in stack and then to the house (William Draper, "Autobiography of William Draper," *Writings of Early Latter-day Saints*, 20; punctuation and capitalization standardized).

Katherine Smith Salisbury

(Threatening notices were tacked to her family's door, warning them to leave town or their lives would be in jeopardy. At the time of the Martyrdom, Katharine, Joseph Smith's sister, left her four children in the care of another family and rushed to Carthage to assist her brothers. The family tending her children fled, leaving the children to fend for themselves. Katharine's daughter Mary recounts what happened to the children.)

Katharine Smith-Salisbury

(Courtesy of the Church Archives, The Church of Jesus Christ of Latter-day Saints)

Her little brood of hungry children crossed the street to a doctor's house. Eight-year-old . . . [Solomon] carried his two-year-old brother, Don Carlos in his arms, the others following. . . . The good woman then told them to come in

... [and] spread some quilts on the floor and told them they could sleep there until morning.... When the doctor came in ... [he] called to his wife, "Whose children are these?" She answered, "They are the little Mormon children from across the street; their mother has gone to Carthage where her brothers have been murdered, and she has not returned." The doctor retorted, "Sure, and we will all be murdered if we keep them here." ... [The] next morning ... [she] fed them again and sent them home saying, "Your mother will surely be back today" (Mary Salisbury Hancock, "The Three Sisters of the Prophet Joseph Smith, part III," The Saints' Herald [January 25, 1954]: n.p.; as cited in Kyle R. Walker, "Katharine Smith Salisbury: Sister to the Prophet," *Mormon Historical Studies* [2002]: 15).

Solomon Salisbury

(Katharine's eldest son recounts other trying experiences the family suffered.)

We soon found that we could not rest here in peace. In a short time it was noised around that my mother ... was a sister to the Mormon prophet, Joseph Smith. What few settlers there were began notifying us that we better be moving along. They refused to let father do their work. We were very poor, and all depended on father's work. They starved us out (Solomon J. Salisbury, "Old Nauvoo Days Recalled," *Autumn Leaves* [April 1924]: 152; as cited in "Katharine Smith Salisbury: Sister to the Prophet," 16).

Kyle Walker

(Speaking of further trials endured by Solomon Salisbury.)

Solomon ... recounted that he had worked for men whose wives would not allow him to eat supper in their houses because of his connection to the Prophet Joseph Smith. In another instance, when Solomon was courting a young woman, the girl's father broke off the relationship. The young woman told Solomon, "Father says you are a Mormon and he does not want anything to do with you." The pain associated with this experience remained with Solomon for life ("Katharine Smith Salisbury: Sister to the Prophet," 21; see also "Old Nauvoo Days Recalled," 155).

Robert D. Foster

(Foster, a member of the mob that participated in the murders, spoke of the inner turmoil he suffered as a result of his actions.)

I am the most miserable wretch that the sun shines upon. If I could recall eighteen months of my life I would be willing to sacrifice everything I have upon earth, my wife and child not excepted. . . . I have not seen one moment's peace since [the Martyrdom]. I know that Mormonism is true, and the thought of meeting (Joseph and Hyrum) at the bar of God is more awful to me than anything else (*History of the Church,* 7:513).

O. S. Democrat

*(*The Democrat, *a St. Louis newspaper, printed the following in regard to the deaths of Joseph and Hyrum Smith.)*

From all the facts now before us, we regard these homicides as nothing else than murder in cold blood—murder against the plighted faith of the chief magistrate of Illinois—murder of a character so atrocious and so unjustifiable as to leave the blackest stain on all it perpetrators, their aiders, abettors, and defenders (*History of the Church,* 7:177–78).

Viewing the Martyred Bodies

Isaac C. Haight

The news soon spread through the city. Mourning was depicted on every countenance; that day was truly a day of mourning with the Saints. About three o'clock in the afternoon the procession was formed in the east of the city to receive the bodies of our martyred prophet and patriarch as carriages were sent to convey them to Nauvoo. We did not wait long before we saw them mournfully winding their way across the prairies. Their bodies were received with tears by the Saints and conveyed to the Mansion amidst the cries and lamentations of the people. The next day, the 29th, the bodies were to be seen at the Mansion from 9 o'clock A.M. till 5 P.M. when they were taken by some chosen friends and buried to await the resurrection morn. The mob, having accomplished their purpose, began to disperse and peace began to be restored and the Saints to return to their different occupations, harvesting having now commenced (Isaac C. Haight, "Autobiographical Sketch of Isaac C. Haight," *Writings of Early Latter-day Saints,* 16).

Joseph Fielding

Their bodies were washed from blood and put into boxes and the next day were conveyed in two wagons, under a guard, to Nauvoo. This was the most solemn sight that my eyes ever beheld. I had often read of the martyrs of old, but now here I saw two of the greatest of men, who sealed the truth which they had held and taught with their blood. Is this an earnest of what has to take place in this last dispensation? Is the blood of the sheep again to be shed like that of the Shepherd, as in former days? Father, if it be possible, let this cup pass from us, but if not, let thy will be done and let us be strengthened to endure to the end.

Joseph and Hyrum Smith were of large stature, well proportioned and had a noble appearance, and this appearance was by no means lost in death, as they lay side by side; for what can make men more noble than to hold the truth of God against his own interest (temporally), to be at war with the world, for the salvation of the upright in heart, and finally seal that truth with their blood? When I think of them and write of them, I feel as though I want to ask their forgiveness that I have not mourned for them more deeply. Joseph had been brought before rulers and judges scores of times, but was never convicted of any crime, neither Hyrum, and although the governor said the burning of the printing press was unlawful, yet the persecutors said they knew the law would not reach him, but powder and ball would, so that they justly are ranked with the martyrs of Jesus Christ (Joseph Fielding, *Diary [1843–1846]* [LDS Church Archives, The Church of Jesus Christ of Latter-day Saints, Salt Lake City, Utah]; as cited in Andrew F. Ehat, "They Might Have Known That He Was Not a Fallen Prophet—The Nauvoo Journal of Joseph Fielding," *BYU Studies* [Winter 1979]: 152–53; spelling, punctuation, and capitalization standardized).

Aroet Lucious Hale

I well remember the day that the bodies of Joseph and Hyrum Smith were brought into Nauvoo. Our parents all went out to the street as the procession passed along the road. The city was in one complete scene of weeping, mourning, and lamentation after the bodies arrived at the mansion house. It was enough to break the heart of a stone, to hear Grandmother Smith and the Saints weep over the loss of their dear Prophet and patriarch, Joseph and Hyrum Smith. Brother John Taylor was brought from Carthage on a sled on account of his wounds. He could not be brought on wheels (Aroet Lucious Hale, "Journal of Aroet Lucious Hale," *Writings of Early Latter-day Saints*, 7).

Joseph Grafton Hovey

Brother Willard Richards, one of the Twelve, was the only one left to gather up the remains of our beloved Prophet and Patriarch. Brother Richards said it was by the power of God that he remained unharmed for the bullets flew in all directions. There was only one family left in the town. They expected the Mormons to come upon them. Brother Richards had great difficulty to get the corpses removed at all. Brother Richards told this family that he would give his life for theirs if they would help him to take care of the bodies. By so pleading he appeased their feelings and they assisted him so that the next day the bodies were brought to Nauvoo. A procession of several thousand people followed the bodies of the beloved Prophet and Patriarch to the Mansion House. The next day at ten o'clock the bodies could be viewed. My wife, Martha, and myself did go and view the corpse[s] of our beloved Prophet and Patriarch. Joseph looked quite natural but Hyrum was so swollen in the face that he did not look natural. We supposed they were buried, but I know not where. The sepulcher was prepared for them but as yet they are not [entered] in there (Joseph Grafton Hovey, "Autobiography of Joseph Grafton Hovey," *Writings of Early Latter-day Saints*, 22; spelling standardized).

Lydia Ann Lake Nelson

Wishing to get closer to the main body of the Saints, we rented another farm within fifteen miles of Carthage and were living there when Joseph Smith and Hyrum were killed, and well do I remember the evening.

That afternoon my father sat reading his Bible; he read aloud the passage, "*The wicked flee when no man pursueth*" and at that time a man rode up to the fence and called out, "Joe Smith is killed." We looked out and saw men, women and children coming with all their might, some in wagons, and others on horses and all were fleeing from the awful scene at Carthage.

My father gathered a few house goods into his wagon and we moved to Nauvoo leaving the beautiful crop for which he never received a cent.

Mosiah Lyman Hancock

I saw the Prophet and the rest when they departed from Nauvoo for the last time; and I went out to meet their martyred bodies when they were brought from Carthage with Apostle John Taylor, who was himself so badly wounded that he could not stir. There were many of the Saints who went out to meet them, and their hearts were full of sorrow. I went to see those noble martyrs after they were laid out in the mansion. Their heads were placed to the north. As we came in at the door, we came to the feet of the Prophet Joseph, then passed up by his left side and around his head, then down by his right side. Next we turned to the right and came to the feet of Hyrum, then up by his left side and around his head and down by his right side; then we filed out of the other door. So the great stream of people continued until the Saints all had the privilege of taking their last look at the martyred bodies.

After the people had gone home, my father took me again into the mansion and told me to place one hand on Joseph's breast and to raise my other arm and swear with hand uplifted that I would never make a compromise with any of the sons of Hell. Which vow I took with a determination to fulfill to the very letter. I took the same vow with Hyrum (Mosiah Lyman Hancock, "Mosiah Hancock Journal," *Writings of Early Latter-day Saints*, 29–30).

Lucy Mack Smith

After the corpses were washed and dressed in their burial clothes, we were allowed to see them. I had for a long time braced every nerve, roused every energy of my soul, and called upon God to strengthen me, but when I entered the room and saw my murdered sons extended both at once before my eyes and heard the sobs and groans of my family . . . wives, children, brothers, and sisters, it was too much; I sank back crying to the Lord in the agony of my soul, "My God, my God, why hast thou forsaken this family!" A voice replied, "I have taken them to myself, that they might have rest." Emma was carried back to her room almost in a state of insensibility.

Her oldest son approached the corpse and dropped upon his knees and, laying his cheek against his father's and kissing him, exclaimed, "Oh, my father! my father!" As for myself, I was swallowed up in the depths of my afflictions, and though my soul was filled with horror past imagination, yet I was dumb until I arose again to contemplate the spectacle before me. Oh! at that moment how my mind flew through every scene of sorrow and distress which we had passed, together, in which they had shown the innocence and sympathy which filled their guileless hearts. As I looked upon their peaceful, smiling countenances, I seemed almost to hear them say, "Mother, weep not for us, we have overcome the world by love; we carried to them the gospel, that their souls might be saved; they slew us for our testimony, and thus placed us beyond their power; their ascendancy is for a moment, ours is an eternal triumph."

I then thought upon the promise which I had received in Missouri, that in five years Joseph should have power over all his enemies. The time had elapsed and the promise was fulfilled (Lucy Mack Smith, *The Revised and Enhanced History of Joseph Smith by His Mother,* ed. Scot Facer Proctor and Maurine Jensen Proctor [Salt Lake City: Bookcraft, 1996], 457–58).

18

Praise to the Man

We sing a hymn in honor of the Prophet that begins: "Praise to the man who communed with Jehovah, Jesus anointed that Prophet and Seer." As we contemplate the life of the Prophet Joseph and the Restoration he was inspired to inaugurate, we also praise the Father and the Son for revealing the gospel of Jesus Christ and the ordinances necessary for our eternal salvation. How long will we praise the Father for His plan of salvation and the Son for His atoning sacrifice? The scriptures declare, "forever and ever" (JST Revelation 5:13). Praise to the Father, praise to His Beloved Son, and praise to the Prophet they called to stand at the head of this final dispensation of the fullness of all times.

D&C 135:3

Joseph Smith, the Prophet and Seer of the Lord, has done more, save Jesus only, for the salvation of men in this world, than any other man that ever lived in it. In the short space of twenty years, he has brought forth the Book of Mormon, which he translated by the gift and power of God, and has been the means of publishing it on two continents; has sent the fulness of the everlasting gospel, which it contained, to the four quarters of the earth; has brought forth the revelations and commandments which compose this book of Doctrine and Covenants, and many other wise documents and instructions for the benefit of the children of men; gathered many thousands of the Latter-day Saints, founded a great city, and left a fame and name that cannot be slain. He lived great, and he died great in the eyes of God and his people; and like most of the Lord's anointed in ancient times, has sealed his mission and his works with his own blood; and so has his brother Hyrum. In life they were not divided, and in death they were not separated!

John Taylor

John Taylor
(Courtesy of the Church Archives, The Church of Jesus Christ of Latter-day Saints)

Joseph Smith in the first place was set apart by the Almighty according to the counsels of the gods in the eternal worlds, to introduce the principles of life among the people, of which the Gospel is the grand power and influence, and through which salvation can extend to all peoples, all nations, all kindreds, all tongues and all worlds. It is the principle that brings life and immortality to light, and places us in communication with God. God selected him for that purpose, and he fulfilled his mission and lived honorably and died honorably. I know of what I speak for I was very well acquainted with him and was with him a great deal during his life, and was with him when he died (in *Journal of Discourses*, 26 vols. [London: Latter-day Saints' Book Depot, 1854–86], 21:94).

Wilford Woodruff

No greater prophet than Joseph Smith ever lived on the face of the earth save Jesus Christ. He was raised up to stand at the head of this great dispensation—the greatest of all dispensations God has ever given to man. He remarked on several occasions when conversing with his brethren: "brethren you do not know me, you do not know who I am." As I remarked at our priesthood meeting on Friday evening, I have heard him in my early days while conversing with the brethren, say, (at the same time smiting himself upon the breast) "I would to God that I could unbosom my feelings in the house of my friends." Joseph Smith was ordained before he came here, the same as Jeremiah was. Said the Lord unto him, "Before you were begotten I knew you" (in *Journal of Discourses*, 21:317).

Brigham Young

Our situation is peculiar at the present time. Has it not been peculiar ever since Joseph found the plates? The circumstances that surrounded him when he found the plates were singular and strange. He passed a short life of sorrow and trouble, surrounded by enemies who sought day and night to destroy him. If a thousand hounds were on this Temple Block, let loose on one rabbit, it would not be a bad illustration of the situation at times of the Prophet Joseph. He was hunted unremittingly. We have the privilege of believing the same Gospel that Joseph taught, and with him of being numbered with those whose names are cast out as evil (*Discourses of Brigham Young*, ed. John A. Widtsoe [Salt Lake City: Deseret Book, 1983], 464).

Brigham Young

Why was he hunted from neighborhood to neighborhood, from city to city, from state to state, and at last suffered death? Because he received revelations from the Father, from the Son, and was ministered to by holy angels, and published to the world the direct will of the Lord concerning his children on the earth (*Discourses of Brigham Young*, 350).

Brigham Young

I can tell our beloved brother Christians who have slain the Prophets and butchered and otherwise caused the death of thousands of Latter-day Saints, the priests who have thanked God in their prayers and thanksgiving from the pulpit that we have been plundered, driven, and slain, and the deacons under the pulpit, and their brethren and sisters in their closets, who have thanked God, thinking that the Latter-day Saints were wasted away, something that no doubt will mortify them—something that, to say the least, is a matter of deep regret to them—namely, that no man or woman in this dispensation will ever enter into the celestial kingdom of God without the consent of Joseph Smith. From the day that the Priesthood was taken from the earth to the winding-up scene of all things, every man and woman must have the certificate of Joseph Smith, junior, as a passport to their entrance into the mansion where God and Christ are—I with you and you with me. I cannot go there without his consent. He holds the keys of that kingdom for the last dispensation—the keys to rule in the spirit-world; and he rules there triumphantly, for he gained full power and a glorious victory over the power of Satan while he was yet in the flesh, and was a martyr to his religion and to the name of Christ, which gives him a most perfect victory in the spirit-world. He reigns there as supreme a being in his sphere, capacity, and calling, as God does in heaven. Many will exclaim—"Oh, that is very disagreeable! It is preposterous! We cannot bear the thought!" But it is true (in *Journal of Discourses*, 7:289).

Wilford Woodruff

Wilford Woodruff
(Courtesy of the Church Archives, The Church of Jesus Christ of Latter-day Saints)

The last speech that Joseph Smith ever made to the quorum of the Apostles was in a building in Nauvoo, and it was such a speech as I never heard from mortal man before or since. He was clothed upon with the Spirit and power of God. His face was clear as amber. The room was filled as with consuming fire. He stood three hours upon his feet. Said he: "You Apostles of the Lamb of God have been chosen to carry out the purposes of the Lord on the earth. Now, I have received, as the Prophet, seer and revelator, standing at the head of this dispensation, every key, every ordinance, every principle and every Priesthood that belongs to the last dispensation and fulness of times. And I have sealed all these things upon your heads (Wilford Woodruff, in Conference Report, April 1898, 89).

Harold B. Lee

President George Albert Smith was about to close one of our general conferences, which happened to be at the time of the furor caused by the book *No Man Knows My History*, one of the scurrilous things published against the Church, and there had been different speakers who had said something about these apostate writings with which the Church was being flooded. Just as President Smith was about to finish, he paused—and it was wholly unrelated to what he had been talking about—and he said:

Harold B. Lee
(Courtesy of the Church Archives, The Church of Jesus Christ of Latter-day Saints)

Many have belittled Joseph Smith, but those who have will be forgotten in the remains of mother earth, and the odor of their infamy will ever be with them; but honor, majesty, and fidelity with God exemplified by Joseph Smith and attached to his name shall never die. (in Conference Report, April 1946, 181)

I never heard a more profound statement from any prophet (Harold B. Lee, *Stand Ye In Holy Places* [Salt Lake City: Deseret Book, 1976], 164).

Doctrine & Covenants 122:1–3

(A revelation from the Lord to and about the Prophet Joseph Smith.)

The ends of the earth shall inquire after thy name, and fools shall have thee in derision, and hell shall rage against thee;

While the pure in heart, and the wise, and the noble, and the virtuous, shall seek counsel, and authority, and blessings constantly from under thy hand.

And thy people shall never be turned against thee by the testimony of traitors.

Index

0 26575 79266 9